DYING WE LIVE

Dying We Live

THE FINAL MESSAGES
AND RECORDS OF SOME GERMANS
WHO DEFIED HITLER

Edited by

HELLMUT GOLLWITZER
KÄTHE KUHN
REINHOLD SCHNEIDER

Translated by

REINHARD C. KUHN

Foreword by

TREVOR HUDDLESTON

Collins
FONTANA BOOKS

First published by The Harvill Press Ltd., 1956
First issued in Fontana Books 1958
Second Impression, March 1960
Third Impression, January 1962
Fourth Impression, March 1965

Published in Germany by Christian Kaiser Verlag
under the title of
DU HAST MICH HEIMGESUCHT BEI NACHT

ACKNOWLEDGMENTS

The Letters and Diaries of Kim Malthe-Bruun,
extracts from which appear on pp. 76-85, have been
published by Random House. Petter Moen's Diary,
sections from which appear on pp. 178-182, has been
published by Messrs. Faber & Faber. The letters
and papers of Dietrich Bonhoeffer, selections from
which appear on pp. 191-197, have been published
by The Student Christian Movement Press.

CONDITIONS OF SALE

Printed in Great Britain
Collins Clear-Type Press
London and Glasgow

EDITOR'S NOTE

THE project of collecting and publishing farewell letters written in the face of death by men and women of the German resistance dates back to the year 1947. At that time Pastor Helmut Gollwitzer, a German prisoner of war in Russia, scanning a parish periodical sent him from his homeland, discovered the farewell letter of Alexis von Roenne, a colonel executed after the unsuccessful plot against Hitler of July 20, 1944, the letter that was to become the concluding piece and resonant finale of our collection. He felt the impact of its message all the more keenly as he happened to be involved in a spiritual crisis. He read the letter to his comrades during divine service and, recalling a few similar farewell letters which had come to his notice earlier, he decided to collect and publish documents of this sort whenever it might be granted him to return to his native land. Not since the time of the martyrs of the early Church, so it seemed to him, had there been such a wealth of testimonials of a faith triumphant in death.

He did come home and his resolve was strengthened when additional letters were made accessible to him, especially those of Pastor Bonhoeffer, Father Delp, and Count Moltke. But his exacting duties as a professor of theology at the University of Bonn hampered the execution of his project. He then invited me to assume the task of compiling the material and of editing it in collaboration with him. Through both my activities as honorary secretary of the American Committee to Aid Survivors of the German Resistance, and my many personal ties, I was acquainted with numerous families of the resistance, and thus felt that a duty was devolving upon me here that I could not shirk. What seemed at first a burden as well as a challenge soon presented itself as a privilege. Tracing unknown documents and collecting material from scattered publications, reading and rereading, copying and editing words vibrating with a life that had been quickened rather than quelled by the death of those who had written them, deciphering a stained original scrawled by a manacled hand on a scrap of paper or on the miserable form sheet supplied by the prison authorities—this was a work that could not fail to leave its mark on the mind of the compiler. Any service rendered in preserving and making available to others such treasures of superlative worth soon came to seem negligible as compared with the benefit conferred upon me by my labour. So while striving to act as a competent editor, I strove even more ardently to become a not too unworthy reader of these documents.

In discharging my editorial duties I have enjoyed the never failing help and advice of my fellow editor, the originator of this volume, Helmut Gollwitzer. Assistance has come from another admired and respected friend, Reinhold Schneider, the poet whose lines had been on the lips of many a prisoner awaiting death at the hands of Hitler's henchmen, and whose voice had brought comfort to the survivors in the disconsolate year of the German catastrophe. Without his encouragement and his advice I should not have been able to finish my work. The chief debt of gratitude, however, is owed to those who made the collection possible through a personal sacrifice—to the owners and recipients of the letters, the widows, children, parents, friends, and relatives of the writers. This volume is a gift of their generosity. They have allowed us to make public property what to them was exclusively their own, a sacred possession. They did so in realisation of the fact that these letters, over and above their personal significance, conveyed a message addressed to men and women of all times and all countries. For such is the miracle wrought by martyrdom: through the mediation of faith, things most intimately private rise to that authentic and unpolluted universality through which the brotherhood of men is gloriously affirmed.

The editors have been rewarded by innumerable expressions of approval and appreciation. In bringing out the English edition we should like to preface it with words from a German reader eminently competent to speak for many. In a letter to me, Gertrud von le Fort has written: " Your gift is a very precious one. No legacy more comforting or more moving could be conceived. That in the days of our deepest humiliation and spiritual darkness these witnesses of Christ, witnesses of a nobler humanity, stepped forth— this fact must fill the mind of every German with infinite gratitude. We may also hope that these documents will plead for us before the tribunal of a world still moved by anger and distrust; surely they will plead for us before God."

KÄTHE KUHN

The spirit cannot die—in no circumstances, under no torment, despite whatever calumnies, in no bleak places.

FRANZ MARC

CONTENTS

FOREWORD

" I TRUST and I pray. I have learned much in this rigorous year. God has become more real and more immediate to me." So wrote one who was to die within a month of having written these words; and who knew what lay ahead of him. And such, too, is the overwhelming weight of feeling amongst those whose writings have been selected for inclusion in this book. " God has become more real and more immediate to me." Yet they were living in the shadow of death: and they were living with that which should, humanly speaking, have produced a dread and a despair in the soul. For nothing, I suppose, in the long story of human cruelty, has exceeded the Nazi concentration camps and the vile philosophy of life which produced them.

It is natural for us to-day to wish to close the door for ever upon those dark and terrible days, when the full horror of Belsen and Buchenwald and Dachau was revealed. It is natural because —after all—this horror was perpetrated by civilised, cultured, Christianised, Western man. It is not easy to escape the horrid fear that *perhaps* it could have happened here. It is natural, too, because we are only too well aware of the fact that the world is still haunted by the fear of another war, and one which would inevitably be more ghastly and more totally destructive than the mind can envisage. And so it is easier to shut the door of memory altogether.

To adopt such an attitude is, I believe, a kind of treason to those who died. But it is also to miss a glorious opportunity of learning what Faith can do. And, I would suggest, there never was a time when Faith was more needed than the days through which we are presently living. We are confronted not so much with a conflict between Faith and Fear. Whatever view we may have of the dilemma in which nuclear power and its misuse has placed us, one thing is sure: to live under the shadow of fear alone is to create a spiritual paralysis which must be deadly. It is for this reason that this book *must* be read. For it states again and again, not in abstract theory but in living, human affirmation the meaning of Faith.

To a generation such as ours, and especially to the young

whose eyes are turned to the future, nothing is more absolutely essential than to grasp this meaning. It is so easy, and so deadly, to write and talk as if Faith were a soft option: to be enjoyed, if you have it; to be regretted if you have not. Whereas, in fact, Faith demands what Love demands: an act of the will; a hold, firm and forceful, upon reality. It is a positive and glorious and flaming thing, which only glows more splendid in the darkness.

It is this Faith that you will find here. Do not turn aside from it, I beg you: for you need it as much as those who suffered so greatly in the winning of it.

Trevor Huddleston, C. R.

1958

A FARM BOY FROM THE SUDETENLAND

February 3, 1944

Dear parents: I must give you bad news—I have been condemned to death, I and Gustave G. We did not sign up for the SS, and so they condemned us to death. You wrote me, indeed, that I should not join the SS; my comrade, Gustave G., did not sign up either. Both of us would rather die than stain our consciences with such deeds of horror. I know what the SS has to do. Oh, my dear parents, difficult as it is for me and for you, forgive me everything; if I have offended you, please forgive me and pray for me. If I were to be killed in the war while my conscience was bad, that too would be sad for you. Many more parents will lose their children. Many SS men will get killed too. I thank you for everything you have done for my good since my childhood; forgive me, pray for me. . . .

PETER, COUNT YORCK VON WARTENBURG

Count Yorck, born in 1904, in Silesia, a jurist by training and a high-ranking official in the German civil service, had much in common with his friend, Count Helmuth von Moltke, and the so-called Kreisau circle, the group of anti-Nazi patriots who had gathered round the latter, counted Yorck among its members. He, too, combined a deep religious faith with liberal ideas in politics. Both as a Christian and as a political thinker, he loathed National Socialism and all its works. Like most of the members of the Kreisau circle, he was close to the group of activists around Count Stauffenberg. After the abortive attempt on Hitler's life of July 20, 1944, he was arrested and sentenced to death. He was executed on August 8, 1944, in Plötzensee.

FROM HIS LAST LETTER TO HIS MOTHER

At the end of a life lavishly blessed with love and friendship, I feel only thanks towards God and humility in face of his will. It is a very deep sorrow for me that I bring this grief upon you after all the suffering you have had to live through. I beg you to forgive me wholeheartedly.

I have had more than two weeks in which to present myself and my actions before God, and I am convinced that in him I shall find a merciful judge. The degree of spiritual distress that people of my sort have had to endure in recent years is certainly incomprehensible to those who are completely animated by their faith, which I happen simply not to share. To you, I may offer assurance that my actions were in no way motivated by ambitious thoughts or desire for power. My actions have been determined purely by my patriotic feeling, by concern for my Germany, as it has grown to be in the last two thousand years, and by efforts directed to its inner and outer development. Therefore I hold up my head proudly before my ancestors, before my father and my brothers. Perhaps the time will come when a different evaluation will be accorded our attitude, when we shall be adjudged not scoundrels but, instead, warning voices and patriots. My ardent prayer is that this marvellous call may provide occasion for giving honour to God.

TO HIS WIFE

We have probably come to the end of the beautiful, rich life we have lived in common. For to-morrow the People's Court will sit in judgment on me and the others. I hear that the army has expelled us: they can take our garments, but not the spirit in which we acted. And in this spirit I feel myself in union with my forebears and my brothers and also with my comrades. That God has guided events as they have turned out, belongs to the inscrutableness of his ways, which I humbly accept. I believed myself to be impelled by a sense of the guilt that is weighing all of us down, and to be pure in heart. That is why I confidently hope to find in God a merciful judge. . . .

The last time we came away after partaking of the Lord's Supper, I felt something of almost unearthly sublimity, I should in fact like to call it the presence of Christ. In retrospect it seems to me to have been a call.

My death will, I hope, be accepted as an atonement for all my sins and as a vicarious sacrifice in expiation of the guilt we all harbour in common. May it also help to lessen, if only by a hair's breadth, the alienation of our era from God. I too am dying for my fatherland. Though in appearance my death is an inglorious, even a shameful one, I tread this last path erect and unbowed, and I hope only that you will not see this as arrogance and delusion. We meant to kindle the torch of life. A sea of fire engirds us—and what a fire!

THREE LETTERS BY UNNAMED AUTHORS

In 1937, Paul Hintz, pastor of the Cathedral of St. Mary at Kolberg, was courageous enough to publish a work entitled *And Praised God: Testimonies of Evangelical Pastors and Laics; Offered to the Congregation for Their Intercession.* The preface states that the book was not meant for general distribution but was intended to be a tribute to those who do not forget the words of Acts 12: 5: " Peter therefore was kept in prison: but prayer was made without ceasing of the church unto God for him."

The little volume brought together letters and other documents written in prisons and concentration camps by persecuted clergymen. The material in the present section is quoted from this book.

June 24, 1937

> But the God of all grace who hath called us unto his eternal glory by Christ Jesus, after that ye have suffered a while, make you perfect, stablish, strengthen, settle you.—I Pet. 5: 10

But I am perfectly certain, and it is becoming clearer to me

all the time, that everything we are experiencing and suffering is a part of something large that God purposes for us.
For us personally, for you and for me, for our Protestant
Church, for all of evangelical Christendom, yes, for our
whole nation, for enemies and for the indifferent, for the
timid and for the " radical," for the scoffers and for the
pious. God has something in preparation for all of us—
quite certainly something different for each individual and
yet for all of us only one thing in common, namely, that his
name be praised and held sacred and that his word be
proclaimed and believed.

And so the time of trial in which we are now living will
last just as long as it takes to attain this, God's actual goal.
That means for each of us the length of time it will take to
learn genuinely the lesson that God has now assigned us.
For man in his natural state this is not easy; yet everything
depends on not evading God's teaching, but willingly
accepting everything that he sends us. Everything comes
from his hands and not at all from those of man; every day
anew God is ready with his aid, both material and spiritual,
for those who really trust in him.

August 23, 1937

> Let us pray in the church with the church for
> the church, for there are three things that pre-
> serve the church and belong to the church.
> First, to teach faithfully; then, to pray diligently;
> and third, to suffer with earnestness.—
> Martin Luther

Now out of my solitude I must send you a greeting to let
you know that I think constantly, with heartfelt prayers,
of you, your dear husband, and your children. For me it is
really a relief that now I too have my little pack to bear and
am allowed to bend my shoulders under the common
burden. Now I too understand something of that peace of
mind with which your husband has borne his imprisonment,

and—as I confidently hope and pray—with which he is bearing it still. We are in the hands of Jesus—here as well as there, and " faith is the substance of things hoped for, the evidence of things not seen." Heard a thousand times, learned by heart, comprehended with the mind, assimilated as a conviction, now at last it becomes " truth " and the only truth that has life and strength in it—enough for to-day, certainly also enough for to-morrow, not because our faith is strong, but because the Lord is true to us.

The tide of suffering that is overwhelming the community of Christ is spreading, but the tide of love is an ocean that takes all this unto itself, lets it become clear and still. I can do no more than echo the words of St. Chrysostom: " God be praised for everything! "

December 4, 1937

The devil may be most wrathful; but let him
not try to tear us from His hand.—Martin Luther

One thing I want to ask of all of you: Let us not give way to apathy! Once again voices are heard trying to persuade us that the suffering of our church is a sign of the perversity of its way. To this we reply confidently that the apostles have given us witness otherwise. Indeed, this we know and affirm: just as our well-being does not bring about nor give us warrant of peace with God, so our suffering cannot do this either. Rather, this peace will always be the work and gracious gift of the One whose suffering began in a manger and was consummated on the cross, in order that we who belong to him might be called God's children. Let us believe in this joyous message of God's to us and by the strength of it continue on the road—in the footsteps of the One—not heeding the censures of man, but with the peace of Christ in our hearts and the praise of God on our lips. To this end may God help us!

PAUL SCHNEIDER

PASTOR

" A martyrdom is never the design of men; for the true martyr is he who has become the instrument of God, who has lost his will in the will of God, not lost it but found it, for he has found freedom in submission to God. The martyr no longer desires anything for himself, not even the glory of martyrdom " (T. S. Eliot). Through faith man puts himself like a tool into the hand of God. It was thus that Paul Schneider, pastor at Dickenschied-Womrath, born on August 29, 1897, near Kreuznach, Rhenish Prussia, became a chosen witness for the faith. When confronted by the antithesis of Christianity—the use of the lie as a political force—he called it by its name and thereby forfeited his life. He could not preach the Word without living it. And this he did in all simplicity, without hesitation, even when he found himself alone and at the mercy of his enemies. God had willed it so, and his instrument, his witness, obeyed. In this way, through a suffering not chosen but endured of his own free will, Paul Schneider was permitted to emulate his crucified Saviour.

It started in the very first year of the National Socialist régime with a disciplinary transfer from his post. An ominous clash took place when Pastor Schneider, at the burial of a child of his parish, denounced the web of pagan mythology that for political reasons was being superimposed upon the Christian concept of the here-after. Now he had a foretaste of the ordeal that was to come. He was not among those who, resigning themselves to anticipated loss, possess as though they did not possess. He loved his wife and children with the unbroken strength of his great heart. No one can measure the abyss of suffering and renunciation through which he must have passed in order to be able to reply as he did to a friend warning him to be careful. " Do you think," he said, " that God gave me children only that I might provide for their material welfare ? Were they not entrusted to me in order that I might safeguard them for eternity? "

For Pastor Schneider martyrdom came as a duty that he could not shirk. But in accepting the duty he made it a voluntary act, completely his own, willed and fought for with all his strength of soul.

He was arrested, then released under an order of expulsion. Despite the order, he preached from the pulpit from which he had been banned, and was arrested again. On July 24, 1937, he was released from prison but at the same time expelled from the Rhineland. He ignored this order and stayed with his parish.

Pastor Schneider did not have to wait long for the final separation, which came on the day of the festival of thanksgiving for the harvest. The congregation was happy to see its pastor officiating as before. The decorated altar, the sermon, the joyful hymns of thanks—everything was as it had been in years gone by. Only a few intimates noticed that, after the blessing, the pastor surveyed his congregation with a look of mingled love and sorrow that gradually faded into detachment, as if the parting had already taken place.

There was still time to say the evening prayer at the bedside of his children.

Then they arrested him.

A LETTER TO HIS CHILDREN

Kirchberg, October 4, 1937

Dear Children: Wasn't it nice that your father could look in on his family and his parish last Sunday? I am always happy when I see that you are being good together and not quarrelling. Without that, God could not listen to you at all when you pray for your father. And continue to do so diligently. I know that God hears you, and that your little prayers help to strengthen the firm wall around us, so that no one can hurt a hair of your father's head unless it be the will of God. Keep on praying that God in his power and mercy may bring your father back and that we may all remain in Dickenschied. Even if God keeps us waiting a while for the fulfilment of our prayers, we must not think that he does not hear us, and we must not tire because it takes so long.

> *Though God helps not in every deed,*
> *He's there in every hour of need.*

For the time being I am not at all far from you, here in

Kirchberg. Perhaps God will cause the authorities to have a change of heart and let your father go free. If not, then you must always remember that this too is good and necessary in order that men may learn to give greater heed to the word of God and to believe in his dear Son, our Saviour. I am glad that you are still living together in peace and safety with your dear mother. And be very good too for your dear mother's sake. You ought to get on a bit every day with reading, writing and arithmetic, and you should also learn some poems and proverbs.

I love you.

Your father

LETTERS FROM PRISON

Coblenz, October 10, 1937

Once again, my dear ones, I have been away from you for a week in the holy crusade of the Church of Jesus Christ. I still do not know what will become of me. It is quite possible that what lies ahead is a concentration camp. In that event, then let us both reconcile ourselves to it cheerfully. In any case, my decisions and my actions have been right: no doubts on that score have disturbed me yet. Perhaps you too, my dear, have found confidence within your heart in the rightness of our course. Perhaps occurrences in the church and the reactions of the brethren have by this time confirmed to you that in this case it was right not to yield to the command of the authorities. Moreover, God will of course stand firm in his promises and will support and aid us, spiritually and physically, according to his omnipotent strength. He will give us his comfort in all our sufferings and the blessing that comes through all suffering.

But those who still want to avoid suffering to-day had better take care lest they be rejected among men and cast off by God. I simply cannot conceive nor comprehend how anyone could obtain from God a remission of the prayers of intercession for the brethren and other required testimonies. Therefore, be comforted and serene, even if we remain the only ones who must descend into the abyss of persecution. " Beloved, think it not strange concerning the fiery trial which is to try you, as though some strange thing happened unto you. But rejoice, inasmuch as ye are partakers of Christ's sufferings." For the time of his coming is at hand; at long last will come the time of rejoicing before the face of our God; then " your sorrow shall be turned into joy."

October 17, 1937

Often, my dear wife, I feel like a most unnatural father and wonder why precisely I had to bring down all this upon your heads, and whether I had the right to do so—and why it had to be I and our parishes that have had to take the brunt of things. Then in a most penitent frame of mind I sit in my cell, which is the perfect place for such feelings. Yet after all we cannot do anything but follow the way along which God leads us, and despite all my reflections I still have thought of nothing else we could have done or any other way in which we could have done it. So we must confidently leave our case to God and trust in him to justify us, justify our faith in our souls and our consciences in all our sin, and also to justify us before the world when the time comes.

The Lord has promised us that he who renounces his kin and all his possessions for Jesus' sake will regain them a hundredfold in this world and win eternal life in the world to come. Let us have faith in this promise. With that the chestnut tree becomes for me God's wide and beautiful world, and the world becomes God's eternity, that even more beautiful world—I am " as having nothing and yet possessing all things." Lord Jesus, let me persevere in this state of mind until I attain thy kingdom.

October 18, 1937

I am sitting in my jolly seat by the windowsill, and enjoying the view into the crown of the chestnut tree, which now in the course of a few days has turned yellow, still holding fast the dying leaves with its last remnant of strength. The fine network of the branches of the crown, which will soon be naked and bare, is already visible. Thus also will the storms of autumn and winter assail the Church and Christianity, and then we shall see how much was only leafage and how much has become pithy and wooden, part of the tree itself. For the tree that fills the world, according to Jesus' beautiful parable, may yet be stripped naked and bare like any tree in winter. Let us therefore not be vexed by the sad and restive branches, which for friends and those who can see have indeed a beauty of their own.

That you were able to write me so cheerfully made me very happy. I am absolutely convinced that the " way of suffering " that I have imposed upon you, and that you endure so calmly and bravely, is bringing you not only sorrow and trouble but also blessing, joy, and the peace " which passeth all understanding." Thus you are contributing more perhaps than I in seeing to it that others do not shrink from the suffering offered to and commanded of us for the sake of our faith, and that they find not pleasure but joy in it. And quite certainly God intends to include our children too in the blessings of our way.

October 26, 1937

You can imagine how I long for the services of our congregations, or for the consolation of hearing the word of God preached by another brother, for " when I remember these things, I pour out my soul in me: for I had gone with the multitude. I went with them to the house of God, with the voice of joy and praise, with a multitude that kept holy day " (Ps. 42: 4). But God's spirit and blessing are not bound, and come to me in a remarkable way even in the quiet and solitude of my cell. In this quiet and solitude, alone with God and his Word, any one of us here has in abundance that of which formerly he had or took too little. Therefore, indeed, we pastors in the prisons can each personally look upon this time of incarceration as a kindly guidance granted by God.

October 31, 1937

In the eyes of God it is the spiritual union in faith that is more important, indeed supremely important, especially in the case of husband and wife, who should " lift each other heavenward." Haven't we now, dearest, in the course of our various separations, discovered this to be true? Your love and your consolation and, I may say, your faith as well, have made me happy and helped me to advance along the way of faith that I, or rather, that the two of us are allowed to follow. Is this not ample recompense for all the outward deprivation and loneliness for each other that we must now bear? That you too are determined not to repine nor grieve over it, that is what made your last letter so precious to me.

This morning I again had my beautiful divine service, with Gospel and Epistle, with prayers and hymns. Then I thought of all of you. The Gospel became so large for me: I thought of how God, since according to the law he must " call us to account," might justly sell us into bondage with wife and child; yet according to his mercy in Jesus Christ he releases us into the glorious freedom of the children of God. I pray only that we may not be found unfaithful stewards in our dealings with our fellow men and our debtors.

October 31, 1937

Once again it is Sunday afternoon. Even here in a prison God fulfils his promise in regard to the Sabbath day and comes with the rich blessing of his Word and with solemn peace into my cell and into my heart, and, I believe, also to my comrades. . . .

Perhaps we may yet have need of the stern words of the Letter to the Corinthians. We are both grateful to God that the time here has given me such peaceful asylum, with the divine blessing bestowed on me therein. But this must not deceive us into thinking—lest we be disappointed after-wards—that my situation is not as serious now as before. A visit Friday evening from Herr O., who interrogated you too, made me aware of this. He urged me once again to sign, to the effect that I accept my expulsion and do not intend to return to the Rhineland. I refused, of course, referring to the duty that binds the shepherd to his con-gregation. Whereupon he said " So you prefer a concen-tration camp." I said that I do not prefer it, but if it is ordained that I bear it, I shall have to be able to bear that also. I know that God, who has been so kind to us up to this time, will continue to stand by us and will not let any situation become too difficult.

The chestnut tree by the window is almost completely bare now; the last few days have robbed it of nearly all its leaves. But the sky shines in the more brightly and more penetratingly in these last lovely autumn days, and the birds still revel merrily in the branches. So also the outlook for our marriage and our family life may become bleaker and barer. Up to this time all has gone undeservedly well and happily with us—now the Cross has come to us in this fashion. But certainly God will cause it to come true that he will let his eternity, his kingdom of heaven, in which we believe, shine all the more brightly through our distress. And he will let our little children, those dear little gay birds, continue to live joyously and safely in the branches of our faith, our love, our hope, and our prayers. " And safely will God keep his children. . . ."

Always think of your prayers, dearest, as most important in all things, and let us never do anything without prayer. In your first letter to me here you wrote about how well sheltered we Christians are under any circumstances. Yes, whenever I call on God and pray, all obstacles give way.

November 2, 1937

Whatever may happen to us now, dearest, rest assured that I bear your suffering too. But let us also both rest assured of this, that the Lord Jesus and the faithful father heart of God have themselves before this borne our pain, and that therefore he cannot let us be tried beyond our strength, but will see to it that the trial comes to such an end that we can bear it.

November 7, 1937

You ask me what I do all day long. Above all I am a student of the word of God, and want to go on being that. . . .

Once again the chestnut tree is preaching a sermon to me. Its bare black branches reach out to me so promisingly the small brown buds for next spring. I can see them close to the window and also in the top branches. They were already there even when the yellow falling foliage was still hiding them. Should we be so thankless and of so little faith that we deliberately overlook among the falling, withered leaves of the church the buds that here too cling tenaciously to trunk and branches?

Dear wife, I believe we know enough out of our own inner experience to speak and to believe for our communities too. . . . The Confessional church—it is truly that—is the tree with the buds; the secret congregations within the congregations are the buds of the church. Wherever a pastor is ready to assume a ministry that no longer is a "ministry," that continues to exist even without assurance of state support (because a "position" thus supported would no longer be a religious post), while all calculations and considerations of church politics are at an end, there the spiritual eye sees even now the coming church and its spring. Of course, the world and the faithless churchmen see the bare tree stripped of its cultural and public significance and judge that, since the world and the state withhold recognition, it will soon die and serve only for firewood. They take refuge in the tangled vine of the false church and the state religion, rankly overgrowing the duly doomed tree of a godless, self-glorifying and self-complacent world—a vine that will collapse and be burned with the tree of such a transient world.

But we abide in the branches of the poor, bare, despised, and defamed church that reaches its buds out to us with so much promise, and we know that it alone carries the promise that the gates of hell will not prevail against it. In it only can we live in safety, " secure in all our ways "; only in that faith which is the indestructible strength of its life and its burgeoning can true freedom and happiness be found. Let us go on holding only ever more firmly and unequivocally to this faith, live by it and act by it, as the richly " comforted," because this faith alone represents the victory over the prison of this world and its lethal power. " Then let the world with all its vain reward dissolve. Faith perseveres, the Cross will lead us to the crown."

Coblenz, November 8, 1937

The life one lives here in one's cell is a very strange one. The external world is almost submerged. Whether it if winter or spring hardly concerns us. Even the events os national and international life have become remote; at least we look at them from a different, I might say a higher vantage point, thanks to the inward life that we are obliged to live and that allows us to look into our own souls, into God, and into eternity. This then is our evangelical monastic life, not self-chosen like that of the Catholics, but ordained for us by God for a time, which as such must be good and salutary for us.

Our letters can be nothing more than short visits, chaperoned as was once the custom for betrothed couples.

But this period of engagement, like any other, will pass and lead us to new joys. At the end of all separations and re-unions, however, there comes for us Christians the ever-lasting wedding feast, when our marriage and our love will likewise find a new blessed consummation in communion with God and with our Saviour. Let us be grateful even for this " ante-nuptial " conversation that is still vouchsafed us.

November 14, 1937

May God give you strength and help according to his promise. He lays a burden upon us, but he helps us too. " And as thy days, so shall thy strength be . . . and under-neath are the everlasting arms." They will carry you and hold you fast. The most difficult thing, you will agree, is the burden of conscience, of taking care always that what we do is right and can meet the test of men and of God. This is the burden that weighs upon us Christians more than upon others, heavier to bear than any external suffering. This burden at least I want to carry with you and for you; sometimes it lies very heavy upon my shoulders and again and again I have scrambled upward laboriously in faith in order to be confident that God will look with mercy on my whole imperfect and sinful doing, accounting, and confessing. In such hours we must trust, therefore, that he will take our sinful human works into his faithful divine hand and sanctify, purify, and bless them for the sake of the consummated sacrifice and work of Jesus. For all our actions and all our life it remains true that " the grace of God and the blood of Christ make all error good." So once again let us place everything in his hands.

November 24, 1937

Now, so it seems, the dice have fallen. Whether it is to be a concentration camp or protective custody, cannot make much difference. What advice can I give you now? It is so cheap and easy to counsel from the outside. Remember

that " it is better to forsake all creatures, than to act in the
least against God's will." And at the same time, put trust
in this promise: " He who fears God has a sure refuge and
safely will God keep his children."

God will give you strength, you dear ones, to go your
way.

Shortly before being transported to the concentration camp
at Buchenwald, Paul Schneider, thanks to the kindness of a
jail-keeper, was able to send a few more lines to his wife. They
read as follows:

Let us continue to put our trust as we have done until now,
in God alone, let us continue in humility and patience to
expect all good to come from HIM alone and to love, fear,
and honour HIM wholeheartedly. Thus God will be with
us, and we shall not be disappointed in our hopes. Be
comforted and faithful; fear not. I hold you close in my
heart. In God we are not separated. Once more, my heartfelt thanks to you for all the love you have shown me while
I was here. Let us be thankful for this beautiful *period of
preparation* for harder trials. New sorrows should bring us
new experiences of our God and a new glory. Christ says:
" I am with you all your days." With love,

Your Paul

Despite the terrible torment of concentration camp life and
the breakdown of his physical strength, Pastor Schneider
brought consolation to his fellow prisoners and, as many of them
acknowledged later, rescue from despair. Even in the camp he
did not cease to speak the truth with his characteristic fearless-
ness whenever such testimony was called for. He endured unspeakable suffering; he was tortured almost to death. Finally
a camp doctor murdered him with an overdose of strophantin.
He died on July 18, 1939. A fellow prisoner, Alfred Leikam, a
lawyer, wrote in retrospect:

In camp life this was for me the greatest of all trials—to
remain silent and passive in the face of the unimaginable

wrongs inflicted upon the people there, or even to be forced to participate in such things, and in that way to become guilty towards them. As far as I know, there was only one man in Germany who did not share in this guilt. That was Pastor Paul Schneider who in both word and deed protested against injustice even in the concentration camp, and for this suffered a martyr's death.

Dean Martin Albertz, a friend, colleague, and brother-in-arms, wrote on July 19, 1939, to Frau Margarete Schneider:

We must really give thanks wholeheartedly that your dear husband has been called to his and our Master and is giving praise to the Lord in the company of the apostles and the martyrs. Through suffering he has attained to glory and is praying with us to Him who called him to His way. Through your husband God bestowed a rich gift of grace on the Confessional Church. It sets up for all of us a symbol visible from afar. We pray for the fruits of such a death. I repeat again and again: the prayers for Brother Schneider have now ended. But our thanks and praise on his account shall not cease.

BERNHARD LICHTENBERG

PRELATE

Bernhard Lichtenberg, born on December 3, 1875, at Ohlau in Silesia, had been Dean of the Cathedral of St. Hedwig in Berlin since 1938. When the great trial of his life came to him, he was well advanced in years, a venerable priest whose body, consumed by long years of self-sacrificing pastoral service, continued to function only under compulsion of a fiery will. In him were combined the tenderness of the ardent worshipper and the hardihood of a crusader battling for injured justice. He was of those who hunger and thirst after righteousness. Thus a conflict with National Socialism was inevitable.

Even before the brown-shirted cohorts seized power, Father Lichtenberg was an object of hatred to them as a pacifist. And when in Germany terror was made a form of government, he could not and would not remain silent, because for a priest silence meant complicity. In October of 1941, the Party disseminated inflammatory pamphlets directed against the Jews; in answer to these, he had the following announcement read from the pulpits of all the churches of the diocese.

ANNOUNCEMENT.—An inflammatory pamphlet anonymously attacking the Jews is being disseminated among the houses of Berlin. It declares that any German who, because of allegedly false sentimentality, aids the Jews in any way, be it only through a friendly gesture, is guilty of betraying his people. Do not allow yourselves to be confused by this un-Christian attitude, but act according to the strict commandment of Jesus Christ: " Thou shalt love thy neighbour as thyself."

No one ever saw him raise his hand in the Hitler salute. When he was asked how he felt towards the Führer, he replied to the Gestapo commissioner: " I have only one Führer, Jesus Christ."

He was denounced for his public prayers on behalf of concentration camp prisoner and of Jews. On October 23, 1941, he was arrested, tried, and condemned to two years in prison. " I knew of the many priests who had been arrested," he admitted at the trial, " and even then surmised what I know to-day, because I have now been having a taste of it these last seven months and have been made to feel it in my own body how hard the fate of imprisonment is even for a priest, and how greatly, in such distress, even he stands in need of strength and consolation from God."

In the prison at Tegel, on January 17, 1943, the " imprisoned Dean, B. L., Carthusian monk," wrote as an enclosure in a letter:

> *I desire nothing more*
> *Than what my Saviour doth will,*
> *And locked behind this iron door*
> *I shall, until the end, be still.*
> *And what the Saviour doth will*
> *Was long ago set down:*
> *The Second Chapter of the Apocalypse*
> *From the tenth verse on.*

The deprivation of freedom was synonymous with a death sentence. Dean Lichtenberg died on November 5, 1943, in Hof, on the way to Dachau, where the Gestapo was sending him after the expiration of his term of imprisonment at Tegel, on the grounds of " jeopardy to public order." His last letter, which

follows, should be prefaced by the words—a line from a prayer—
to which he once planned to dedicate a book: *Deus, Deus meus,
ad te de luce vigilo.*

Prisoner Book No. 717   *Berlin-Tegel, September 27,* 1943
Tegel Prison, Berlin

Praise be to Jesus Christ in eternity. Amen.

Reverend Sister and Mother Superior: The dear Lord has
sent me to the prison infirmary for the third time. And so
I must write in bed what will probably be my last letter
from prison. When I look back upon the last two years, I
desire and am obliged to thank God with all my soul, as
well as all who have been instrumental in carrying out his
holy will upon me. It is my firm resolution to keep, with
the help of God, the vows that in his presence I made at
the end of the thirty-day spiritual exercises. That is to say,
I shall consider everything that happens to me, joyful or
painful things, elevating or depressing, in the light of
eternity. In my patience I will possess my soul. By neither
word nor deed will I sin, and I will do everything out of
love, and out of love I will suffer everything. I have enough
courage to live for another twenty years, but should the
dear Lord will that I die to-day, may his holy will be done.

A thousand greetings to my right reverend Bishop, to the
cathedral chapter, to the parish house, to the rectory, to the
congregation of St. Hedwig, to all who have given me
comfort by writing to me and by praying for me.

May the most just, sweet, and holy will of God, inscrutable
in its heights and in its depths, be accomplished, praised,
and honoured in eternity, now and for evermore, Amen.

A prisoner in the Lord,
Bernard Lichtenberg
Dean of the Cathedral of St. Hedwig

EWALD VON KLEIST-SCHMENZIN

LANDED PROPRIETOR

" A National Socialist régime can end only in chaos." The author of these words, appearing in a pamphlet published in 1932 under the title *National Socialism—A Menace,* was Ewald von Kleist, born on March 22, 1889, in Pomerania. He belonged to the group of influential personalities that made up the conservative elements in Germany, but his Christian tenets and his statesman-like discernment forbade his sanctioning the opportunist alliance that men of his rank and party had formed with the National Socialist movement. He knew Hitler, and saw through him; and on the occasion of an audience with Hindenburg, he warned the aged President of the Reich in the most forceful terms. Hindenburg conceded that he was right, but six weeks later assented to the appointment of Hitler as Chancellor of the Reich.

From that moment on Kleist withdrew from national politics, and was heard among friends to declare repeatedly that there was no longer any hope of averting catastrophe. Where need was most pressing, he gave his help. He found places of refuge in his district for persons outlawed by the government. Meanwhile those in power were pursuing him with a well-founded hatred. He was arrested on May 1, 1933, and released a few days later; arrested again on June 23, he was held in custody for weeks. He escaped the bloody liquidation of the enemies of the Party on June 30, 1934, by fleeing from Pomerania. On July 21, 1944, the day after the unsuccessful attempt on Hitler's life, the manor house of Schmenzin was surrounded, and Kleist, arrested by the Gestapo, was taken first to Stettin, then to Berlin. There he committed his thoughts on life and the principles of his Christian faith to a testament that is presented here with only minor omissions. In this time, confined in a prison cell and face to face with death, Kleist, like Boethius, came into merciful certitude of eternity. He died on April 15, 1945, in Plötzensee, at the hands of the hangman.

LAST NOTES

Begun October 6, 1944

To-day, as the twelfth week of my imprisonment begins, I want to start writing down some things that have moved me here in prison. I do so in order to while away the long hours and unburden my soul of these matters, and also because perhaps some day these lines will reach you, my dear Alice —you, to whom they are dedicated first and foremost. For obvious reasons I can put only a few things on paper, but I hope that what I say will be plain. I am writing down simply whatever happens to come to my mind.

My mood has often vacillated between hope and the most gloomy anticipations; these shifts have usually been determined not by rational considerations but often by quite trivial things. In Stettin we comrades in suffering hoped for early release; this feeling was encouraged by the pronouncements of the local Gestapo. But on one point my state of mind till now has remained constant, serene, and firm: I have resigned myself unconditionally to the will of God. Not once have I been assailed by any doubt that what God wills even in this situation is just and good. Not for one moment have I contended with HIM. Therefore, despite some very gloomy hours, despair has remained far from me. Another thing that has helped is that I have not given way to the temptation of self-pity. I have also kept in check melancholy and wistful thoughts about my dear ones and about Schmenzin. Only occasionally have I allowed myself to picture in my mind what you were doing, and then in fancy I heard the singing at vespers, the voices of the two little ones playing before the house, asking daddy for " sweeties," or coming in their night clothes to say " Night-night."

But the hardest thing of all for me has been to envisage you, Alice, consuming yourself in sorrow and anxious love. And it has been hard also to look out into the lovely autumn days—in my first cell here I had an unobstructed, broad view of trees—and to think of the rutting time. I longed to be with you again up in the hide, watching the stags and hearing them bell in the beautiful autumnal woods, experiencing all this magic with you once more, perhaps for the last time! But to have lost oneself too deeply in these enticing, bitter sweet imaginings would have been wrong. Perhaps strongest of all was the longing to be with you at Advent and at Christmas time, hearing the old dear songs.

But, strange as it may sound, I have learned one thing in prison—to be joyful.

October 7, 1944

In my former life I was absorbed in what transcends the individual, in the universal; I might almost say that I had become somewhat estranged from my own consciousness. And so I usually did not feel either greater or lesser human joys as profoundly as I could and should have felt them. This realm of experience was simply eclipsed. It was for all that an idealistic and—at least I hope so—a selfless attitude, but it had a typical masculine one-sidedness, in that it was somewhat impersonal. For how meagre life would be if there were no complement to this—how lacking in warmth, love, tenderness, and intimacy.

In these last years, in which I have lived withdrawn from all public life, a change has set in. Here, in the desolation of an eleven-week-long solitary confinement, the little things and the purely human have gained a completely different meaning for me. I can find such deep and lasting joy in seemingly insignificant things as I would never have known before.

October 8, 1944

Yesterday my letter stopped at the matter of finding joy. My first great joy was your first letter and the picture of you with the two little ones. Every day I have had it in my hands many times; it has been a consolation to me so

often! And then the news that we should be able to see each
other on the seventeenth of August. For a week I counted
the days and the hours. When the eve of the seventeenth
brought the heavy air attack on Stettin, my first thought
was that train connections would be disrupted and that you
would not be able to come. And that is just what did
happen, and we did not see each other.

The first weeks here in Berlin were not pleasant—cut off
from every, really every, connection with the outside world.
Not a sign of life from you. I assumed that Hermann had
been killed. I was tormented by thoughts of Ewald-
Heinrich; I knew that he was in prison too, since we were
by chance both taken at the same moment and thus saw
each other. Again and again I pleaded to be permitted to
have some news of you and Hermann, to hear whether you
were still alive. All in vain. Not even a rejection of my
request came. Nothing. It was as though I lay alive in my
coffin. Those days were hard, but now that they are behind
me, I would not wish to have done without them, for they
too embodied the merciful guidance of God. In those days
I became absolutely sure of my faith: it withstood all trials
unimpaired. There was not a single moment of wavering
or despair. Even in those days I was able to thank God.
Sometimes it was as if I could almost physically feel the
hand of God leading me and drawing me closer to him.
And in all this there was nothing of exaltation or ecstasy.
The certainty that this life is only a very short period of
trial and that death will lead us as a friend and redeemer
out of all sorrow into happiness, nearer to God, helped me
safely over everything.

And then, quite unexpectedly, came the day when the
cell door opened and the greeting in your handwriting,
together with the provisions, was brought in to me. I do
not believe that you can really imagine how overjoyed I was.
And after that a parcel every day. The whole day, before
the moment and after it, was illumined from then on. . . .
The most precious thing about the gifts was your love,
which shone through all of them, and not the least was your

separating yourself for so long from the children. On the nineteenth of September you sent me the first roses. I still have one of the petals from those roses.

November 10, 1944

A long interval of no writing.

One more thing I have learned—to be thankful to my fellow men even for insignificant kindnesses, but above all thankful to God. Despite all hardship, God has given me so much good, and with this the best thing that man can have: from the first moment of my life to this very day, loyal and selfless love has accompanied me in unusual measure. And I have always had a few true friends. That indeed means more than the fulfilment of many a far-reaching wish or plan. Every day it becomes clearer to me that we human beings—especially we people of the white race, we Europeans—put false valuations on everything, because we have become estranged from God. The world of to-day no longer has a true scale of values. Men chase after fleeting goals and no longer know what happiness is, nor where it lies; they really no longer even know what they should be thankful for. But precious beyond all else are the love and mercy of God, who will save everyone who believes in him from all distress and all pain, and who even in this earthly life gives help through his Spirit. God has revealed to us everything that we need for living and for dying. I have actually experienced it: " Nevertheless I am continually with thee: thou hast holden me by my right hand. Thou shalt guide me with thy counsel, and afterwards receive me to glory. . . . And there is none . . . that I desire besides thee." I have experienced it with an indescribably blissful certainty. I have learned to thank God, and learned what is meant by the precept, " And thou shalt love the Lord thy God with all thine heart." He has never let me fall by the way. In his loving-kindness he has always drawn me to himself again.

My attitude towards prayer, too, has changed. I had come close to the position that urgent prayer actually should be offered for spiritual gifts only, because God gives or withholds in his wisdom, and cannot be influenced by prayer. In my youth I sometimes smiled at my grandmother a little (but in this smile there was still respect, because at that time people were not as disrespectful as they are to-day) when with childlike faith she prayed and gave thanks for the most trivial things. Now I have completely changed my mind. I do not know, and indeed probably am not to know, to what extent God grants our prayers. However, only a dull mentality would simply deny the possibility.

> And where the wisdom of the wise man fails
> The childlike heart's simplicity prevails.

Surely a prayer with the inward addition of " But thy will be done " bears blessing in itself and gives comfort and strength. I believe also that an earnest prayer may be granted, even though our poor reason cannot envisage such a thing. Once again I pray constantly for many things, especially on behalf of my loved ones. Man should turn with all his troubles and joys to God, lest he lose the loving contact with him. It should be done with concentrated, earnest absorption; it should be an opening of oneself to God. In praying one should hear and be willing to hear; God does not remain silent. This I know.

It is of the greatest importance that children learn many hymns and Bible verses, and in such a fashion that they retain them for the rest of their lives. That is more important than explanations of the catechism. Adults also should not spare effort in re-learning hymns and proverbs. They really help.

Formerly, I always stressed faith, obedience, and trust, and perhaps put too little emphasis on the love of God and of one's fellow men. Of course I do not mean that insipid love, that so-called charity or " social consciousness " which concerns itself only with material things, the things of this world, thus running counter to the will of God, since it turns the thoughts, wishes, and endeavours of man away from God and the eternal things, and actually teaches him to violate the commandment, " Thou shalt not covet."

November 16, 1944

For some time now I have known that I shall be sentenced to death. Only the thought of you and the children, especially the thought of your sorrow, makes it difficult for me. My daily most fervent prayer is that God may lead you and the children in his mercy and comfort and strengthen you. Apart from this, I shall gladly die when God calls me away.

You know that I have always regarded death as a friend and saviour and not as a frightful thing nor a punishment. Only the certainty of death makes life bearable. Only through death can we find happiness. Happiness is exclusively in God. Everything earthly is transient and vain (Ecclesiastes). Of course, we should not live turned away from the world; rather, we should labour with all our strength in earthly affairs—politics, economics, cultural matters, etc.— in an attempt to shape them, according to our best convictions, in conformity with the will of God. We may and should rejoice in the earthly gifts of God. But we should never set our hearts on any earthly thing. For all these things, and even states and nations, will pass. But the soul is immortal. How infinitely brief is the duration of even the most powerful world empire, as compared with this immortality!

Only one thing really matters, namely, that our souls should go to God—only this, only this, and nothing else. It is allowable to mourn the loss of earthly things, the ruin of something for which one has worked all one's life long. But we need not and must not despair. It is a loss for only a short moment, as short as the duration of life, and our happiness is not in the least affected by it. Happiness lies in the hands of God alone. It lies beyond life, and the gate that brings us to it is death. Even the loss of a most beloved one does not rob us of happiness. After a short period of trial we shall be reunited with our loved ones in the Glory of God, and he will wipe away all our tears. This is certainly true. We must believe it, must struggle through to believing it, be it ever so difficult, and even though we fall back again and again. God will give us the strength to do so if we pray for it with all the power of our hearts, if we open our hearts to him: " Thy will be done." God does not remain mute, even if there are times when we do not hear HIM. God is mercy, God is love. Everything that HE does, or enjoins upon us, is good, everything. " Blessed is the man that endureth temptation "; " Be not afraid, only believe "; " I have redeemed thee, I have called thee by thy name; thou art mine "; " I have loved thee with an everlasting love: therefore with loving kindness have I drawn thee."

Think at all times of the very beautiful hymn, " Though I know not the way, Thou knowest it well." Therefore have no sadness if God frees me from this life and calls me to him. This is my great plea.

November 22, 1944

To-day, my dear Alice, I was supposed to see you. My joy at the prospect was indescribable. And then came the news of Wilfried's serious illness. Once again something has interposed on the eve of a reunion awaited with so much longing. Am I going to see you once more? May God preserve Wilfried. But " thy will be done." What God does, is well done. He puts a burden upon us, but he also helps. In his own good time God will end this short life of ours and take us up into his eternal home, into blessedness.

Poor Alice, you have so much to bear, and you bear it so bravely. God's power is much stronger in you than you know. In all your sorrow you hold your head high and think lovingly of others. Be of good cheer; God will some day reward you. You are, without knowing it, a person who leads others to God also. Yes, this is a very sad day, but God has stilled and pacified my heart. In all my

sorrow I have been able to read the psalm, " Bless the Lord,
O my soul." Besides my concern about Wilfried, it is my
concern about you that weighs upon me. The day on
which you learn that I am dead! Now you still have hope.
How hard this blow will be for you! May God in his mercy
support you. He will do so. For all of us these verses hold
true:

> Hence I wait silently,
> Thy word holds no deceit.
> Thou knowest the way for me:
> That doth suffice.

" Be not afraid, only believe."

November 27, 1944

Are you at some point going to find yourselves completely
penniless in these frightful times? Only God knows. But
I can leave you a legacy that is imperishable and beyond all
earthly goods, and that is my baptismal verse: " But seek
ye first the kingdom of God." Let this saying be your lode-
star throughout life; then no evil can befall you, then you
will be blessed. He who does the will of God abides in
eternity. You must fulfil your earthly tasks with all earnestness and according to the will of God. In these transient
things man must labour as God wills. But all this will pass;
only what you do for your souls and for the souls of others
will not pass. And this is my bequest to you, my last will,
that in faith, obedience, trust, and *love* you keep God before
your eyes and in your hearts your whole life long. We
should love God above all else. You must completely free
yourselves of those attitudes, ruling the lives of nearly all
people nowadays, which place far too much value on the
things of this world. Just remember that this earth on
which we live, compared with that part of the universe
which we little people know and whose extent is measured
in countless millions of light years, is only an infinitesimal
mote of dust. And how can events on this mote of dust have
any importance in God's infinite creation ?

How short even the longest human life is when measured against that eternity to which we are called. It is really only a short moment. Even the severest trial will pass, even the severest burden is bearable for him who prays to God for strength. And even when obedience to God brings on the most fearful afflictions, we must not hesitate one instant in obeying God for our own sakes, that is to say, for the sake of our souls. Earthly suffering passes, but the soul is immortal. When all the present nations of the earth shall be no more, we—that is, our souls—shall still exist. I know how difficult it is to believe, to obey, to fight the evil within us. I know how difficult it is to free the heart from all earthly bonds. Time and time again man will stumble and fall—time and again. Do not lose courage in this struggle. For God will lend you help.

From your youth on, remember that you must die. Prepare yourselves constantly for this moment. Open your hearts daily to God in praying and in listening to him. Time and time again he will help, he will give his strength and his comfort. Seek your happiness in God and you will find it. He holds us by the hand and leads us and finally receives us in glory. Give yourselves up completely to the will of God: he will take care of everything. Never, absolutely never, not even in the most secret chamber of your heart, rebel against what God has inflicted upon you, and you will see how incomparably easier it will be to bear anything. I have written no single word that does not stand for something I have experienced myself, with gratitude towards God. It is truth for all eternity. But all this does not simply fall into one's lap. It must be fought for in a constant struggle with oneself, a daily and some-times even hourly struggle. But the inward sense of blessed-ness, which compensates for everything, will not escape you. Believe me: I have experienced it. Read and learn by heart Paul Gerhard's song, " I am a Sojourner on Earth."

You know me and won't misunderstand me as meaning that you should become hypocritical, disconsolate, joyless bigots. You know how much I dislike such unctuous so-called piety.

My dear, dear Alice, I thank you for your great love and for everything that you have been to me. My heart is always with you, and my most heartfelt prayers have been for you. Just think—I shall be with God, in his happiness. This should comfort you. God's will is holy and good. And it is my consoling belief, which must console you too, that we shall find each other again in the presence of God. After a short period of trial, you and I will be reunited before God. Through God's grace we can really say: " O Death, where is thy sting; O hell, where is thy victory? " But thanks be to God who has given us the victory. Against our faith, all baseness and all human might are powerless. Every sorrow will with all certainty be changed into blessedness. May God give you strength and comfort. Yes, he will do so; you will feel it. May he bless you and keep you, from now to eternity, until you too, by aid of our friend and liberator, death, pass from faith to vision, from hope to fulfilment. All life has only a single meaning, a single goal—" Nearer to God." God will reward you abundantly for all your selfless love and kindness.

December 2, 1944

Yesterday I was served with a warrant of arrest for high treason.*

Now it is only a matter of time.

It is after all a relief to me to have made these notes. I hope indeed that they will come to your hands.

The worth of a nation is determined only by the extent to which it is directed to God. A non-Christian people may be much closer to God than a Christian people. The Christian peoples of to-day are very far from God. But a new and better time is coming for the world. I believe that in what I have written there is much that, in the hands of

* Up to this time Kleist's imprisonment had been termed " protective custody." It became a legal detention through the warrant of arrest issued by a court (translator's note).

men who will understand it with their hearts, and who are gripped and dominated by the same faith, could be further developed in beneficent ends. Some day this faith will raise its head in triumph in the world.

And now once again: dear, dear Alice, do not give yourself over too profoundly to grief over my death. It would not be right. For indeed, the best of treasures remains to you, namely, God.

December 7, 1944

Yesterday at last I saw you and spoke to you. That was my last great desire. I was always in apprehension that something would again thwart our meeting. Now I have experienced this last great joy. I thank God for it, and also for having kept you safe during the heavy air attack. How happy you made me in that short half-hour! Now I have probably seen you for the last time in this life. The farewell was indeed very difficult for me. I marvelled at you, at the strength with which you kept yourself in hand, not showing your pain. God has given you much strength. That is such a great consolation to me.

According to human reckoning, I shall never see any of you again—never. Nevertheless, " thy will be done."

December 10, 1944

The second Sunday in Advent. Once again I held a quiet hour of observance. Many remembrances of my life are emerging. They are actually always happy memories. Now that no worldly concerns or cares distract my gaze from the inward and upward direction, I see more and more clearly what happiness on earth consists of. It consists of the love of God and man, of unselfishness, kindness, and friendliness, which are thoroughly compatible with earnestness, austerity, keenness, and militant alertness. How much I have fallen short in these things. I had always thought that it must be a great misfortune to become totally blind.

I do not think so any longer. I can understand how, even blind, one could be very happy. I should like to have a great many people hear and understand that happiness lies within one and not in outward things—solely in the living union with God.

December 17, 1944

The third Sunday in Advent. With hymnal, Bible, and your proverbs and songs, I have spent another pleasant, peaceful morning. Men—and religions too—are so closely bound in their thoughts to this little earth. I am convinced that there is going to be a religious revival—the ground is even now being prepared for it—that will put an end to the megalomania of man and force upon him a consciousness of the minuteness and insignificance of the earth. Such a revival will be an immeasurable blessing for humanity. Not that I believe that mankind can be fundamentally transformed. Alas, no. But an era of terrible decline in faith will be followed by an era of resurgence of faith. However, we must want to listen to the voice of God: he reveals himself and speaks in exactly the same way, and no other, in which he has spoken at any other time to pagan or Christian. There are those who say that God revealed himself once in the past, and that any revelation, every communication, must come through the medium of the earlier one, which has been recorded and can be read; but with this idea they disrupt the living connection between mankind and God.

December 27, 1944

Once again the Christmas festival lies behind us. On Christmas Eve I had a curious experience. I looked forward to that evening, the Christmas tree, and the heaping up of the gifts with such eager suspense as I had known only as a child. I believe I had hardly ever before been as happy over the presents as I was this time. The thoughts that wandered to my beloved ones were, of course, very yearning thoughts. But no sadness assailed me. I read the Christmas story and all the songs that you sing in Schmenzin. It became such a lovely, quiet evening.

I begin now to grasp the truth and blessing contained in the admonition that we should not feel troubled without cause. I also have been too greatly concerned for the morrow. Even though I think that my heart was relatively not much bound to earthly things, there was still too much of this and too little trust in God. One should do one's duty in earthly affairs, but with greater trust in God leave the future in his hands. With this one will be much happier— and a better individual. Would that all who read this may take it to heart and pass it on. For we are here not in order to keep for ourselves the truths that we have recognised. And we can hand them on with success only when we live in accordance with them.

> Enjoy whatever God allots to thee,
> What thou hast not, in gladness learn to spare.
> Each station has its own tranquillity,
> Each station has its load to bear.

Mother impressed this stanza on my memory. It contains one of the most important truths. Only he who lives in this thought can know contentment: and without contentment one knows no happiness. " Thou shalt not covet ": disregard of this commandment is the mark of our times.

December 31, 1944

New Year's Eve. In love and gratitude my heart is with you, with the children, and with Mother. Now you are all probably in the drawing-room round the Christmas tree, singing the beautiful Christmas songs. Every previous New Year's Eve I have known passes before my eyes. I believe that in thirty years I have never looked forward to a new year with such inward peace as I do to-day. " Thou hast holden me by my right hand. Thou shalt guide me with

thy counsel, and afterwards receive me to glory"; "The
Lord is my shepherd; I shall not want." May all of you
remain free of too great heaviness of heart. As so often
before, my whole life is passing before my eyes. Only now
do I see wholly how thankful I should be to God. How
much good and happiness he has given me and is giving
me daily!

And now I consign myself and all of you into the faithful
hands of God. May he unite us all in his kingdom, our
home.

January 6, 1945

For the first time in a long while I am again feeling a little
depressed. But communing with God in prayer keeps this
mood from becoming too dominant. I have experienced so
very often how God holds us by the hand and helps us on.
Through these days I have been praying from the depths of
my soul—but always with the stipulation, "Thy will be
done."

I do not believe that you realise just how much you have
given me during this time with your unselfish love. Above
all, you have throughout the period of our marriage given
me one thing: you have made me a better man and helped
me forward on the way to God. That is the highest gift a
human being can give.

Yes, God is love and he is merciful; he helps those who
seek him and believe blindly in him. He is just as you wrote
in your last letter: "Fear not: for I have redeemed thee,
I have called thee by thy name. Thou art mine." Further,
"Nothing can befall us that he has not foreknown." And
his will is good. The help of God is such that I can still
thank him even when I am depressed. The certainty that,
on the far side of death, happiness awaits us in the kingdom
of God, is our most precious possession. And the feeling of
union with God can confer blessing even while we are still
in this life. But as long as we are bound to our bodies, this
feeling of blessedness is obstructed. How glorious it will be
when we have left our bodies! Here on earth we must learn

patience, much patience. But the day will come when God will wipe away all our tears. It is really so—the more willingly we bear the burdens laid upon us, the lighter they become. The oftener and the more intimately we turn to God, the closer will he come to us.

January 12, 1945

To-day the lawyer told me that judgment will probably be passed upon me in about a fortnight, and that the death penalty is an absolute certainty. I was prepared for this, but I am nevertheless surprised at how slight an impression this information made on me. The reason is probably that the only thing that still holds me to this earth is my love for you, for the children, and for Mother. Except for this, I believe, my soul has freed itself completely from earthly concerns. Only the thought of you gives me pain. Otherwise I am completely calm. My way leads to the Father. It is strange that on this road I can still take carefree pleasure in eating, smoking, or a book.

January 19, 1945

It was lovely to be speaking to you to-day. Am very happy about it. And so to-morrow the verdict. I consign everything to God's hands.

FRANZ REINISCH

PRIEST

Born on February 1, 1903, at Feldkirch-Altenstadt in the Tyrol, Father Franz Reinisch joined the Pallotine order in Untermerzbach on November 3, 1928. He was condemned to death by a court-martial on July 7, 1942, for refusing to take the military oath of allegiance, and beheaded in Brandenburg-Görden on August 21, 1942. In his explanation of his refusal to take the oath, he declared, among other things:

The present government is not an authority willed by God, but a nihilistic government that has attained its power only through force, lies, and deceit. . . . The National Socialist principle, " Might before right," has forced me into a position of self-defence. Hence for me there can be no oath of allegiance to such a government.

FAREWELL LETTER TO HIS PARENTS

April 14, 1942

My dear parents: Once again, in farewell, I want to say, with all my soul, God reward you for everything you have done for me. You brought me into life, in order that I might give honour and glory unto God. You had me baptized and reared me in the Catholic faith, in order that I might mysteriously be drawn in my own person to partake of the life and suffering and glorification of Christ. Finally, I was allowed, thanks to you, to receive priestly orders as a pure and undeserved gift of grace from the hands of the one true High Priest through the intercession of the blessed Mother of God, so that I could for fourteen years celebrate the holy sacrifice of Mass and administer the sacraments for the salvation of many souls.

Thanks be to the Holy Trinity, thanks be to the beloved Mother of God. Thanks be to the angels and the saints, thanks be to all my benefactors in matters spiritual or material, whether living or dead.

Finally, I want to make mention of the great gift of grace bestowed on me in being called into the order of the Pallotines, so that above all I might work with the monastery of Schönstatt through the thrice-blessed Virgin to extend the Marian kingdom of Christ throughout the world.

May you then join with me in a glorious and joyful *Magnificat* and *Te Deum*, when you hear that my mission has ended in this world, only really to begin in the other. May sorrow and joy be reconciled in the boundless love of the Father, the Son, and the Holy Ghost.

Once again, receive the blessing of your grateful

Franz

My blessing also upon my dear brothers and sisters and their children, as well as all of my country, the Tyrol.

LAST STATEMENT

With regard to the court-martial sentence passed on Franz Reinisch, soldier, on July 7, 1942, in Bad Kissingen, the condemned prisoner requests permission to make a last statement as follows:

Since we are at this time engaged in a struggle against bolshevism for the preservation of the Christian faith and the German fatherland, and, as the President of the Senate has himself declared in the General Assembly, for the preservation of a *Christian* Europe, the subject under sentence believes it imperative to abide unflinchingly by his previous demonstration of principle.

For in our country this time of war is being used chiefly to tear from the hearts of the people, and especially from the hearts of youth, the belief in God incarnate, Jesus Christ. This seriously undermines the will to fight of the men at the front. Soldiers on leave and wounded men, all of them fathers, on coming back from Russia have said to me: " What is the point of our fighting? We fight *against* the bolshevism of foreigners and *for* bolshevism in our nation "—as instanced in the removal of crucifixes from the schools, the suppression of monasteries, and the closing of churches. The prisoner under sentence is not a revolutionary—that is to say, an enemy of the state and of the people, fighting with his fists and by use of violence; he is a Catholic priest, using the weapons of the spirit and of faith. And he knows what he is fighting for.

It would therefore seem an obvious first step to render impotent and condemn to death those who are bringing about the disintegration of the armies. But since indeed the present government does not restrain these forces in the least, but on the contrary actually favours them, the prisoner under sentence believes that in refusing to give his oath of allegiance to the present government, he is more genuinely " loyal to the German nation in its fight for survival " than he would be in taking the opposite course.

He is therefore ready and willing to sacrifice his life for Christ the King and for the German fatherland, in order that Christ the Lord may defeat the anti-Christian and bolshevist powers and principalities not only abroad but also especially at home, that our people may become once more a strong and free nation of God amidst the nations of the Occident.

Franz Reinisch

ULRICH-WILHELM, COUNT SCHWERIN VON SCHWANENFELD

LANDED PROPRIETOR

Count Schwerin was born on December 21, 1902, in Copenhagen. He was executed on September 8, 1944, because of his connection with the abortive plot against Hitler, of July 20, 1944.

The wife of a political prisoner reports:
I was standing at the heavy iron inside door of the prison, trying to talk an SS man into taking in a parcel for me. Suddenly the prison door opened, and through it strode calmly and erectly a man with his hands bound behind his back, followed by a little Gestapo man who looked to me like a reptile. The SS man whispered to me: " That is Count Schwerin—Plötzensee." I knew what Plötzensee meant, and through my mind there flashed the realisation, " This is a man who knows how to die."

FAREWELL LETTER TO HIS WIFE

Berlin-Plötzensee, September 8, 1944

My darling: Now the last hour has come.

I can give you no further counsel, I can ask you only to make the youth of our children as happy as possible under all the present restrictions. Think of your own childhood. Let the boys study a great deal and adopt professions suited to their capabilities and fitting them for advancement. That is . . . not vocations disagreeable to them, to which they would not be adequate. . . .

I go to my death unbowed, with the firm conviction that I have wanted nothing for myself, and everything for our fatherland. This must remain for ever a certainty to you, and something you must tell our sons over and over. You know that my actions were at all times directed to the welfare of Germany, in the family tradition of an ardent patriotism outweighing all else. New times may bring changes in custom and outlook as regards particulars, but the love of one's country will always remain that prime constituent of life which governs everything else. Bring up our sons to be Christian noblemen, with neither narrowness nor slackness in their convictions. And finally, from my overflowing heart, thanks to you for your love that made my life beautiful. Be brave, and preserve your love for me to the end of your life.

I must stop. Greet all those whom I love and who loved me and cherished me.

I embrace you and the boys in thought, with eternal gratitude to you.

Your Ulrich-Wilhelm

FROM HIS WILL

Further, it is my desire that in that part of the gravel bed in my forest of Sartowitz where the victims of the massacres of the late autumn of 1939 are laid to rest, a very high oaken cross be erected as soon as the conditions of the time permit, with the following inscription:

Here lie from 1,400 to 1,500 Christians and Jews
May God have mercy on their souls and on their murderers

CAESAR VON HOFACKER

LIEUTENANT COLONEL

Dr. Caesar von Hofacker, born in 1896, belonged to the staff of
the German High Command in Paris, and there became the actual
head of the resistance movement in the West. Failure of all
attempts to elicit from him, after his arrest, information about the
conspiracy to assassinate Hitler on July 20, 1944, was followed by
his execution on December 22, 1944.

FROM A LETTER WRITTEN AT THE TIME OF THE
CONFIRMATION OF HIS TWO ELDEST CHILDREN
(APRIL 2, 1944)

My dear confirmands: Why is it that just at this time we
have reason to confess our Christian faith with special
fervour?

Because we feel more than ever that every one of us is in
the hands of God, that He guides individuals and nations,
and that therefore we must be devoutly humble. Because
we feel that human beings need to feel humility and awe in
the face of something higher, purer, and greater than themselves, if they are not to fall prey to pride, to megalomania,
and to crime.

Because we feel that there are certain eternal laws of
goodness, of magnanimity, and of justice that cannot be
transgressed with impunity and that men obey only when
they believe not merely in the possible existence of such laws,
but in the existence of a God who wills the good and
opposes evil.

Because we feel that God, in the unique and great person
of Jesus Christ, our Saviour, has made a gift to mankind,
has granted us a revelation for which we can never be
thankful enough. Through Jesus' words, through his life
and work and suffering, God has revealed to us those great
eternal precepts and principles to which we on earth must

adhere, according to which we must live and strive if we want to become better, purer, and happier.

The teaching of Christ is the greatest and most profound testament that God has given us human beings up to this time. For nearly two thousand years it has determined the development of mankind, especially in Europe, and again and again it has prompted and spurred on the best and noblest among men to try to lift humanity to a higher plane of morality. In times when the teachings of Christ have been falsified by small minds or misused for earthly purposes, there have always been men—such as Martin Luther, for example—who arose to free it from dross and to reduce it to its pure essence.

And there have always been serious setbacks and catastrophes when men thought they could get along without religion—that is to say, without an inner tie to God, without respect for a higher power.

The fact is that in all history up to this time there has appeared no spiritual force that has been able, as Christianity has, to bring man to a realisation of his own limits, to make him desire the good and resist evil.

And should we deny our reverence to such a faith, which has brought about so much good, to which all our ancestors have clung, and which cannot be offset by anything of equal worth? Rather, should we not adhere to it with conviction and joy—especially in these days, when it is so crucially necessary to bring inward stability, confidence, and calm strength once more to millions of despairing people?

It is possible to be a good Christian and still a good German. The two do not contradict each other, but on the contrary complement and enhance each other. We Germans shall win all the greater respect from other nations if our actions do not run counter to those Christian laws which they too revere.

To confess the Christian faith, to be a good and strong Christian, to make of the great eternal teachings and admonitions of the Saviour, as set forth in the New Testament, the guide of one's own actions—this is not at variance with the duties that you, Eberhard, will some day have to fulfil as a German man and combatant, or that you, Annele, will have to meet as a German woman and mother. Rather in these times more than ever before, it provides everything that is needed for a personal example in leading our poor German nation, bleeding from a thousand wounds, back to the right road.

This day is for you a new foundation for your whole life to come. May you, like the long line of your forebears, profess your commitment to it always with courage and pride.

I embrace you with love and trust.

Your father

THE MUNICH STUDENT GROUP

" There is nothing more unworthy of a civilised nation than to allow itself to be ruled by a clique of irresponsible overlords dominated by sinister passions, and to offer no resistance." This sentence occurred in the *Pamphlet of the White Rose,* one of a number of leaflets disseminated in Germany in 1942. In bold language these anonymous pamphlets called upon the German people to shake off the yoke of a criminal dictatorship and to agitate for peace. This was at the time when the catastrophe of Stalingrad had shaken the confidence of even the blindest of Hitler's followers. Those responsible for the framing of the texts, the printing, and the circulation were a group of students at the University of Munich, guided and assisted by Dr. Kurt Huber, a professor of philosophy. The chief members of the group were Christoph Probst (born 1919), Alexander Schmorell (born 1917), Hans and Sophie Scholl (born 1919 and 1921), and Wilhelm Graf (born 1918). After Hans and Sophie Scholl were caught on February 18, 1943, while dropping their leaflets from a gallery into the main lobby of the university, the group was speedily annihilated. There was a hasty trial, at which the redoubtable Freisler presided, on February 21: Christoph Probst and Hans and Sophie Scholl were executed on February 22, Professor Huber on July 13, Alexander Schmorell on August 13, and Wilhelm Graf on October 12.

CHRISTOPH PROBST

Munich, February 22, 1943

My dearest Mummy: Don't be frightened by what you may have heard since my Sunday leave was cancelled because of " service requirements," or by what you will learn from me now. On Saturday, instead of handing me my pass, they put me under guard and took me to Munich. Through an unlikely sort of mishap, I have got into a difficult situation. But I am not glossing over anything when I tell you that I am in good health and quite serene. They treat us well, and prison life seems bearable enough, so that I am not at all afraid of a long term of imprisonment.

The only thing that depresses me is that you are all suffering more because of my situation than I am, and worrying a great deal too much. Hard as the external separation from my dear little wife and the darling children is, I feel myself inwardly more closely bound to them than ever. This inner bond is a source of great strength to me, and your love is also much more precious to me now than before. I am unspeakably sorry that I must give anxiety to you, my dear ones. What other thoughts and feelings most profoundly occupy me, I'll tell you later some time. Above all else, I cannot stop thinking of my darling little ones and of my fatherhood. Fate has played such a large role in this whole matter that I must entreat you most earnestly not to reproach me with lack of responsibility. You know that I should like best to live only for you all, my mother and sister, my wife and children, I am infinitely grateful to you for all the kindnesses you do for me. I am doubly thankful when I know that you are just as calm as I am, that you are not consuming yourself in sorrow, that you never lose faith and hope in the face of difficulties.

For you are my one and only, my best, my dearly beloved little mother; it would be hard for me if I were to know that I had brought bitterness into your life. Our fate is *sent* to us human beings, and there is nothing we can do except to bear it without rebelling against it. Mother, my feelings are so loving, thankful, and strong that no words can express them. Never before have I felt so powerfully the indestructibility of love. To-day I know less than ever what the future will bring; but I am also less than ever seeking to know. I have no fear for myself. I am concerned only for you, for my wife and little children. I hope that I shall always be able to help them when there is need. But if this should become impossible for a time, I must not despair, and I hope that with your love and protection they will fare as well as if I were with them. Even if something were to happen to me, I should be glad that these innocent little beings are alive, for I cannot imagine that things should ever go ill with them. How everything is going to turn out, I do not yet know. I know only that nothing is so difficult that it cannot be borne.

I do not feel at all separated from you; I feel you always close to me, and I am so glad that I have such a peerless dear mother. I embrace you and remain for ever and ever

Your son,

Christel

Munich, February 22, 1943

My dearest darling sister: On Saturday, as I was going to pick up my pass to go to Tegernsee, I was arrested and taken to Munich. Now for the first time in my life I'm sitting in a cell and do not know what the morrow will bring. But being in prison isn't as bad as I thought, and I'm glad that I haven't lost my peace of mind; in fact, I'm often in very good spirits. Don't worry, my dear, and have no anxiety about me. These days are difficult, but those that preceded were no less so. You know how hard the separation from wife and children is for me. But my faith and hope are strong, and they help me. I feel as if I were especially close to you, to all who are dear to me, and I know that the bonds of love are indestructible. I know that there is nothing for me to do now but to shoulder whatever may come and to bear it. And don't think that I'm not capable of bearing it or that fear is robbing me of sleep. My strength grows with the burden. What I cannot bear is that I am necessarily causing you anxiety. That is why I beg you from the depths of my heart not to worry. Even here there are some nice people, and the secret police don't treat us too badly. . . .

My little sister, you dear half of my life and being, don't be distressed—it isn't worth while. Don't be sad or despairing. One does not fashion one's own fate, and can do nothing but bear it.

I see your warm brown eyes (which had better not be wet with tears), I see your lovely face, from which so much love always shines out to me, I hear your voice, saying so many dear things to me. And when I see your whole image before me, I feel much more than words can tell, and then my heart turns over. I am yours, you are mine!

Your Christel

Probst wrote the preceding letters on the day of the hearing before the People's Court; on the afternoon of the same day he was beheaded. His mother and sister were permitted to read his fare-well letters in the presence of a Gestapo official, but the letters were not handed over to them. The following are some lines set down from memory shortly afterwards.

TO HIS MOTHER

I thank you for having given me life. When I really think it through, it has all been a single road to God. Do not grieve that I must now skip the last part of it. Soon I shall be closer to you than before. In the meantime I'll prepare a glorious reception for you all.

TO HIS SISTER

I never knew that dying is so easy. . . . I die without any feeling of hatred. . . . Never forget that life is nothing but a growing in love and a preparation·for eternity.

ALEXANDER SCHMORELL

Munich, May 1, 1943

Dear parents: There is of course not much that is new to write you about; here one day is much like another and time passes very rapidly. Dear father, dear mother, if I have to die now, you must know that I am not at all afraid of death—regarding that you need have no concern. After all, I know that a better life awaits us and will bring us all together again. The thing that is hard for me is to have to leave all of you whom I have loved so much and who have loved me so much. How much I have loved you I realise only now at the parting, when I must lose all of you. Try to overcome the pain of losing me, do not forget that there is a fate, that this fate did not allot a longer life to me, and that therefore this had to come about as it did. And nothing happens contrary to the will of God.

My greeting to everyone, my most heartfelt greeting to all. I embrace you and kiss all of you many times over.

Your Schurik

Munich, May 30, 1943

My dear parents: There is nothing new here to report to you. Everything is as it was. But there are a few things that I still want to tell you, in order to ease your sorrow somewhat. In case my plea for mercy is rejected, remember that

" death " does not mean the end of all life, but actually, on the contrary, a birth, a passing over into a new life, a glorious and everlasting life. Hence death is not a fearful thing. It is the separation that is hard, and heavy to bear. But it becomes less hard and less heavy to bear when we remain mindful that we are indeed not parting for ever, but *only for a time*—as for a journey—in order afterwards to meet again *for ever and always* in a life that is infinitely more beautiful than the present one, and that then *there will be no end* of our being together. Remember all this and your burden will surely become lighter. I embrace and kiss you.

Your Schurik

Munich, June 18, 1943

My dear parents: I can tell you nothing new about myself. I am healthy and in good spirits. Recently I read in a very good and significant book a passage that applies very well to you: " The greater the tragic element in life, the greater our faith must be; the more we seem forsaken by God, the more confidently must we give our souls into the Father's hands." And the holy abbot Theodore of Byzantium wrote: " And therefore I have given thanks to God for misfortune and bowed to the unfathomable decrees of his providence, which from the founding of the world has purposefully foreseen the time and place of each man's death." That is just about what I have already written you. It would make me very happy if you thought likewise: it would take so much sadness and sorrow from you. But I haven't died yet—so pray and don't lose hope.

Heartiest greetings to all from

Your Schurik

A LETTER TO HIS SISTER

Munich, July 2, 1943

My dear, dear Natasha: You have surely read the letters

I have written to our parents, so that you are fairly well
posted. You will perhaps be surprised when I tell you that
I am day by day becoming calmer inwardly, even joyous
and glad, and that my mood is nearly always better than
it used to be when I was free. How does this happen? I'll
tell you at once. This whole terrible " misfortune " has
been necessary, to show me the right way—and therefore
it has actually not been a misfortune at all. Above all, I am
glad, and grateful to God for it, that it has been granted to
me to understand this sign from him, and thereby to find
the right way. For what did I know before this of faith,
of true deep faith, of truth, of the ultimate and only truth
of God? Very little! But now I have progressed so far that
I am happy and calm and confident even in my present
situation—come what may, I hope that you have experienced a similar development and that you too, after the
deep sorrow of separation, have reached the point of
thanking God *for everything*. This misfortune was necessary;
it opened my eyes—not only my eyes but the eyes of all
those to whom it has befallen, our family included.

I hope that all of you have likewise understood correctly
this sign from God. My sincerest greetings to all, but
greetings especially to you from

                                    Your Schurik

                                    Munich, July 13, 1943

My dear Mother and Father: It was indeed not to be
otherwise, and by the will of God I am to conclude my
earthly life to-day, in order to enter upon a new life that
will never end, and in which we shall all meet again. May
this reunion be your comfort and your hope. Unfortunately,
this blow is harder to bear for you than for me, for I leave
this life with the knowledge that I have served my deepest
conviction and the truth. All this permits me to face the
approaching hour of death with a *calm conscience*. Think of
the millions of young men who are giving up their lives
on the battlefield—their fate is also mine. In a few hours

I shall be in the better world, with my mother;* I shall
not forget you, and shall intercede with God for your
comfort and peace. And I shall wait for you. One thing
above all I urge upon you: do not forget God!!!

Your Schurik

CATO BONTJES VAN BEEK

Cato Bontjes van Beek was born on November 14, 1920, in
Bremen. She was arrested on September 20, 1942, condemned
to death on January 21, 1943, and executed at Plötzensee on
August 5, 1943.

Brought up amid heath and moor in Fischerhude, near Bremen,
Cato van Beek was gifted with the sensibility of a child and of an
artist, and inspired by a great, selfless love for suffering humanity.
Because of her aversion to the current régime, she allowed herself
to be drawn into a group of political activists. But their ambitious
scheming repelled her. " I am not a political being," she said.
" There is only one thing I want to be, and that is a *human being*."

After only two months she left the group—but it was too late.

TO HER MOTHER

My dear, very dearest Mama: I still cannot grasp the fact
that this must be a letter of farewell—farewell to you and
to all of you whom I hold dear, farewell to life.

My dear, dear Mama, how am I going to tell you that I
am calmer than I have ever been before? I feel nothing
but love for you and for all the rest of mankind. I am
completely free of ill will or anything like hatred—it is as
if all things had taken on a kindly aspect. For I am always
with you and in you. In spite of the disaster these three days
have brought down on us, they have been marvellously
beautiful days. Now I know that man is good; I know it
with complete certainty, and that makes dying much easier
for me.

* His father remarried after the death of his first wife, Alexander
Schmorell's mother (translator's note).

In the night between the eighteenth and nineteenth of January I wrote an appeal for clemency. I have so great a love for mankind and for life, and for me the most wonderful thing is to be always able to help others: this is what I wrote, and also what I said, in my last words before the court. I shall think of you and be with you to the very end; nevertheless I shall also to the very last put my faith in a miracle—a miracle that will give me back to life. Give a greeting from me to everything that I loved. At the present moment I am not conscious of any great guilt, and the great question within me is why all this must be. Even here in prison all persons have been full of kindness towards me.

"Try to reconcile yourself to it"—that is what Heinz wrote and said to me at the last. Believe me, my dearest Mama. I can do it—truly I can. Only it is all so incomprehensible to me. Yet I harbour no ill will; rather, I go on loving mankind to the very end—all men, all.

My dearest Mama, I have inflicted such great sorrow upon you. Oh, if only all of those who are in the same situation as I could feel as I feel! That is my wish for them.

Good-bye, my dear, dear Mama, and give my greeting to everyone and everything.

Always,
Your Dodo

February 9, 1943

My dear, dear Mama:* I want quickly to send you a greeting. Will it reach you? It would be wonderful.

I do not know whether you have heard what my sentence is. It is the severest verdict possible—I have been condemned to death!

If you could see me, you would not suppose that I am a person condemned to death. I think about it so rarely; all my thoughts are altogether in the future, and I believe quite, quite firmly that none of this will take place.

I wait and wait, and am otherwise of good cheer. Nobody

* From a smuggled letter found in a laundry bundle.

could tell by looking at me that I had received such a severe sentence. My dearest Mama, you yourself and all of you together must hope with me—surely it will not happen. In the first few days after the verdict I was in a most extraordinary mood. I was completely ready to die—for what, I really did not know—but death in itself did not seem horrible to me and does not now. There is no death—that I am absolutely sure of. I shall be with you, in you, and about you, even if my hope should be in vain and I should have to die. I can reflect on this quite clearly. The most terrible thing is the thought of your sorrow. For me everything actually still has a benign aspect, and inwardly I am totally free of hatred or ill will towards anyone. I feel a great lightness within me, and it lifts all weight from me.

I embrace all of you and kiss you many times, I am still alive; surely it won't happen. It is so incomprehensible.

Always your loving

Dodo

TO HELMUT NIEWERTH, IMMEDIATELY AFTER THE VERDICT

Dear Helmut: It is already quite dark outside and I am writing by candlelight. I can write you neither a sad nor a gay letter. Everything has taken on a benign aspect to me, and my wish for all those who are to meet the same fate as I, is that they may be serene.

I do not want to lament because now it's all over with me. But it is not very easy—" Try to reconcile yourself to it." I do not die as a fighter, but perhaps there is a purpose in my death. There is so much in man that is immortal, and this is a marvellous thing.

Oh, if only all men would love one another as I love them all. And so I shall die without the slightest ill will or any hatred. The only thing that affects me is my inability to understand why it must all really be so.

Dear Helmut, you must live on. Enjoy life, which is so

lovely, and do not be too sad on my account. I think often of Chang-Tse and of one of his songs:

> *Into the infinite*
> *rise the joyous clouds.*
> *Hardly does man sense*
> *what is meant by boundlessness.*
> *Good and evil are requited,*
> *be it soon or be it late.*
> *Wherefore do earth's children strive*
> *perversely after goods and power?*
> *Everything is foreordained.*
> *Not until the end do they perceive*
> *the great delusion.*

Dear Helmut, you have always been so good. Can it be that the thought that I must die has not yet penetrated to my inmost being? I do not know—I am indeed still hoping for a miracle.

Farewell, my dear Helmut. Who knows——

> Most affectionately,
> Your Cato

Berlin, Alexanderplatz, March 2, 1943

My dearest Mama: It is now six weeks since the verdict, and I am still alive. Had they taken me away at the beginning, I should have gone willingly, but now the great will to live has welled up powerfully again within me, and I can almost no longer picture to myself that to-morrow, the day after, or in a few weeks perhaps everything will be over. Now my thoughts are so very much concerned with things of this earth. We follow world events with excitement, and everything seems animated by a great hope. Perhaps we shall all be lucky, as a result of petitions for clemency or by reason of other factors.

The only sad thing is that I have not the slightest idea what I am to die for. Ten or even only five years in the penitentiary would have been senseless in relation to the deed. But through this extreme penalty the thing somehow becomes transfigured, and I take this as my consolation.

If only this letter reaches you some day! I should be so, so grateful to the intermediary. I go on believing and hoping to the last, and I sense your love and the love of all those whom I love, and that gives me much strength.

I embrace and kiss you.

Your Dodo

Kantstrasse 79, Berlin-Charlottenburg, April 26, 1943

My most dearly beloved Mama: I was just sitting down to write to you when two letters were brought in to me. My joy is so exceedingly great, for you write of all the things that move me so much just at this time. No doubt you know and feel that in my thoughts I am with you, Tim, and Meme in Fischerhude, and that we are celebrating Easter together. Can you picture to yourself that I am filled these days with a marvellous inner joy that permits me to forget everything around me, everything that has been, everything that I hope will never be again? Beside me on the table are the pictures of you and of our house, and in the salt cellar the little flower, your precious Easter greeting. At night I place the salt cellar in front of the barred window, so that the little flower may surely go on blooming for a long time.

I feel all of you so close to me, and I am happy and joyful with all of you together. Why? Because you exist, and because I know that you are all there. Last night I went to bed very early and read in the Gospel of John, and read it to my cell mate. We were both overwhelmed by the tremendous power that radiates from those words.

Continue to be brave, my dearest Mama, and to believe in our return. That will help Tim in Russia and me here.

I embrace you.

With deepest love,
Your Dodo

Plötzensee, August 5, 1943

My dear, dear Mama: I had hoped that this would be a birthday letter, but now it will be the last letter I shall ever write you. My Mama, the time has come, and I shall be among the living for only a few more hours. That I cannot tell you this in person, that you are not with me, Mama, that is hard. But I am quite collected and have completely reconciled myself to my fate. I have really found the peace I hoped I would have in these last hours; it gives me much strength to let my thoughts dwell with you, with Tim in Russia, and with Meme and with all those I love. In our last conversation I told you that I take it as a gift of grace that in my dreams each night I am with you in Fischerhude. If only I could give this peace to you. My heart is so over-full in the effort to thank you, and I shall leave behind me the love I bear all of you.

My beloved Mama, I hope so much that you will overcome the sorrow that I am inflicting upon you by my death, and that through this pain you will become even greater in your art. There is so much that I still want to tell you, but now there comes to me, as so often before, the realisation that all of it is already said. For we are so close to each other—you know and sense everything that I am thinking. It is a pity that I leave behind on this earth nothing but the memory of me. It is all much simpler than one thinks, and I know that I owe my strength to you and I am so grateful to you, and I should like to make return for everything to you a thousandfold. Keep my love, my dear, good Mama. Paint beautiful pictures; may much joy come to you through Meme and Tim. Recently in church I heard a little Bach composition on the organ, and you know what that meant to me. Meme and Tim will still be a great joy to you.

Give my greetings to all good people—people are all sweet and good, I know and think of that.

Actually I do not have to write you as much as this, for

I feel you so vividly present, and you know always everything that has been said.

I am always with you, my dearest Mama.

Your Dodo

FROM FAREWELL LETTERS TO HER BROTHER
AND SISTER

August 5, 1943

My beloved Meme: It is my greatest wish that you will always remain with Mama and never leave her. You must be a strong support for her now. . . . Do you know, you ought to read the four Gospels through systematically. You have no idea how much strength one gains through such a systematic reading. Do not mourn much that I shall no longer be on this earth with you, but only living on in you. You must leave aside in life everything that does not carry you forward spiritually. There is so much that is useless; unfortunately one comes to know this a bit too late. You will believe me, won't you, when I tell you that I am calm and collected? I know that it would be the same way with you, and that we all have the same ideas about death. There is no spatial separation, and what is time? Some day we shall all be together again.

In my thoughts I embrace you and am always with you.

With deepest love,
Your sister, Dodo

August 5, 1943

My dearest, my good Tim: I really don't have to keep telling you how dear you are to me and how much my thoughts have always been with you. It was so wonderful to be able to see you once more. How tall you have grown and how strong! Perhaps I can help you too, in seeing that you are protected and that you return to Mama and Meme in Fischerhude. Then continue to live in your music: I

know perfectly well that some day you will accomplish a
great deal. A while ago I sang the theme of the Fifth
Brandenburg Concerto to myself, and I still remember all
your many Bach pieces.

My good Tim, I am not at all sad and love you all so
very much, and may God always protect you.

Much, much love

Your sister, Dodo

JAROSLAV ONDROUSEK

Jaroslav Ondrousek was a student from Ricany near Brünn. He
was born on June 23, 1923. He had been engaged in illegal
activities since 1939. Betrayed by an informer, he was arrested
in 1941 and held prisoner in the Kounic Student House, which,
during the German occupation of Czechoslovakia, was used as a
Gestapo prison. He was executed in Breslau on May 23, 1943.
After the sentence was passed, he wrote a last letter to his parents.

Breslau, May 10, 1943

Beloved ones: In a little while now I shall be with you,
together with you, my precious ones. My life is coming to
an end, and my soul feels so light. So beautiful. I am
almost happy at being allowed to die in such a beautiful
mood. I have forgiven everyone, and I pray that everyone
whom I have hurt in any way will forgive me too. Mother,
on your name day I thought of you, kissed you, and wished
you a happy life. Be happy, my dear.

Father, do you know, it is beautiful to die hoping for a
better future for mankind. Marushka, I wish you a long
and happy life. Be a good member of the community
of man, obey our parents, and love them as I have loved
them.

My beautiful fatherland, how dear you are to me, sweet
homeland! To-day I die: it is May, there are four of us
here in the room, we are waiting to say farewell. I shall be

with you, in your midst; I shall be sitting with you on the garden bench, and my spirit will always be with you. I shall waken you in the morning with laughter, and I shall greet you with the evening star. May love reign on earth, not hate.

I thank you for all the good you have bestowed on me. Father, mother, little sister, my heart burns with love for you, in unending hope and happiness. I send you the most beautiful remembrance and take leave of you.

I send you my greetings and kiss you. I rejoice that I shall soon be with you. Ask for my ashes.

MARIE KUDERIKOVA

Marie Kuderikova, born on March 24, 1921, at Vnorovy in Moravia, went to work, after leaving secondary school, in a factory at Brünn. She was active in an illegal organisation, was betrayed in December, 1941, arrested, and executed in Breslau on March 28, 1943.

Breslau, March 26, 1943

My dear parents, my beloved little mother and little father, my only sister, and my little brother. Dearest grandmother and aunt, my friends, dear and cherished acquaintances. My family. All of you who are precious to me in what is dearest to my heart. I take leave of you, I send you greetings, I love you. Do not weep; I am not weeping. I depart without lamentation, without trembling, without pain, and even now, yes, even now, I am attaining to that which should indeed be the goal, not the means—to parting from you and at the same time to full nearness to you and complete union with you. I can convey so little of my love, nothing but the most earnest assurance of its depth and sincerity. My sincerest thanks.

To-day, the twenty-sixth of March, 1943, at half-past six in the evening, two days after having reached the twenty-second year of my life, I shall draw my last breath. And yet, up to the last moment—to live and to hope. I have always had the courage to live—moreover, I am not losing it in face of what in human speech is called death. I should like to take upon myself all your sorrow and all your pain. I feel in myself the strength to bear it for you too, and the desire to take it with me. Please, please have that strength too, do not suffer, do not weep. I love you, I cherish you so very much. Whenever I have read your words, I have grown wings. You have done everything that is within the power of human love. Do not reproach yourselves in any way. I know everything, I feel everything, I read everything that is in your hearts.

To-day is a beautiful day. You are somewhere in the fields or in the little garden. Do you feel as I do that fragrance, that loveliness? It is as though I had had an intimation of it to-day. I was out walking, I was in the open air, which was full of the essence of spring, of warmth, the shimmer and scent of memories. The naked nerve of the soul was stirred by the poetry of the commonplace, the smell of boiled potatoes, smoke and the clatter of spoons, birds, sky, being alive—the everyday pulse beat of life. Love it, love one another, learn love, defend love, spread love. So that you may perceive the beauty of the obvious gifts of life as I do—that is my wish for myself. So that you may be able to give and to receive.

The afternoon to-day is beautiful too; I feel so much warmth and love, so much faith, so much resolution, that I spread out my arms and stretch out my hands, that you may feel it too, that you may receive it. I am not afraid of what is coming. Always, even when I have failed and hurt others, I have felt an urge to the good, the sublime, the human. My whole life has been beautiful. Ardent, believing, fighting, winning. And you have been the blessing of my life. You, my little mother, my little lamb, my father, my sister and Jozinek, my little grandmother, auntie. All of you whom I have loved and who have held me dear. Beloved people, dear life, and dear world. I kneel before you, you most precious beings in my life, and ask for love and forgiveness. I ask forgiveness for everything and of everyone whom I have ever injured. On the road towards the ideal of humanity I have often gone astray—but faith remained in my heart, and longing in my eyes. I kiss your hands and thank you with all my heart, with all my soul, in this, the most solemn hour of my life. I shall not becloud it with tears—no, I shall bedew it with a smile of love, of thanks, of reconciliation, and ask for a smile in return. I place a kiss upon your lips—yours, little mother and little father, yours, beloved little girl and boy, yours, little grandmother and auntie. Be happy, love one another. My greetings to you, I greet you all and, deeply and sincerely, I wish all of you human happiness. " Thanks be to you, and love to you—oh, that they might resound like bells."

Your loving daughter,
Marie Kuderikova

PETER HABERNOLL

Peter Habernoll, born in 1924, was recruited for military service at the age of seventeen. Arrested on March 27, 1944, on the basis of a denunciation by a comrade with whom he had talked in December, 1943, he was condemned to death on July 14, 1944, and executed by a firing squad on September 20, 1944.

Litzmannstadt Prison, May 12, 1944

Dear little Mama: Thanks for your half-sad, half-cheerful spring letter. And I want to answer it right away, even if only briefly. Things don't move as fast as little mamas like you think they should. But that is not instantly a reason for worrying and being unhappy. Not to mention the fact that I don't always feel like writing. Not that I am always terribly sad; nevertheless, I am dependent on what is called " mood " and on the general atmosphere in a building like this one and in such a cell as this. Sometimes these flat grey walls stare at me so idiotically that I can't find anything to say any more.

I have received the books and reproductions. I really cannot very readily express my joy. And I almost think that in this long silence, one becomes too unaccustomed to the use of words. At the moment I am communing with Schiller. Of late the atmosphere happens to be propitious for reading, and one must of course take advantage of such a time. Moreover, the daily event of a one-hour " leisure period "—with May in the air, spring sunshine, and a sky speckled with small white summer clouds—together with the smell of young green trees, has recently quite distracted me. Despite all the patience I have gained, a little throbbing of the heart could not be completely suppressed. A little touch of spring like this always goes to the very marrow of my bones. Well, now you have a bit of news from me and know that I am still alive and well. Most heartfelt greetings to all of you!

Berlin-Tegel Prison, June 6, 1944

Dear little Mama: Forgive my long silence—this time it wasn't my fault. And even now only a " concise, easily readable " letter as a sign of life from me. And it will have to do for four weeks. Yes, we'll just have to put up with that now. I have been here ever since the twenty-seventh of May—after a trip that, thanks to intelligent company, afforded me a refreshing change—and am beginning to get used to the conditions here, which are very different from those at Litzmannstadt.

Unfortunately you won't any longer have to provide for my spiritual well-being with books, etc. About food too it isn't at all here as it was at Litzmannstadt. Please, please remember that. I can't waste more words on this subject. You don't have to worry about me, no matter what happens. Franz Marc's line about the " spirit . . . that cannot die . . , under any torture," transcends everything and remains alive within me. So things really can't become too bad for me. In this spirit——

As for a visit here, I wouldn't advise it unreservedly. The place doesn't offer a very pleasing impression to anxiety-ridden mamas. But I leave that wholly to you. May all go well with you, as well as possible; and be brave as possible, no matter what may come. I shall do the same.

Berlin-Tegel Prison, July 7, 1944

Little Mama! Like the old fisherman of Hiddensee, I should like to cry out, " Yes, yes—life's not easy, but one stands it." Being condemned to spiritual inactivity isn't fun. I could use a good history of art or literature—then I'd feel better. Adolf Hitler wrote his *Kampf* as a prisoner in the fortress at Landsberg. I should like to do the same— but a struggle for what? Against what? Not to know this, simply to have no excuse for one's suffering, makes the matter something of a torment.

Yet there are always some little gleams of sunshine, like your letter of the twenty-seventh, which I had of course not yet received when you visited me here, with the two Gauguin reproductions and the extraordinarily, wonderfully beautiful passage from Nietzsche about " the man who wills his fate." In association with that many things come into my mind that I should now have to tell you about in a long letter. In a " concise " one of this sort it's impossible to express these things. Therefore I can only advise you, if you ever find a quiet hour, to read " The Grand Inquisitor," a chapter in *The Brothers Karamazov*. It would have to be a very quiet hour. And when you feel a longing to speak with me a bit and to invoke my spirit, then above all play the slow movement from the Italian Concerto of Bach. Then I'll be altogether with you. Do!

Thanks again for your visit. I hope it didn't just make you more miserable to see me in these surroundings. The fact that I am, however, not pervaded with a sense of my " guilt " will not, I hope, seem to you a sign of immaturity or superficiality. Your visit made me all the more happy in that now I have something to look forward to once more. I can count on seeing you again in a fortnight. The things you brought with you, moreover, gave me enjoyment beyond any possible description and altogether beyond your imagining. Most heartfelt greetings to all of you. And for you, a great big hug.

AFTER THE VERDICT

Berlin-Spandau, August 2, 1944

You dear ones—dear little Mama! My life has not been so easy and carefree that I could be completely shattered by misfortune now. It hasn't come like a bolt of lightning from the blue, but into a life that has been full of obstacles and physical and spiritual torment for me. I haven't just gone on living without a thought or a care; rather, fate has taught me to seek my God in good time. I have found him, in so far as man can ever find and recognise him— and he is close to me and helps me.

I fear death as I fear God. I love life as only a nineteen-year-old can—but I know that death cannot be a punishment for me. It is hard not to be able to defend one's life nor fight for it any more. That is what you must do now, so far as it is at all possible.

No, I am no longer as full of hope as I was, but I am far from despair and calm. And as long as the sun goes on shining and I still see the sky above me, I want to believe in life, in my life.

External conditions have improved compared with what things were like recently in Tegel. I have the opportunity of working intensively at French with a comrade. My reading consists alternately of *Faust,* Grillparzer's master-pieces, and the Old and the New Testaments. On the side I do a little pasting of paper bags.

Do whatever is possible to alleviate my plight and to ward off the fate that menaces me. For the rest, remain strong, steadfast, and believing—I'll do the same.

I greet everyone who is on my side, and embrace my poor little Mama

Spandau, September 7, 1944

My dear little Mama! Thanks for your long, sweet, consoling letter—so full of optimism and vital courage. And I really don't know how to answer you. For the sky above me is so heavy and grey, and the sun shines all too feebly into this environment and on the experiences amid which one lives here. And yet I go on living with all the strength I still have, summoning all my will power. Prayers and pleading are not for me; the will to live expresses my trust in God. And my thoughts are with all of you, with those who share this will with me.

The sun stands very low in the sky and shines blood-red into my cell, as if it were coming from a faraway other world.

At the next visiting hour please come *by yourself*—and don't be shocked at my clean-shaven skull.

Spandau, September 20, 1944

You dear ones—my dear little Mama! The hour has struck—and I am calm as I have never before been in my life, and full of confidence. I have known it for days and weeks, even if I could not admit it to you nor to myself. The Lord is close to me and has stretched out his hand to me—and he has given me strength. He will not withhold it from my poor little Mama. You mustn't lose courage, you must live on, now more than ever. My execution by a firing squad to-day must not be kept secret from anyone.

Be comforted, as I am.

I hug and kiss my little Mama.

Peter

A LETTER TO PETER'S MOTHER AFTER HIS DEATH

Berlin-Gatow, September 25, 1944

Dear Frau Karen Habernoll: Your son Peter wanted me to write you something about his last moments. He died fully composed, brave and calm. You are not to mourn, he died willingly: this is what he said. When I said to him a few minutes before his death that life is a vale of tears and that our real life begins after death, he said that for him life had not been a vale of tears. He went to eternity about 4.50 o'clock. The verdict was read to him at 4.30. A few seconds before his death I said farewell to him and told him quietly to pray. In reply he said to me, " God is with me! " Looking towards heaven, erect and composed, he collapsed. It was as if the breath of God were about him. His wish was that you should not mourn. May he find in God the fulfilment of his young life. And may God take him up into his eternal dwelling.

Sincerely yours,

G. Jurytko, Catholic Chaplain

KIM

CABIN BOY AND SEAMAN

The press bureau of the chief of the SS and the police force in Denmark on Sunday, April 8, 1945, issued the following announcement:

Condemned to death: Seaman Kim Malthe-Bruun, born on July 8, 1923, in Saskatchewan, Canada, resident in Copenhagen, because, as a member of an illegal organisation, he annexed a revenue service boat and took it to Sweden. In addition he procured arms for his organisation and took part in transporting arms. The death sentence was carried out by a firing squad.

TWO DAYS AFTER HIS ARREST

December 21, 1944

Dear Mother: Conditions here are excellent, and my new life is far better than I expected. These are undeniably completely new surroundings and impressions, but they undoubtedly contribute to my development. . . . I sit in my cell with five others, and discussion runs high about everything under the sun. . . . You must all be perfectly calm now. It probably won't be too long before I'm home with you again.

A very merry Christmas and a happy New Year. Be of good cheer and don't let the thought of me cloud your joy. I assure you that the hardest thing for me is the thought of you.

Your Kim

(Censored)

January 13, 1945

The Gestapo is made up of very primitive men who have gained considerable skill in outwitting and intimidating feeble spirits; if you observe them a little more closely during one of their interrogations, you will see them displaying a look of violent dissatisfaction, as if they were obliged to muster all their self-control and as if it were an act of mercy on their part not to shoot you down on the spot for not telling them more. But if you look into their eyes, you see that they are enormously satisfied with anything they have succeeded in squeezing out of their victim. The victim himself realises only much later that he has allowed himself to be led by the nose.

Now listen, in case you should find yourself some day in the hands of traitors or of the Gestapo, look them—and yourself—straight in the eye. The only change that has actually taken place consists in the fact that they are now physically your masters. Otherwise they are still the same dregs of humanity that they were before you were captured. Look at them, realise how far beneath you they are, and it will dawn upon you that the utmost that these creatures can achieve is to give you a few bruises and some aching muscles. . . .

You come into a room or a corridor and you have to turn your face to the wall. Don't stand there trembling at the thought that perhaps now you must die. If you are afraid of death, then you are not old enough to take part in the fight for freedom, certainly not mature enough. If this obsession has power to frighten you, then you are the ideal subject for an interrogation. Suddenly and without cause they slap you. If you are soft enough, then just the humiliation of such a slap is such a shock that the Gestapo has the upper hand and puts such terror into you that they can have their own way with you.

Confront them calmly, showing neither hatred nor contempt, because both of these goad their over-sensitive vanity beyond endurance. Regard them as human beings and use their vanity against them.*

Western Prison [No date]

Nothing is happening to me. I sit here within four walls, behind a locked door, and nothing happens. I keep saying that I live for the day, and I do, but in the same way as the winter seed does. It lies very quiet under its blanket of warm earth; it lies and waits, perhaps it dreams. For the grain, the rich harvest, will not be reaped until after the warm summer.

It is a strange feeling of security that has descended upon me, while I sit inside these four infinitely strong walls. For here nothing can happen, everyone knows that, at least nothing surprising, and this induces a certain numbness and lethargy—a state, I imagine, much like that of the winter seed as it lies resting in preparation for the coming struggles and deeds.

* This letter was smuggled out.

January 22, 1945

During the last few days I've been thinking a good bit about the present-day Pharisees and how much the Bible has been misused, and how well I understand this. Suppose that I am reading the Bible—I am speaking now of the New Testament—and suddenly, behind a couple of lines, I see Jesus clearly and sharply; then he disappears again behind the flooding wordiness of the evangelists. Slowly their ponderous words pile up on top of me. Slaves that we all are, we are numbed by this flattening weight, and we trot along, submitting to it, with the result that it becomes part of us.

To-day I was standing on my bunk and looking out of the window, and suddenly it seemed as if all the thoughts that I had recently expressed were returning to me, just like the landscape before me. When I saw it last it was grey and monotonous; there was nothing special that would catch the eye. But to-day the whole scene lies so radiant in its snow-white covering, with a blue sky sparkling in the cold above it. Suddenly, just as in raising one's eyes, I saw my old thought in a completely new light. I understood it thus (remember that every season has its garb): the teaching of Jesus should not be something that we follow just because we have been taught to do so and permit ourselves to be influenced by this. We should live not *by the letter* of his precepts, but rather *in conformity with* them, complying with a deeply felt inspiration that should come not as an influence from without, but from the heart, from the innermost depths of the soul, as is the case with every inspiration. At this moment there comes to me, as one of the profoundest truths I have learned from Jesus, the perception that one should live solely according to the dictates of one's soul.

On March 2, after being tortured, Kim was carried back unconscious to his cell. The next day he wrote:

March 3, 1945

Since then I have been thinking about the strange thing that actually has happened to me. Immediately afterwards I experienced an indescribable feeling of relief, an exultant intoxication of victory, a joy so irrational that I was as though paralysed. It was as if the soul had liberated itself completely from the body, as if soul and body were gambolling like two detached beings, the one in a completely unfettered supernatural ecstasy, the other, severely earthbound, writhing in a passionless convulsion. Suddenly I realised how incredibly strong I am. When the soul returned once more to the body, it was as if the jubilation of the whole world had been gathered together here. But the matter ended as it does in the case of so many other opiates: when the intoxication was over, a reaction set in. I became aware that my hands were trembling, that there was a tension within me. It was as if a cell in the depths of my heart had short-circuited and were now very swiftly being discharged. I was like an addict consumed by his addiction. Yet I was calm and spiritually far stronger than I have ever been.

However, though I am unafraid, though I do not yield ground, my heart beats faster every time someone stops before my door. This must be something purely physical, even though it is indisputably a sense of perception that evokes it.

Immediately afterwards it dawned upon me that I have now a new understanding of the figure of Jesus. The time of waiting, that is the ordeal. I will warrant that the suffering endured in having a few nails driven through one's hands, in being crucified, is something purely mechanical that lifts the soul into an ecstasy comparable with nothing else. But the waiting in the garden—that hour drips red with blood.

One other strange thing. I felt absolutely no hatred. Something happened to my body; it was only the body of a boy, and it reacted as such. But my soul was occupied with something completely different. Of course it noticed the little creatures who were there with my body, but it was filled so with itself that it could not closely concern itself with them.

March 27, 1945

Since then I have often thought of Jesus. I can well understand the measureless love he felt for all men, and especially for those who took part in driving nails into his hands. From the moment when he left Gethsemane, he stood high above all passion. . . .

Jesus felt how his whole life was burning itself out of his own fiery force in a last concentration of everything that was strongest in him. Fear is something that comes from within. And if someone tries to instil fear in too great a degree into a man, he may easily succeed in driving out all fear, in projecting his victim into a state in which he stands out of reach of everything and untouchable to anything.

A LETTER OF FAREWELL TO HIS SWEETHEART

Western Prison, German Section, Cell 411

April 4, 1945

My own little sweetheart: To-day I was put on trial and condemned to death. What terrible news for a little girl only twenty years old; I obtained permission to write this farewell letter. And what shall I write now? What notes are to go into this, my swan song? The time is short, and there are so many thoughts. What is the final and most precious gift that I can make to you? What do I possess that I can give you in farewell, in order that you may live on, grow, and become an adult, in sorrow and yet with a happy smile?

We sailed upon the wild sea, we met each other in the trustful way of playing children, and we loved each other.

We still love each other and we shall continue to do so. But one day a storm tore us asunder; I struck a reef and went down, but you were washed up on another shore, and you will live on in a new world. You are not to forget me, I do not ask that: why should you forget something that is so beautiful? But you must not cling to it. You must live on as gay as ever and doubly happy, for life has given you on your path the most beautiful of all beautiful things. Tear yourself free; let this joy of joys be all for you, let it radiate as the strongest and clearest force in the world, but let it be only one of your golden remembrances; don't let it blind you and so prevent you from seeing all the glorious things that lie still before you. Don't give yourself up to melancholy. You must become mature and rich, do you hear, my own dear sweetheart?

You will live on and meet with other marvellous adventures. But promise me one thing—you owe this to me because of everything for which I have lived—promise me that the thought of me will never stand between you and life. Remember that I am in you a reason for being; and if I leave you, that means merely that this reason lives on by itself. It should be a healthy and natural thing, it should not take up too much room, and after a while, when larger and more important things take its place, it should fade into the background and become nothing more than a small element in a soil full of promise of development and happiness.

You feel a stab at the heart; that is what people call sorrow. But you see, Hanne, we all have to die, and if I have to go a bit sooner or a bit later, neither you nor I can say whether that is good or bad.

I think of Socrates. Read about him—you will find Plato telling about what I am now experiencing. I love you boundlessly, but not more now than I have always loved you. The stab I feel in my heart is nothing. That is simply the way things are, and you must understand this. Something lives and burns within me—love, inspiration, call it what you will, but it is something for which I have not yet found a name. Now I am to die, and I do not know whether I have kindled a little flame in another heart, a flame that will outlive me; nonetheless I am calm, for I have seen and I know that nature is so rich that no one takes note when a few isolated little sprouts are crushed underfoot and die. Why then should I despair, when I see all the wealth that lives on?

Lift up your head, you, my heart's most precious core, lift up your head and look about you. The sea is still blue —the sea that I have loved so much, the sea that has enveloped both of us. Live on now for the two of us. I am gone and far away, and what remains is not a memory that should turn you into a woman like N.N., but a memory that should make you into a woman who is alive and warm-hearted, mature and happy. You must not bury yourself in sorrow, for you would become arrested, sunk in a worship of me and yourself, and you would lose what I have loved most in you, your womanliness. Remember, and I swear to you that it is true, that every sorrow turns into happiness—but very few people will in retrospect admit this to themselves. They wrap themselves in their sorrow, and habit leads them to believe that it continues to be sorrow, and they go on wrapping themselves up in it. The truth is that after sorrow comes a maturation, and after maturation comes fruit.

One of these days, Hanne, you will meet a man who will become your husband. Will the thought of me disturb you then? Will you perhaps then have a faint feeling that you are being disloyal to me or to what is pure and holy to you? Lift up your head, Hanne, lift up your head once again and look into my laughing blue eyes, and you will understand that the only way in which you can be disloyal to me would be in not completely following your natural instinct. You will see this man and you will let your heart go out to him —not to numb the pain, but because you love him with all your heart. You will become very, very happy because you will have found a soil in which feelings still unknown to you will come to rich growth.

You must greet Nitte for me. I have had it much in mind
to write to her, but don't know whether I'll still have time.
I seem to feel that I can do more for you, and you are after
all the essence of all living life for me. I should like to
breathe into you all the life that is in me, so that thereby
it could perpetuate itself and as little as possible of it be lost.
That is willy-nilly what my nature demands.

Yours, but not for ever,

Kim

FAREWELL LETTER TO HIS MOTHER

Western Prison, German Section, Cell 411

April 4, 1945

Dear Mother: To-day, together with Jörgen, Nils, and
Ludwig, I was arraigned before a military tribunal. We
were condemned to death. I know that you are a courageous
woman, and that you will bear this, but, hear me, it is not
enough to bear it, you must also understand it. I am an
insignificant thing, and my person will soon be forgotten,
but the thought, the life, the inspiration that filled me will
live on. You will meet them everywhere—in the trees at
springtime, in people who cross your path, in a loving little
smile. You will encounter that something which perhaps
had value in me, you will cherish it, and you will not forget
me. And so I shall have a chance to grow, to become large
and mature. I shall be living with all of you whose hearts
I once filled. And you will all live on, knowing that I have
preceded you, and not, as perhaps you thought at first,
dropped out behind you. You know what my dearest wish
has always been, and what I hoped to become. Follow me,
my dear mother, on my path, and do not stop before the
end, but linger with some of the matters belonging to the
last space of time allotted to me, and you will find something
that may be of value both to my sweetheart and to you, my
mother.

I travelled a road that I have never regretted. I have

never evaded the dictate of my heart, and now things seem to fall into place. I am not old, I should not be dying, yet it seems so natural to me, so simple. It is only the abrupt manner of it that frightens us at first. The time is short, I cannot properly explain it, but my soul is perfectly at rest. . . .

When I come right down to it, how strange it is to be sitting here and writing this testament. Every word must stand, it can never be amended, erased, or changed. I have so many thoughts. Jörgen is sitting here before me writing his two-year-old daughter a letter for her confirmation. A document for life. He and I have lived together, and now we die together, two comrades. . . .

I see the course that things are taking in our country, and I know that grandfather will prove to have been right, but remember—and all of you must remember this—that your dream must not be to return to the time before the war, but that all of you, young and old, should create conditions that are not arbitrary but that will bring to realisation a genuinely human ideal, something that every person will see and feel to be an ideal for all of us. That is the great gift for which our country thirsts—something for which every humble peasant boy can yearn, and which he can joyously feel himself to have a part in and to be working for.

Finally, there is a girl whom I call mine. Make her realise that the stars still shine and that I have been only a mile-stone on her road. Help her on: she can still become very happy.

In haste—your eldest child and only son,
Kim

CARL FRIEDRICH GOERDELER

MAYOR OF LEIPZIG

Carl Friedrich Goerdeler, born on July 31, 1884, at Schneidemühl, Posen, was mayor of Leipzig. In the year 1937, at a time when he was absent from the city, a statue of Felix Mendelssohn-Bartholdy was removed by vandals from in front of the great concert hall of Leipzig. On finding it impossible to effect the restoration of the monument, he resigned his office. This act of protest was an index of the man, and likewise the prelude to his activity as a leading personality in the German resistance. His sense of right and decency, rooted in Christian piety and in the tradition of civic service, gave him a clear perception of the fate that had descended upon Germany with the advent of the National Socialist régime. The tragedy in the situation of this great fighter was that he was forced into the career of a conspirator, a role incompatible with his nature. It suited his temperament, abhorring deception and secrecy as he did, to go from place to place as an indefatigable preacher, stirring men's consciences, encouraging the weak, and drawing in the hesitant.

In this missionary activity as an apostle of conscience, he wore himself out and daily put his life in jeopardy. It was only with effort in face of his Christian scruples that he could bring himself to consent to the plot against Hitler's life. The failure of the attempt of July 20, 1944, meant the death sentence for him too. After unspeakable torture at the hands of his National Socialist jailers, he died on February 2, 1945, at Berlin-Plötzensee.

THOUGHTS OF ONE CONDEMNED TO DEATH

From the Cell

Is there a God who takes a part in the personal destiny of man? It becomes difficult for me to believe so, for this God has now for years permitted torrents of blood and suffering, mountains of horror and despair, to be engendered against mankind by a few hundred thousand bestialised, spiritually diseased, and deluded individuals—men in any case incapable of any normal human feelings. He has allowed millions of decent people to suffer and die.

Is this a judgment? How unjust that would be, for the majority of mankind wanted none of this degeneracy. Was it that He sought to lead mankind back to Him, because man had turned away from Him? But many had remained true to Him. How imperfect such a method of teaching would be; it is a collective method, like that of punishing a whole class because two or three pupils have offended against order. And a teacher dares to inflict such collective punishment only when he cannot identify the culprits. But God is omniscient; he knows who are the criminals and the rebellious. And does he nevertheless punish the upright? No, that cannot be. Such a God would not let matters go so far that finally the good and the pious would be made callous by an excess of suffering.

Pursuing these thoughts, I stumbled upon the fact that in none of his commandments does God make mention of the idea of nation. He binds man to God himself, to his parents, to his neighbour, to the truth, to property, but by no injunction does he bind man to his nation. Have we not erred in calling upon the aid of God for national purposes, even those of us who believe firmly and deeply in him? Is it not indeed the curse of the Jewish nation that it has regarded itself as the chosen people? Certainly it remains the unique achievement of the Jewish people that they have at all times linked their history to God, that they have believed that they were successful when they obeyed God, and have attributed all their failures to defection from God. Never except in the Old Testament has such a noble and profound concept of the destiny, mission, and vicissitudes of a people become written history. Is it not in the over-weening idea of being " exclusively chosen " that the sinful error lies? Did not Christ himself lay bare this error in that he addressed his teaching to the gentiles too, sent his disciples into all the corners of the world? He did not teach love for one's fellow countryman, but for one's neighbour. " Honour thy father and thy mother," but not the head of the nation. To the latter, render what is Cæsar's, a material sacrifice, but not a sacrifice, but not a sacrifice of the soul. God addresses himself to men and their human ties. The God revealed through Christ takes no heed of races, peoples, or nations.

Is it not possible that with our arbitrary nationalism we have affronted God and practised idolatory? Yes, in that case the things that are happening would have meaning:

God desires to root out thoroughly in all nations the propensity to harness him to their national ambitions. If this be true, we can only beg God to let it suffice, and in the place of tears and death, to give ascendancy to the apostles of reconciliation who have recognised this spirit in God and this purpose in his judgments. For this I pray to him.

FOUR WITNESSES

On November 10, 1943, four clergymen from Lübeck—three Catholic chaplains, Johannes Prassek (born in 1911 in Hamburg), Hermann Lange (born in 1912 at Leer in East Friesland), Eduard Müller (born in 1911 in Neumünster, Prussia), an Evangelical Lutheran pastor, Karl Friedrich Stellbrink (born in 1894 in Münster)—were beheaded in Hamburg. They had spoken from the pulpit of the burning of Lübeck after an air raid as a judgment of God. When JOHANNES PRASSEK learned of his death sentence, he wrote into his New Testament: "The name of the Lord be praised! To-day I have been condemned to death!"

HERMANN LANGE wrote from his prison cell at Hamburg on July 11, 1943, as follows:

Personally I am perfectly calm, facing steadfastly what is to come. When one has really achieved complete surrender to the will of God, there is a marvellous feeling of peace and a sense of absolute security. . . . For men are only tools in the hand of God. Hence, if God desires my death—his will be done. For me, it means that my life in this vale of sorrow is at an end, that I am entering upon that life of which the apostle says, "Eye hath not seen, nor ear heard, neither have entered into the heart of man, the things which God hath prepared for them that love him." For, after all, death means homecoming. The gift we thereupon receive is so unimaginably great that all human joys pale beside it, and the bitterness of death as such—however sinister it may appear to our human nature—is completely conquered by it.

FROM A FAREWELL LETTER TO HIS PARENTS

November, 10, 1943

When this letter comes to your hands, I shall no longer be among the living. The thing that has occupied our thoughts constantly for many months, never leaving them free, is now about to happen. If you ask me what state I am in, I can only answer: I am, first, in a joyous mood, and, second, filled with great anticipation. As regards the first feeling, to-day means the end of all suffering and all earthly sorrow for me—and " God will wipe away every tear from your eyes." What consolation, what marvellous strength emanates from faith in Christ, who has preceded us in death. In him, I have put my faith, and precisely to-day I have faith in him more firmly than ever, and I shall not yet be confounded. As so often before, I should like now also to refer you once again to St. Paul. Look up the following passage: I Corinthians 15:43 f., 55; Romans 14:8. In truth, look where you will—everywhere you will find jubilation over the grace that makes us children of God. What can befall a child of God? Of what, indeed, should I be afraid? On the contrary—rejoice, once more I say to you, rejoice. And as to the second feeling, this day brings the greatest hour of my life! Everything that till now I have done, struggled for, and accomplished has at bottom been directed to this one goal, whose barrier I shall penetrate to-day. " Eye hath not seen, nor ear heard, neither have entered into the heart of man, the things which God hath prepared for them that love him " (I Cor. 2:9). For me believing will become seeing, hope will become possession, and I shall for ever share in Him who is love. Should I not, then, be filled with anticipation? What is it all going to be like? The things that up to this time I have been permitted to preach about, I shall now see! There will be no more secrets nor tormenting puzzles. To-day is the great day on which I return to the home of my Father; how could I fail to be excited and full of anticipation? And then I shall see once more all those who have been near and dear to me here on earth!

From the very beginning I have put everything into the hands of God. If now he demands this end of me—good, his will be done.

Until we meet again above in the presence of the Father of Light,

Your joyful Hermann

From prison in Hamburg, EDUARD MÜLLER wrote in April 1942:

It is especially during this period of fasting, so rich in grace, that we should entreat the Lord to give us the grace to understand at least something of the mystery of the Cross, so that we too, like St. Paul, should " glory . . . in the cross of our Lord Jesus Christ." If it is too difficult for us, the people of the present time, to bear our suffering, to take upon ourselves the cross that the Lord sends us, the reason surely lies in the fact that the meaning of the Cross and of the Passion is by now lost to us. All these things have become mere theory for us: in practice we set up reservations all too quickly. Otherwise we too should glory in suffering for Christ and in taking upon ourselves with utmost willingness every repugnant task. In the past I have always been greatly stirred by the heroes of our holy Church, by their readiness for sacrifice, and by their perfect devotion to Christ. Only now do I begin to apprehend their greatness, and I am filled with awe at their unsurpassable heroism. How far removed we are from their attitude! And now our Lord and Master receives us into his rigorous school; now he gives us a slight taste of what it means to follow Christ!

> *Lord,*
> *Here are my hands.*
> *Place in them what thou wilt,*
> *Take from them what thou wilt,*

Lead me where'er thou wilt,
In everything—Thy will be done.

KARL FRIEDRICH STELLBRINK wrote from prison in Hamburg, just before he was sentenced:

"Do not be afraid, only have faith!" I greet you with II Corinthians 1:3-12 and Mark 5:36. "He for whom time is as eternity and eternity is as time, that man is freed from all suffering."

AFTER THE VERDICT. . . .

"O eternity, beautiful eternity, accustom my heart to thee; my home is not in this age of men." Truly, no one can determine the limits of his life. But thanks be to God that our lives may rest in his hands: he has said it, and on this my heart relies, happy and undaunted and unafraid. I Corinthians 15:19 and I John 2:25, 26. Somewhat later: "My times are in thy hand"; let me find only mercy before thy throne.

"In nothing has his dominion ever erred; nay, in what he does or suffers to be done, the end is good." How beautiful it must be indeed when the gates of eternity are opened.

THE STETTIN CASE

On November 13, 1944, at four o'clock in the afternoon, three men were beheaded in the penitentiary at Halle: Dr. Carl Lampert, fifty-year-old Vicar-General of the diocese of Innsbruck; Friedrich Lorenz, a forty-seven-year-old Oblate Father; and Herbert Simoleit, a thirty-six-year-old chaplain.

These three priests were natives of different parts of Germany and belonged to different ranks in the church hierarchy. For years they had performed their work as priests in Stettin,* where, in February, 1943, in the aftermath of a large-scale Gestapo drive

* Dr. Lampert had been forced out of his diocese by the Gestapo and ordered to take residence in the province of Mecklenburg.

against the clergy of Mecklenburg and Pomerania, they were arrested and, after a long period of suffering, condemned to death —" not because they were criminals," as one of the judges at the main proceedings in Torgau asserted, " but because it was their tragedy that they were Catholic priests."

FATHER LAMPERT wrote to his brother two hours before his execution:

The hour has now come—the hour so " terrible " for you and for all who love me, the hour of liberation for me. On the Way of the Cross I am approaching the last station; there has been darkness, but the " day " is dawning. " In thee, O Lord I have hoped. Alleluia! "

I can give you nothing further but my brotherly love and care, enduring beyond the grave. For love after all does not die, and now I am carrying it to the fountainhead of all love, to God, and there it will become even deeper, purer, firmer, and more potent. . . . Oh, how glad I am that all this bitter suffering is finally coming to an end—I'm on my way home, and nevertheless I remain with you.

I have just received the supreme visitation—my last Communion. So I enter upon the final sacrifice at four o'clock, with the *confiteor* of my heart's faithfulness. With the *Kyrie eleison* of a poor sinner, with the last *Gloria in excelsis* and *Credo in unum Deum*, my last *Suscipe* and *Orate fratres*, my last adoration of Christ in the Eucharist—oh, how thankful I am to him—and now this last Communion before the great final one. And so, rejoicing, I recite my *Ite, missa est—consummatum est;* and once more I bless all of you, all who are bound to my heart by ties of blood, love, vocation, and especially suffering. *Nunc dimittis servum tuum. . . . Magnificat anima mea!*

HERBERT SIMOLEIT'S

LETTER OF FAREWELL

My beloved parents, brothers, and sister: Before throwing myself into the arms of the just and merciful God, I want to embrace you all once more here on earth. Forgive me for the weight of sorrow that I must inflict upon you and please do not weep and lament for me, for I am going to the Father, to God, who made my youth so joyful. . . . For twenty-two months I have been cut off from the whole world, and at last I can say: *Laqueus contritus est et nos liberati sumus*—" The net has been rent and we are freed."

My beloved Mother! I owe everything to you, everything that has been great and beautiful in my life. Now this sorrow. I have felt you close to me all day long. . . . O Mother, how greatly blessed we have been, and how happy too, despite many tribulations. Now let us accept whatever burden our Father lays upon us, the cross of his beloved Son: " If anyone wishes to come after me, let him take up his cross and follow me." I want to try to do that now, for the most efficacious thing in the world is suffering. Farewell until we meet again there where all tears dry up, until we meet again in the presence of our heavenly Father—Mary, who stood beneath the cross of her Son, is standing at my side, helping me in my weakness. . . .

My dear ones all! I spread my hands wide over all of you and in my priestly function I send you my priestly blessing: " In the name of the Father and of the Son and of the Holy Ghost. Amen." In my blessing in this hour I include all of you, together with our holy Church and my beloved fatherland, that peace, blessing, and happiness may reign everywhere. How happy I was when I was told, " Now we are going into the house of the Lord! " Farewell until we meet again in God.

With heartfelt love for you all, your son and brother,
Herbert

MY TESTAMENT

God's will be done. He has willed that I live for no more
than forty-eight years, that I should be a priest for no more
than twenty years. I commend my soul to the mercy, goodness, and love of God. My body I leave to the earth from
which it came. Blood flowed on the cross; blood flows on
our altars in a renewal of the sacrifice on the cross. My
droplet of blood mingles with this blood for the adoration,
honour, and glorification of God, whose servant I have been,
as a thanksgiving for all the mercies and favours I have
received, especially those of birth, of holy baptism, of the
first Holy Communion, of the Holy Eucharist, and of the
sacrament of holy orders, in expiation of my sins and the
sins of the whole world, especially those sins which I did
not prevent or of which I may be guilty, and in petition for
mercy for me and for all whom I love and hold dear. I die
as a Catholic priest and as an Oblate of the Immaculate
Virgin Mary, in the name of the Father, the Son, and the
Holy Ghost. Amen. Praise be to Jesus Christ and the
Immaculate Virgin Mary. Amen.

P. Friedrich Lorenz
Halle a. d. Saale
November 13, 1944, 4:00 P.M.

LUDWIG STEIL

PASTOR

Ludwig Steil was born on October 29, 1900. He was pastor of the
Evangelical community of Holsterhausen, Wanne-Eickel, and died
on January 17, 1945, in Dachau.

Ludwig Steil came very early into conflict with National Socialism.
He made no secret of the fact that he considered it to be the
ruin of Germany. As early as December, 1933, a plan was set
on foot to disrupt an assembly of his parish with the help of Storm

Troopers brought in from elsewhere, and to assault the pastor. But his congregation protected him. As a member of the Westphalian Council of Brethren and as a collaborator with its president, Pastor D. Koch, he was especially suspect in the eyes of the Gestapo. In 1938 no fewer than five criminal procedures were instituted against him. In the summer of 1944, he lectured before audiences of hundreds in Westphalia on behalf of " persons under attack." Because of these lectures he was arrested on September 11, 1944, and taken to Dortmund.

TO HIS LITTLE DAUGHTER BRIGITTE

Dortmund i. d. Steinwache October 2, 1944

As an addition to the evening prayer:

> *Make mother strong and father free*
> *Until in Holsterhausen we*
> *Shall once again together be*
> *To offer thanks and songs to thee*

On October 5 he wrote to his wife:
At my meal just now I was gladdened by the beautiful design of a laurel leaf floating in my soup. I let it lie on the edge of the plate while I was eating, and marvelled over its tracery of veins and its perfect form. Thus does God remind us of the beauties of his kingdom even in an environment lacking in everything that is " lovely and harmonious." Not a day has passed on which I have not had reason to give thanks. Even though now I have to prepare my pallet on the floor as early as six o'clock in the evening because of the darkness, and have to lie on it for twelve hours, I find joy in the prospect of arising. But even the long hours of wakefulness between brief stretches of sleep are refreshing. " For Thy sustenance declared Thy sweetness unto Thy children " (Wisdom of Solomon 16:21).

He was kept locked in his cell even during air-raid alarms. On October 7, he described a heavy air attack:

Yesterday, Friday, from half-past eight in the evening on, we spent an hour in hell, or at least in a furnace, but the Saviour was with us. He heard our supplications. It still seems like a miracle to me. After the attack, when everything was burning around us, we were allowed to go into the cellar, where the smoke was no longer as corrosive as upstairs. That led to offering words of consolation and cheer to many a one. About midnight we were taken upstairs again. We praised God and went to bed amidst crackling flames, collapsing walls, and exploding time bombs.

October 14

To-day is the thirty-fourth day of my imprisonment, and every day I still have reason enough to give thanks for the ways of God with his children. I have peace and quiet enough. K. has been here, and I was moved by his report about the bombing of Holsterhausen, which caused so much damage on Thursday while you were here. I want to pray for all who suffered injury. I know that you will minister in my place to the people whom you visit. God grant that you be permitted to weep with the tearful, and yet, as one of the consoled, to give consolation. In face of all the misery and the great number of casualties, the words from Lamentations still hold true: " It is of the Lord's mercies that we are not consumed, because his compassions fail not." Preservation and perseverance go hand in hand. Both come from God, even if it looks as though the second were our affair. And as long as the picture of you and Brigitte remains constantly before my inner eye, I have no anxiety about your ways or my ways, for we go in the peace of God.

October 16

This difficult time, which has separated us just when we needed each other most, will—may God grant it so—bring about a time of real blessing. Then we shall be able to say with Job, but conversely: "What? Shall we receive evil at the hand of God, and shall we not receive good?" Everything comes from him. Never before has he led me to adore him and praise him as he has since the sixth of October, when that happened visibly which you expressed in the words of R. A. Schroeder—"inviolable, garbed in light." That is just how it was, and it is for me also a promise of blessings of God still to come for you and for me. Great as was my joy when you told me, on a return journey from Herne, that you understood my way—and that even before I had set out upon it—("if they ever come to get you, we shall know at all events that the church has sinned more through its silence than through its words"), I have an equally great certainty now that we three are sheltered in the hands of God.

October 17

They cannot take from us anything of that which God has given us, and this makes me very calm and happy. It would be indescribably wonderful if we could be with each other again on our wedding anniversary, and we may indeed urgently pray for that. But if it is not to be, let us in this too recognise the will of God and wait further for the day on which he will open the gates. "It will not be much longer, persevere a little while."

October 26

During the night the stanza, "When all my strength was shattered, I felt Thy helping hand," kept running through my mind. How marvellous a hymn indeed is "I Will Ever Sing Thy Praises." In the hymns we are with those whose lives are already consummated, and give praise with the heavenly hosts. But the hymns of praise that come from those who live in need and misery are certainly more beautiful than those of the angels, who never walked in the

D

" valley of the shadow " except on an errand of God. You cannot imagine what an advantage we Christians have in prison over those who have no hope. Some of them are brave, but somehow still despairingly sad.

October 31

Up to now I have been able to give thanks to God for every one of the fifty days of my incarceration. To-day is Tuesday, the Feast of the Reformation. And when I think that a week from to-day on Tuesday, God will perhaps open the gates, my heart pounds with longing for you, for my parish, for freedom. And then I begin to pray once more for serenity, for the strength to assent in case God says No again and continues to require service in prison, perhaps in the harder form of Dachau, from me and from you. But that does not detract from my prayer for the opening of the gates, nor even from my great anticipatory joy.

November 1-1

Last night I lay awake for an hour and had many questions to put to God. They were posed not in the spirit of challenge, but only out of longing for an answer. And suddenly the verses of a long-forgotten hymn sung in East Berlin rang in my ears and silenced me: " Oh that thou couldst believe, then wouldst thou wonders see, for by thy side for evermore, thy Saviour then would be."

TO HIS DAUGHTER

November 23, 1944

It is now a week since I wrote to you two, and to-day it is almost too dark to write, because the sun is not willing to come out. Nevertheless, I want to begin this letter and to thank you for your chatty letter of November 3, which gave me great pleasure. In it you tell me about the gymnastics at Aunt E.'s. You must not be downcast when, in the process of learning, something that is new to you does not go easily right away. A thing that is difficult at first gives all the more pleasure later, even writing in ink, or arithmetic. For learning is not playing. Your father is being reminded of that once more, now that he must learn anew, as a prisoner, to maintain a cheerful heart and to say to the good Lord, " Hence I wait silently, Thy word holds no deceit. Thou knowest the way for me: That doth suffice."

LETTER OF FAREWELL*

Herne, Middle of November, 1944

Dear Friend: Since it has become perfectly clear in these last days that my way will lead me to the brethren in Dachau, I want to take time to send you some indication of my thoughts and prayers for you.

When I was arrested ten weeks ago, I gave thanks to God that the motive and reason arose from my utterances, namely, the series of lectures on behalf of " persons under attack " that I had delivered some time before in Herne and Wanne. As regards that, I could joyously stand by every single incriminating word, with good conscience before God and man.

The first difficulty was that the work in my parish and in the church as a whole had to be left to its fate. But God gave me strength to lay it all at the foot of the Cross and to assent wholly to the way he was commanding me to take in the imitation of Christ. Thus I was made totally free to devote myself to the tasks of endurance and of patience— more than that, I found myself enveloped in an inexpressible peace, so secure that no external trouble could assail it. I shall never be able to forget the long night hours in which I lay awake on my pallet on the floor: time stood still, my thoughts went in mediating prayer to my parish, to my

* This letter was addressed to a friend, but intended as a communication to all the pastors of Westphalia (translator's note).

fellows in the struggle, to the battle fronts. This was the service imposed upon us prisoners before the throne of God in his inexpressible glory.

Only now does it dawn upon me *how much* easier God makes the way for those who for long years have borne the ordeal of their imprisoned brethren within their hearts as they prayed, when they themselves enter upon the same condition. All of it has been fought through beforehand, even the all too human and the inhuman. Therefore, during this wandering in the desert there is never lack of water—it springs from the rocks—nor of men suddenly rendering angelic services. " The day will bring it forth. . . ."

This report is of consequence to me only because it shows that our hymns of praise have not been silenced. And this, my dear friend, is the task that God has given to you and to all who are still permitted to serve the Gospel: " All ye who hearing join me in glad adoration." Take care of those among the brethren who are lonely, those who cannot entrust their concern for the sufferings of others to God, because they themselves do not entrust anything to God. Rally those who, in the midst of God's judgments, perceive that he desires to be merciful to our nation. As you follow the way of the Confessional Church, do not contemplate the failures of man—contemplate God's miracles. I close with a verse from Zinzendorf:

> *Hence do not say good-bye*
> *As though it were for ever.*

Give my regards to all the brethren.

> Sincerely yours,
> L. Steil

On November 14, Pastor Steil's wife inquired of the Gestapo whether there was any prospect of her husband's release. She was obliged to convey to him the reply that his way led to the concentration camp. Thereupon he wrote, on November 15:

If for a time now we are outwardly to be completely

separated, let us not forget that the shortest road by which we can meet passes before the heart of God. "God's children journey inviolable, garbed in light "—even to Dachau.

November 16

One thing in your letter was not correct. You wrote that you bring me affliction. No, you brought me an order from God. Did not Jesus say, " Let him take up his cross "? Despite disturbances, the night was restorative.

> *Do as a child and seek your Father's arms,*
> *Entreat the help his mercy e'er bestows.*
> *His spirit will, by ways now dark to you,*
> *Through well-won struggle, free you from all woes.*

How fortunate we were in possessing together our treasure of hymns. Even if I had to go on without a Bible or hymnal, I should be sufficiently provided for many a year.

December 2

I wish you an Advent for which you will still be able to give thanks in your old age, full of little stars in the night, full of helpfulness, and full of little joys. And if for a time then I should disappear physically from your side, I wish you, transcending that, a security filled with the spirit of Advent, as in Philippians, chapter 4. " And again I say, Rejoice." You must never worry about me, do you hear?

In the beginning of December, Pastor Steil was placed in a convoy headed for Dachau, along with other prisoners. On December 5 he wrote from Bochum:

It does not look as though it would still be possible for you to meet me here on Thursday morning, for we shall be moved on at once to-morrow, somewhere in the direction of Dachau. Therefore on Monday, without either of us knowing it, you restored and strengthened me with your last visit for the time being. Amid the miseries of the November bombings, God nevertheless gave us a fruitful moment, in that we could bear the suffering together, and in that together we could also discuss the problem of what the future holds for you and the child.

For the first time in my three months of imprisonment, I have to-day (for one night) had a nice solitary cell all by myself. How different it was in Dortmund, where we were three in a cell, and in Herne, where we were six—just because of the people. To-day I am enjoying the opportunity for silence; moreover, one must also prepare oneself for the none too easy mode of travelling. I place that with confidence in God's hands, for he has made of these difficult three months of initial imprisonment a time of blessing. Because God comforted you, you were able in turn to give comfort. And because you bore affliction, you were given sufficient strength.

TO HIS DAUGHTER

Leipzig, December 15, 1944
(*on the way to Dachau*)

Dear Brigitte: We are still on the long journey. . . .

You must be looking forward to Christmas as eagerly as I, for you too know the words of the angel, " For unto you is born this day a Saviour," and the song, " Oh, let us come a-running . . ."

Even though separated, we shall be celebrating Christmas together before the manger.

HIS ONLY LETTER FROM THE CONCENTRATION CAMP

Dachau, January 9, 1945

May God bless your decision to return to Holsterhausen.

At the holiday all our hapless journeyings were behind us. It was good to have Wilm and Reger coming to my aid, as soon as possible, with friendly services. But they themselves were my greatest comfort.

I am greatly consoled to know the three of us to be sheltered in God's hand. He has preserved you thus far, and you will maintain your position as long as it is inwardly possible. Greet my congregation for me. . . . Where will God's way lead us now? But HE himself stands always at the end of the road. That restores us. Write me about Brigitte too. Greetings and kisses to you and to her.

Your Ludwig

AN EXTRACT FROM THE DACHAU DIARY OF
K. A. GROSS
(*Prisoner* 16-921)

Pastor Steil of Westphalia is dead! Friend Reger told me about it at twilight this evening in the roadway of the compound. Brought in only recently, he became ill with a fever and was put into the infirmary. Reger visited him only three days ago. He was lying quiet, wrapped in his blankets, and full of an inward happiness. " I cannot communicate with the Russians," he said, " and yet I do not feel alone. My heart is completely at rest in the peace of God." These were the last words Reger heard him say. When he wanted to repeat his visit, he learned that his friend had passed away. *Lux aeterna luceat ei!*

ALFONS MARIA WACHSMANN

PRIEST

Father Wachsmann was born on January 25, 1896, in Berlin. He had been serving as a priest at Greifswald, in Pomerania, when he was arrested on June 23, 1943, at Zinnowitz, on the charge of undermining the morale of the armed forces. He was executed on February 21, 1944, in Brandenburg-Görden.

LETTERS TO HIS SISTER MARIA

Stettin Prison, August 1, 1943

In my thoughts to-morrow, on my name day, I shall be with you alone. I know that your thoughts are here, and that your best wishes are for me alone. Even if I should have no mail to-morrow, I know that we are more united than we have ever been. Affliction and sorrow join our hearts so firmly. I am so glad that you are so brave, thus helping me to bear affliction. If only I could repay all your kindness very soon. . . .

I say the prayers of Guardini's book on the rosary every day, and a part of the rosary itself. Never before have I held such a contemplation. If only the Lord will consent to be merciful to me, and to hear our ardent prayers. I must shed everything in me that has been hollow and luke-warm. I want to find my initial zeal again. Never in my life have I experienced so deeply the strength and grace and, moreover, the concentration of prayer as I have in these weeks. Nonetheless there are hours of deep depression, which have to be borne in this complete solitude.

Now, dear Maria, how are you? I know that you are much braver than I. For that you have not only my brotherly love, but also my great respect. Do not grieve, take care of your health, save all your love and kindness for the day of grace when God will reunite us.

Gollnow Penitentiary, August 15, 1943

This unending loneliness is very painful for me. I am allowed to write you only once a month. How are you, my most dearly beloved sister? I am so much with you and should like so much to help you, yet in my great distress I can do nothing for you. About my health you need have no concern. Spiritual ills are far harder to bear than physical ones. Now we must go about in convict garb. I haven't received a line from Berlin in reply to my letter. How much trouble I have shouldered for others! Nothing remains really except God and prayer. And so I fill my whole day with my breviary, my rosary, and very earnest prayers and silent thoughts about you. We must reckon with a wait of from ten to twelve weeks before there is a hearing. . . .

Now, dearest Maria, console me with your love, with your prayers, with visits and letters. Daily I realise more and more how unpractised I am in suffering and how far ahead of me you are. Don't think that I am letting myself go. But believe me—these fifty days are a hard discipline, and even so only the beginning.

Stettin, September 19, 1943

As far as health is concerned, I am fine. Spiritually I am often depressed. My day is filled out with ardent prayers of entreaty and with repeating, "Thy will be done." I alternate between hope and fear. I am completely isolated. Your communications and Sister Amata's are the only things I hear. . . . Since August, no holy Mass, no sacraments, no priest! The thing that brings me the most consolation is when your great love comes to me in your letters. How much longer? Oh, my dearest Maria, if only I could tell you how dear you are to me and how in the future, apart from my holy calling, I should like to live only for you and with you. I am so glad that the spiritual exercises have made you strong and happy. The only thing that still sustains me is prayer, especially the rosary. . . .

Stettin, October 17, 1943

Recently I have become much calmer. I have placed my fate completely and *absolutely* in the hand of God. As a matter of fact I had done this from the beginning, but it was only in the school of the Cross that I received the grace to do it not only through words of prayer but through a total commitment of my life. My whole day consists of prayer—rosaries, the Way of the Cross, the litany. And I read the Holy Writ ; Mark 11:24 is for me a source of unshakable confidence. How God will help I do not know, but I firmly believe that he will help. Read Hebrews 11:1. My motto is Romans 8:35, with II Corinthians 7:10. How often have I read all these words of Scripture, and now for the first time, in the darkness of my own life, they shine like stars. . . . If God, in his mercy, ever allows me to step before the altar again, I hope to do it as a priest coming from the Mount of Olives who has been initiated into the mystery of sin, and likewise into the mystery of salvation and grace. Only in the school of the Cross, a schooling gained through *personally* experienced suffering, and only through the exercise of ardent prayer, can one attain that knowledge of Christ which no study will unlock. By now I have come far enough to thank God sincerely and ardently for the grace of this period of suffering, although at the same time I pray that it may be shortened. From the end of July on, no more sacraments. God often gives consolation so wondrously, just when it is wholly unexpected.

Berlin-Tegel, December 1, 1943

What I have lived through during the past week can hardly be put into words. The air attacks came so close and were so heavy that during every one of the first nights I thought that I should never see you again. Since the twenty-second,

of November no window-pane in my cell has been intact.
Splinters of glass in my face, but nothing happened to me.
Thursday, moved to Tegel. In the night between Thursday
and Friday, the terrible attack on Tegel. More panes
shattered. The cells remained locked. Trusting in God, I
preserved calm in my heart and mustered all the strength of
my mind. The great anxiety that consumes me is this:
Are you alive? Did you travel home at once on Monday?

The defence counsel has still not been here to see me.
So I remain in a torment of uncertainty. But I have confidence that God, who has protected me so wondrously,
holds all of you in his hand. I pray for you hourly. During
the attack my most ardent prayers were for you. Every
evening our question is: Will they come to-night? Despite
the increased dangers I have become still calmer. . . .

Now I am reading the *Imitation of Christ* in the Latin and
Guardini's *The Lord*. I have ample opportunity to prepare
myself well for Christmas—hunger, cold, daily danger of
death. I hope confidently that God will be merciful to us.
. . . What fate may still await us? Sometimes I feel I can't
go on—and then I am forced to keep going nevertheless.
I embrace you and thank you from the bottom of my heart
for your love and loyalty; I carry you in my heart as the
only person I love.

Berlin-Tegel, December 23, 1943

I have a great anxiety about how you will spend Christmas
Eve. At Christmastime in 1897 we lost father, and it was
at Christmas two years ago that God called our beloved
mother. This year you have been deprived of your brother,
who among all people on earth has loved only you and who
now reverences you. For me the frame of the festival is
clearly defined—the walls of my prison cell. Never have
I knelt at the manger in such poverty as I do this year;
everything has been taken away—my home, my honour,
my life. So I want to kneel at the manger of Him who
had no place to lay His head, who as a friend of His people

was condemned to death, who poured out his blood like a libation, in sacrifice for the salvation of His people and of the entire world.

As gifts I bear to the manger hunger and cold, loneliness and forlornness. Shining chains are my only ornament. So I want to give my life, previously placed in the service of the King of Christmas, to him who saved me with his precious blood. With copious tears of penitence I want to wash away everything that has turned to guilt and remorse in me. It is in this spirit that I am going to make my pilgrimage to the manger. I hope through grace to celebrate Christmas deep within my heart and mind as I never have before in my life. No gift, no festive meal will distract me, no candle will gleam, no fir tree will emit its fragrance; not even a holy Mass is granted me. But the Infant Jesus in the Eucharist will, as a glorious reality of Christmas, irradiate me with eternal light and fill me with the warmth of compassionate love. I shall recite the breviary so slowly, so inwardly, that I shall taste the sweetness of every word; quietly I shall chant the *Primo tempore*. I shall say many prayers of the rosary and read in the Holy Scriptures. In this way, I hope, the peace of Christ will be my portion and his grace will be my glory. I am without any bitterness; I bear everything with the patience that only Christ gives. I hope that my prayer and the prayers of so many others will be heard; I hope that I may at some time intone the Gloria at the altar once more. I wish you the grace of Christ, so that you may with strength and love drink with me the myrrh that God's love offers us this year. Be assured that I am always with you and that I implore God hour by hour to reward you bounteously for everything that you have done and borne for me in loyalty and love. You are the only human being who never for one second has failed me. And so, rich blessings on your heart. The thorny crown of sorrow entwines our hearts inextricably.

Brandenburg-Görden, January 6, 1944

Recently there has been an alert nearly every night. Thank God, the windows here are unbroken and so it is warm. To-day I took great joy in the breviary. *Illuminare, Jerusalem!* From now on daily I shall recite as my prayer the *commendatio animae* from the breviary, at the back. . . . It shall be my daily preparation for death. And I read the New Testament a great deal, at this moment the Epistle to the Hebrews. It is marvellous. I have just read the First Epistle of John in Greek. The chaplain will come often to give me Holy Communion. So I live completely in the realm of the intellectual and the spiritual. My most faithful companion is the rosary. . . .

When I had the words, *Et iterum venturus es,* engraved on the high altar, I did not surmise that I should at some time be looking towards the door every day to see whether the Lord was coming. Just as I now day by day await the advent of Christ, so should every Christian. I keep vigil and pray that I may hear the summons of Christ: *Ecce sponsus venit.* Despite the glory of the eternal life (Apocalypse) that flames like lightning at the transparent horizon, the casting off of the old raiment, the taking leave of earth, becomes difficult. I am a human being! Hence I hope and pray that God's mercy will lead me back to the altar, if that be pleasing to the will of God. Give my greetings to all who pray for me. Tell everyone that there is only *one* misfortune, namely, sin.

Brandenburg-Görden, January 29, 1944

On the twenty-seventh of January it was fifteen years since I came to Greifswald. I celebrated the day quietly in my heart. As I did so, it became really clear to me how much I love the parish. I have explored my conscience. Certainly I have committed errors and have been guilty of omissions; nevertheless, I must be thankful for all the good that God has deigned to bring about through me. . . .

I am now studying Augustine's *City of God* and Tertullian. I live more strictly and more silently than a Carthusian. I am reading the New Testament in Greek with much joy. Yesterday John, chapter 10, concerning the good shepherd, and to-day John, chapter 11, about Lazarus—" He who believes in me, even if he die, shall live." How often have I read and meditated upon these great holy texts. And still what eternal illumination, what divine radiance flashes forth when I read them as one standing on the rim of the world and recognising in the mortuary candle the presence of Christ, the Light of the World. Now my whole day consists of prayer. Whether I read or meditate, whether I weep over my sins or give thanks for mercy, always I stand before God. I hope that when my hour comes, Christ will snatch me up to the Father. Should God hear our ardent prayer that I be permitted to stand at his altar again, I shall praise his mercy eternally. In that case I should like to live somewhere very quietly offering sacrifice, praying, and working.

Now, dear Minka, I must tell you that I pray for you unceasingly, and that from my overflowing heart I give thanks to God that he gave you to me. I have not shown you much tenderness in my life, in word or in deed, but I have loved you and have been proud—and still am—of my devout, good sister. Oh, if only I could once more adequately thank you. Now all that remains to me is our daily meeting before God.

Brandenburg-Görden, February 11, 1944

When you receive these lines, it will be Lent, the season of fasting. The manner of observance of it this year is predetermined by the situation. For I have been fasting for over eight months already, and so have training for it. Therefore I want to consecrate this fasting particularly in prayer. Sometimes I feel myself getting weary, like one who cannot go on. Then God helps with his grace. As a special penance I shall bear in patience the chains that I have worn for over seventy days now, and that torment me and hurt me terribly. How I must have sinned with my hands! To console and fortify myself, I often think of how Christ bore chains, and of how Peter and Paul lay in chains. I know that you are bearing all my suffering with me, but please, do not fast. See to it that you stay well. Let us pray together for God's mercy.

I have become used to loneliness and begin to love it. Gradually I am discovering in myself an aptitude for the monastic life. As a consolation and as a motto for the week, note the words of Bloy: " There is only one sorrow, that of not being a saint."

In my heart I am becoming still calmer. My life lies in God's hand. My existence is sheltered in the grace of Him who was put to death on the cross. The pattern of my life consists in hoping for God's mercy and faithfulness. The Passion is the means by which man is mercifully led from intellectual perception to feeling Christ as a reality. A painful and yet a sweet way. The most difficult thing for me is patience. Oh, how impatient my prayers still can be! All my anxieties, sufferings, and prayers are offered as a sacrifice on behalf of the congregation.

To you the sincerest greetings and halting thanks of your brother, who no longer possesses anything, not even life.

HIS LAST LETTER

Brandenburg-Görden, February 21, 1944

Dear Minka: At three o'clock I am going to die. Now the hour has come that God in his eternal love has ordained for me. Scholz, that good man, has heard my confession and given me the viaticum. In one hour I shall pass over into the glory of the living God. I have given myself over wholly, completely, and without reservation to God. In his hand I am sheltered. In his holy heart Christ will carry me up to the Father. Mary will protect me, and St. Joseph will accompany me.

Now I still have to say farewell to you. Receive my heart-felt thanks for all the kind things you have done for me in life. Blessings on you for the love you have given me, and for the forbearance and patience you have shown me. It is with particular feeling that I beg your forgiveness for having caused you so much suffering in these last eight months. I commend you to the heart of Christ. God will care for you. Do not lose courage. Trust in God. He has not forsaken me. The eight months of my preparation for eternity have been difficult, yet very beautiful. Now I must go home through the narrow gate of the guillotine. I am convinced that Mother and Father are waiting for me. . . .

Dear Maria! May the almighty God, the Father, the Son, and the Holy Ghost bless you.

Until we meet again in heaven,

Alfons

HARMEN VAN DER LEEK

DUTCH RESISTANCE WORKER

The main contribution of the Dutch resistance consisted in rescue work and in the protection of individuals persecuted by the Nazis. Many thousands lost their lives in this sacrificial service. In commemoration of the liberation of Holland, the Dutch newspaper *In de Waagschaal* published the last letter of one of the members of the resistance, Harmen van der Leek. In 1951 the letter was republished in the German monthly *Die Neue Furche*, but no further information about the writer is available.

LAST LETTER BEFORE HIS EXECUTION BY A FIRING SQUAD

Amsterdam, November 17, 1941

Beloved Pastor and Friend: What an experience we have had again! On Friday four of us were first taken to Amsterdam by car, and we were in very high spirits. One of us had been told that we were to have another hearing, and, since the death sentence had already been pronounced, this could have meant a favourable turn of events. But the blow that came after was all the harder.

We still had three hours to live, and we could write our last letters. I did that and then waited for your arrival. I spoke to Pastor Ferwerda for a moment and was able to assure him that all was well with me. There was nothing else that I could say, for I was infinitely calm and full of courage. How could I otherwise have been so gay? I was able to take leave of everyone and everything—and with that the last tie that still bound me to earth was severed. But then, a quarter of an hour before the scheduled time, came the report—postponement. That completely crushed me. With death before my eyes, I was never for a moment troubled; my trust in God remained strong. When I was shut up in the terrible, heavily barred death cell, I even had an impulse for an instant to sing out loud. I looked at all the iron with a smile. And then when the door was locked behind me, I thought: Now the door of life is closing for ever for me. But immediately the thought came to me clearly and firmly: If God so wills, he can still free me, even from this place. But I had not the slightest feeling of hurt or disappointment, nor the slightest desire that he do so.

However, to be flung from the certainty of death back into fear and doubt and new anticipation made me inwardly weak. Of course I remained certain of God's infinite goodness in Jesus Christ, and certain that he knows better than I; yet I had to implore his special help, screaming and sobbing, to be able to bear this new shock. For two days I together with my cell mates suffered under it; at times we were able to speak with one another about God's great mercy, but the certainty that I should be saved was gone. This did not cause me to revolt against God—in the first sleepless night between Friday and Saturday I fought the last fight and learned anew to pray, " Thy will be done." I said: " Lord, I am finished. Here you have me, completely, impotent and beaten. Now I await nothing more but your mercy."

But my faith was not shattered. I only came to this conclusion, that God's plan for me in relation to this time or to eternity was not yet completed. During the night I awoke and felt that my whole faith had returned. I still feel pain and fear, for now I know what probably lies before me; but this also serves to calm me, for it is no longer unexpected. However, I am certain that even in this God will help us through. We are now prepared for the end. At the same time, I still possess my full belief in God's miraculous power; even now he can still save us and bless the last efforts that are being made for us in Berlin. But I feel that I no longer want to grasp at this possibility; I only want to wait quietly, like a child, for my Father's decision. I must suffer, but not as one who is without hope. Whatever comes will be good, even of unexpected splendour. We pray that we may be allowed to live as powerful witnesses for the Saviour; more than that we do not ask. As you see, a clear, unalloyed attitude is not within my capacity, but I wait for the Lord. . . .

Your devoted
Harmen van der Leek

HELMUTH JAMES, COUNT VON MOLTKE

Helmuth James, Count von Moltke, was born on March 11, 1907, at Kreisau in Silesia. He was the eldest son of a grand nephew of the great field-marshal; his mother came of a family that had settled in South Africa. He was a jurist, devoting himself in addition to the management of his estate, Kreisau. He represented, as no one else could, the " other Germany," as opposed to the National Socialist rulers. The " Kreisau circle," the group that formed around him, included many of the most outstanding representatives of the German resistance, of all convictions. Both as a Christian and as a statesman Moltke disapproved of the assassination plot against Hitler. He wanted to prepare the rebirth of Germany after the catastrophe that he foresaw as inevitable. He was arrested in January, 1944, because he had warned a friend of the imminence of his arrest. In January, 1945, the People's Court condemned him to death, and the sentence was carried out on January 23, at Plötzensee.

Bishop Hans Lilje, who met Moltke in prison, says: " Without any self-deception as to his probable end, he lived in a serene clarity of spirit—a shining example of idomitable firmness based on faith."

FROM HIS FAREWELL LETTER TO HIS SONS

My whole life long, from my school days on, I have been fighting against a spirit of narrowness and violence, arrogance, intolerance, and absolute, merciless consistency that is latent in the German and that has found its expression in the National Socialist state. I have also worked towards the overcoming of this spirit, along with its evil consequences, such as excessive nationalism, racial persecution, irreligion, and materialism.

FROM LAST LETTERS TO HIS WIFE

Tegel, January 10, 1945

Dear heart: First I must tell you that quite evidently the last twenty-four hours of one's life are no different from any others. I had always imagined that it would come as a shock to say to oneself: " Now the sun is setting for the last time for you, now the hour hand will make only two more revolutions before twelve, now you are going to bed for the last time." Nothing of the sort. Perhaps I am a little cracked. For I cannot deny that I am in really high spirits. I only pray to God in heaven to sustain me in this mood, for surely it is easier for the flesh to die in this state. How merciful the Lord has been to me! Even at the risk of sounding hysterical—I am so full of thanks that there is actually no room for anything else. He has guided me so firmly and clearly during these two days. The whole courtroom might have roared, like Herr Freisler* himself, and all the walls might have rocked—it would have made no difference to me. It was just as is written in Isaiah 43:2: " When thou passest through the waters, I will be with thee; and through the rivers, they shall not overflow thee; when thou walkest through the fire, thou shalt not be burned; neither shall the flame kindle upon thee." That is to say, upon your soul. When I was called up for my last words, I was in such a frame of mind that I nearly said, " I have only one thing to add to my defence. Take my goods, my honour, my children and wife; the body they may kill; God's truth abideth still, his kingdom is for ever." But that would only have made it harder for the others; therefore I said only, " I do not intend to say anything, Herr President."

There is still a hard stretch of road ahead of me, and I can only pray that the Lord will continue to be as merciful to me as he has been. For this evening Eugen had noted for us Luke 5:1-11. He had intended a different application, but it remains true that this day has brought me a great draught of fishes, and that to-night I can truly say, " Depart from me; for I am a sinful man, O Lord." And what beautiful words we read last night, my beloved: " But we have this treasure in earthen vessels, that the excellency of the power may be of God, and not of us. We are troubled on every side, yet not distressed; we are perplexed, but not in despair. Persecuted, but not forsaken; cast down, but not destroyed; always bearing about in the body the dying of the Lord Jesus, that the life also of Jesus might be made manifest in our body." Thanks above all, dear heart, to the Lord, thanks to you, dear heart, for your intercession, thanks to all others who have prayed for us and for me. Your husband, your weak, cowardly, " complicated," very average husband has been granted this experience. If I were to be rescued now—and so far as God is concerned this is neither more nor less likely than it was a week ago—I must say that I should first of all have to find my bearings

* President of The People's Court.

again, so overpowering has been the demonstration of
God's presence and omnipotence. He can make this
demonstration, make it indeed quite unmistakably, when
he does exactly what does not suit us. All else is rubbish.

Therefore I can say only one thing, dear heart. May God
be as merciful to you as to me—then even the death of a
husband matters not at all. For He can demonstrate His
omnipotence even when you are making pancakes for the
boys, or when you have to take Puschti out of the room
(although I hope that isn't necessary any more). I should
be saying farewell to you—I can't do it. I should be
mourning and regretting the drabness of your everyday life
—I can't do it. I should indeed be thinking of the burdens
that will now fall upon you—I can't do it. I can say only
one thing to you; if you attain to a feeling of supreme
security—if the Lord gives you that which, had it not been
for this period in our lives and its conclusion, you would
never have had, then I am leaving you a treasure that
cannot be confiscated, a treasure compared to which even
my life is of small account. These Romans, these wretched
creatures, this Schulze and Freisler and whatever the names
of the pack of them may be—they would not even understand how little they can take away.

To-morrow I shall write more. But, since one never
knows what may happen, I want to be sure in this letter
to have touched on every topic. Of course I do not know
whether I shall be executed to-morrow. It may be that I
shall be questioned further, beaten, or shut up. Please
scratch on all the doors—for that may make them refrain
from beating me too severely. I know in view of to-day's
experience that God can also make these beatings seem as
nothing, even if I should have not one sound bone left in
my body when they hang me. Thus at the moment I have
no fear; still, I should prefer to avoid the ordeal. And so
good night; be of good cheer and undaunted.

January 11, 1945

My dear: I am in the mood only to chat with you a bit. I really have nothing to say. We have already discussed the material consequences thoroughly. As regards this you will struggle through somehow, and should someone else take over Kreisau, you'll still manage. But don't let anything assail you. It really isn't worth while. I am absolutely in favour of your seeing to it that the Russians learn of my death. Perhaps that will make it possible for you to remain in Kreisau. Moving about in whatever remains of Germany would, in any case, be horrible. Should the Third Reich survive, despite all expectations—something that even in my wildest fantasies I cannot imagine—you must find a way of saving our little sons from this poison. Of course I do not oppose your leaving Germany in that case. Do whatever you think is right, and don't think that you are bound in one way or another by any wishes of mine. I have told you over and over again that a dead hand cannot rule. . . .

I think with unclouded joy of you and our little sons, of Kreisau and all the people there; leave-taking is, at the moment, not at all hard for me. Perhaps that is yet to come. But in this instant it is no effort. I do not feel at all like bidding farewell. Why that is, I don't know. But it is not an onset of the feeling that came upon me so powerfully after your first visit in October—no, it must have been November. Now an inner voice tells me that (*a*) God can lead me back there to-day just as readily as he could have done it yesterday, and (*b*) if he should call me to himself, I accept it. I have not at all the feeling that has sometimes overcome me: " Oh, if only I could see it all just once more! " And yet I don't feel at all " other-worldly." Indeed, you see that I am fondly conversing with you rather than turning to God. There is a hymn that goes, " And he for death is ready, who living clings to Thee." That is just how I feel. Since at the moment I am alive, I must living cling to him; more than that he does not ask. Is that pharisaical? I don't know. But I think I do know that I am now living in his mercy and forgiveness, and possess nothing of my own acquisition, can do nothing of my own strength.

I am babbling, dear heart, saying whatever comes to my mind; therefore, something completely different now. In the last analysis, the dramatic thing about the trial was this. In the course of the proceedings, all concrete accusations proved untenable, and indeed were dropped. Nothing remained of them. However, the one thing that has put such fear into the Third Reich that it must put to death five people—or rather seven, as will prove to be the count later—is, in fine, as established by the evidence, just this: A private citizen, namely, your husband, together with two clergymen, one of each faith, with a Jesuit father superior and several bishops, *without any intention of doing anything concrete*—this is established—discussed matters " that are the exclusive concern of the Führer." The discussion turned on no organisational problems, not even on reconstruction of the Reich—all that fell away in the course of the trial, and Schulze said it explicitly in his summing up. (" This case differs completely from all others in that during the discussion there was question neither of violence nor of any organisation.") What we had discussed were questions of practical-ethical demands of Christianity. Nothing more; it is for this, and this alone, that we have been condemned. In one of his tirades Freisler said to me, " We and Christianity resemble each other in only one respect: we claim the whole man! "

I don't know whether the people sitting there took all this in, for it was a sort of dialogue between F. and myself—a spiritual one, for I was not allowed to say much—in the course of which we came to know each other through and through. Of the whole pack only Freisler understood me, and of the whole pack he is also the only one who knows why he has to do away with me. There was no talk of " complicated individual " or " complicated ideas " or

" ideology "; rather, " The mask is off." But only for Herr
Freisler. We were talking to each other in a vacuum, so to
speak. He did not crack a single joke at my expense, as he
did with Delp and Eugen. No, it was all in grimmest
earnest: " From whom do you take your orders? From the
world beyond or from Adolf Hitler? To whom do you owe
loyalty and faith? " All rhetorical questions, of course. . . .

Dear heart, your very precious letter has just arrived.
The first letter, dear heart, in which you have not understood my mood nor my situation. No, I do not occupy
myself at all with God or with my death. He is unspeakably
gracious in coming to me and occupying himself with me.
Is this arrogant? Perhaps. However, there is so much that
he must forgive me to-night, that I may after all ask forgiveness for this last bit of arrogance too. But I hope of course
that it is not arrogance, for I do not glory in the earthen
vessel—no, I glory in the precious treasure that has availed
itself of this earthen vessel, this totally unworthy dwelling.
No, dear heart, I am reading exactly the same passages in
the Bible that I would have read to-day had there been no
trial, namely, Joshua, chapters 19 to 21, Job, chapters 1 to
12, Ezekiel, chapters 34 to 36, Mark, chapters 13 to 15, and
our Second Epistle to the Corinthians all the way through,
together with the brief passages that I noted on a slip for
you. Up to now I have read only Joshua and our passages
in Corinthians, ending with that so familiar, beautiful verse
heard from childhood on: " The grace of the Lord Jesus
Christ, and the love of God, and the communion of the
Holy Ghost be with you all. Amen." I feel, dear heart,
as if I were authorised to say these words to you and to
our small sons with absolute authority. And so may I not
with full justification read Psalm 118, which was the
selection for this morning? Eugen related it to himself in
connection with a different situation, but it became much
more truly applicable than we ever thought possible.

Dear heart, that is why too, despite your request, you are
getting your letter back. I am taking you with me, and for
that I need no sign, no symbol; I need nothing. It is not

even as though I had been promised that I should not lose
you. No, it is much more: I know that I shall not lose
you. . . .

The decisive pronouncement in that trial was: " Count
Moltke, Christianity and we National Socialists have one
thing in common, and one thing only: we claim the whole
man." Did he realise what he was saying? Just think how
wondrously God prepared this unworthy vessel of his: at
the very moment when there was danger of my being
drawn into active preparations for the coup—Stauffenberg
came to see Peter on the evening of the nineteenth—I was
taken out of it, so that I am free and remain free of any
connection with the use of violence. In addition, God had
implanted in me that socialistic trait which freed me,
although owner of a great estate, from any suspicion of
representing vested interests. Then he abased me as I have
never been abased before, so that I have had to give over
all pride, so that after thirty-eight years I finally understand
my sinfulness, so that I am learning to pray for his forgiveness, to entrust myself to his mercy. Then he caused me to
come here, that I might see you standing fast, and that I
might be freed of all thoughts of you and the boys, that is
to say, all anxious thoughts. He is giving me time and
opportunity to put in order everything that can be put in
order, so that all earthly cares can fall away. Then he
permitted me to experience, to an unheard-of depth, the
anguish of parting and the fear of death and the terror of
hell—so that this too is over and done with.

Then he endowed me with faith, hope, and love, all this in
a plenitude truly lavish. Then he gave me a chance to speak
with Eugen and Delp and to clear up things. Then he
allowed Rösch* and König to escape, so that the matter did
not suffice for an indictment of the Jesuits, and so that at the
last moment Delp was joined to us. Then he caused
Haubach and Steltzer, whose cases would have introduced

---

* Moltke, who was in Plötzensee, did not know, at the time when he
wrote this letter, that Father Rösch had been arrested and imprisoned
in Moabit.

extraneous material, to be set apart from us, and finally with practical purpose placed Eugen, Delp, and me together as a separate group. And then through hope, through the human hope they cherished, he gave Eugen and Delp that weakness which led to making their cases only secondary, with the result that the denominational factor was removed. And then your husband was selected to be attacked and condemned, as a Protestant, above all because of his friendship with Catholics. And thus he stood before Freisler not as a Protestant, not as a landed proprietor, not as a nobleman, not as a Prussian, not as a German—all that was explicitly eliminated in the main hearing (for example, Sperr said: " I thought, what an extraordinary Prussian ")—but as a Christian and as nothing else. " The mask is off," said Herr Freisler. Yes, all categories were cancelled out—" A man who would naturally have to be repudiated by his peers," said Schulze.

For what a tremendous task your husband had been chosen! All the labour that the Lord God had spent upon him, the labyrinthine ways, the intricate zigzags, all these found their explanation quite suddenly in one hour on the tenth of January, 1945. In retrospect everything has gained a meaning that previously was hidden. Mama and Papa, my brothers and sisters, my small sons, Kreisau and its problems, the labour camps, the refusal to hoist the swastika flag or to join the Party or any of its organisations, Curtis and the English journeys, Adam and Peter and Carlo—all of it finally became comprehensible in the light of a single hour. For the sake of this one hour the Lord had taken all these pains.

And now, dear heart, I come to you. I have not listed you anywhere, because you, dear heart, stand in a place completely different from that of all the others. For you are not an instrument of God for making me what I am; rather, you are myself. You are my thirteenth chapter of the First Epistle to the Corinthians. Without this chapter, no human being is truly human. Without you I would have accepted love, as, for example, I have accepted it from Mama, thankful and happy, thankful as one is for the sun because it is warming. But without you, dear heart, I should " have not charity." I will not say that I love you; that is not at all correct. You are rather that part of me which would simply be lacking were I alone. It is a good thing that I in myself lack it. For if I possessed it, this greatest of all gifts, as you possess it, I should never have been able to look upon the suffering that I have had to witness, and much else would have been impossible. Only we two together are a human being. We are, as I wrote symbolically a few days ago, a single idea of the Creator. This is true, literally true. Therefore, dear heart, I am certain that you will never, not for a single moment, lose me on this earth. And in the Last Supper we partook of together, which now has become my final one,· we have indeed been allowed to symbolise this fact.

Just a moment ago I cried a little, not sadly, not pensively, not because I want to go back, but out of gratitude and awe at this documentation on the part of God. It is not granted us to see him face to face, but we cannot but be overawed when suddenly we recognise that throughout life he has gone before us as a cloud by day and as a pillar of fire by night, and that he is allowing us suddenly, in a single instant, to perceive this. Now nothing further can happen. . . .

Dear heart, my life is finished, and I can say of myself: " He died old and sated with life." But that doesn't alter the fact that I should like to live a little longer, that I should like to accompany you a little farther on this earth. But that would require a new mission from God. The mission for which God made me is fulfilled. If he wants to give me another mission, we shall learn of it. So continue serenely to make efforts to save my life, in case I should live through this day. Perhaps there will be another mission.

I am going to stop, because there is nothing more to say. I have indeed not named anyone whom you are to greet or embrace. You know of yourself for whom the messages I have charged you with are meant. All our beloved sayings are in my heart and in your heart. But by virtue of the treasure that has spoken through me and that fills this humble earthen vessel, I say to you in concluding:

The grace of the Lord Jesus Christ, and the love of God, and the communion of the Holy Ghost, be with you all. Amen.

ALFRED DELP, S. J.

The life and thoughts of Alfred Delp, born on September 15, 1907, in Mannheim, were determined by his devout concern over the estrangement of modern man from God. This anxiety vibrates in his theological writings; it opened his eyes to the political depravity of his time and brought him into the Kreisau resistance group. He was arrested on July 28, 1944, and sentenced together with Count Moltke. On February 2, 1945, he suffered death by hanging.

NOTES BEFORE HIS ARREST

July, 1943

It is glorious now, this midsummer ripening. From the fields comes the enchanting song of the swishing sickles and scythes. I like this so much, the ripe fields and then the harvest itself. Somehow or other, this of course is the meaning of our lives—becoming ripe, and then being cut down and stored in the barns. The world is full of beauty and goodness, and after all it is the goodness and beauty of God that gives the world all this. . . .

I have let myself be tempted by this bucolic way of life. I have just been mowing for a whole hour, and now my hands are full of blisters, and my unpractised arms are full of tremors. But it was lovely. This sweeping motion has a peculiar and meaningful rhythm that somehow touches on the meaning of life. Remain wakeful and happy and confident, and once in a while say a little prayer for me.

I am doing it for all of you too. It is good praying here under the ægis of Mother Earth—and also in the direct encounter with the calm, true, vitalising forces of nature. But this vitalising and impelling radiance is really only an intimation and likeness of the Lord God. All things are encompassed in the one. It will be the great, consummating moment of existence when at last the word of God means everything and confirms and embraces everything and at the same time draws it all back to the centre. At least I should like to die thus, if it should not be granted me before death.

FRAGMENTS FROM HIS DIARY

December 31, 1944

The outcome of this time can be only a great inner desire for God and for his glorification. I must meet him in a new and personal way. I must beat down the walls that still stand between him and me. The tacit reservations must be completely cleared away. I must live the prayer of Nikolaus von der Flüe.* The divine life existing in me in the form of faith, hope, and charity must grow, intensify. All this, together with my life, my temperament, my capabilities, my mistakes and prejudices, as well as things external, must solidify into a new mission, into the idea of a new order, to be brought to realisation through my work.

In a quiet hour to-night I want to meditate on the events of this year and gather up my personal experiences into a prayer of repentance, thanks, and dedication, into an expression of trust and love.

Over and over again I have to ask myself whether I am not a dreamer deceiving himself. The gravity of the situation is an inexorable fact, unreal and dreamlike

---

* My Lord and God, take all from me that blocks my way to thee. My Lord and God, give all to me that speeds my way to thee. My Lord and God, take this my self from me and give it as thine own to thee.

though it often seems to me. But the words of the Lord have
been spoken, and he himself has urged upon us this faith
that moves mountains, this trust that he does not forsake.
Those are facts determined by him, which can and must
be taken seriously. Except for the time when he drove the
money changers out of the Temple, he was angry only once;
that was when the disciples were unable to cure the epileptic
boy because they did not trust in their own powers. And
surely we shall be able to remove the sole obstacle involved
here by means of faith and prayer. Up to now so much
guidance and mercy have been discernible, in spite of all
ordeal and all destruction.

New Year's Eve

In my inward being this year there has been much vanity
and self-assurance and presumption and untruthfulness and
deceit. This occurred to me when, during the beating, they
called me a liar, because once again they had discovered
that I had given them no names they did not already know.
I asked God why he let them beat me like that. I realised
that it was because of the ambiguity and insincerity of my
nature.

Thus a great deal has been burned away on this mount of
lightning, and a great deal has become purified. That the
Lord God so miraculously made it possible for me to take
my vows, stands as a blessing as well as a confirmation of
my inward existence. He will also confirm my outward
existence once more, as soon as it has freed itself for a new
mission. The external task and the enlarging of the inner
light must kindle a new passion—the passion of bearing
witness for the living God. For I have come to know him
and have felt him. *Dios solo basta:* this proves true. The
passion of the mission to man, who must be made capable
and desirous of living. These problems are to be attacked
—*in nomine Domini.*

January 1, 1945

JESUS—I want to write the name of the Lord, and of my order large upon the beginning of the new year. It attests what I pray for, hope for, and believe in—inward and outward salvation. A breaking down of the blockages and limitations of the ego in free dialogue with God, in free partnership, in unconditional dedication. And a speedy deliverance from these miserable shackles. The situation is based on sham. I am held prisoner here by things I have neither done nor known about.

The name of Jesus furthermore attests what I still seek in the world and among men. To lend myself to the work of salvation, of help. To love mankind and to do good. I remain indebted for many things to many persons.

And finally, the name stands for my order, which now at last has taken me unto and into itself. In me it is to be bodied forth. I want to associate myself with Jesus as a faithful companion and lover. Lastly, however, his name is to designate a passion—a passion of faith, of dedication, of striving, of service.

January 2, 1945

It seems that the final decision is to be made next week. I am of good hope. The Lord has lighted a Christmas candle within me that fortifies me in my hope. I even dream of the journey home, lighthearted fellow that I am. . . .

I trust and I pray. I have learned much in this rigorous year. God has become more real and more immediate to me.

January 6, 1945

By dint of a kindly favour on the part of the Lord God, I was chained so loosely for the night that I was able to slip out of my fetters. And so, just as on Christmas Eve, I was able to say Mass with my hands completely free.

My lawyer was here again to-day. There are three ifs to be surmounted if all is to go well. I have firm confidence. My friends likewise will not leave me in the lurch. This is a moment in which all existence seems to be caught up into a single point, and all reality with it. I must put all my cards on the table. The reality of God, things and their interrelations, justification of and responsibility for one's words and deeds, compassion and militancy as elements of existence—all this presses to be realised simultaneously. I have boldly asked God for the two freedoms. And now I shall do so again.

January 7, 1945

In a moment now the man will come with the shackles. And to-morrow I go to the house of silence.

In nomine Domini. I have written no letters of farewell, since everything within me resists doing it.

MEDITATIONS

Universal fate, my personal condition, the decision to come within the next few days, the message of the Feast—everything coalesces into this one precept: Man, give yourself up to your God, and you will find yourself again. Now others possess you, they torment you and frighten you and drive you from one tribulation to another. Then it is freedom that sings: No death can kill us. Then it is life that moves out into boundless space. *Adoro* and *Suscipe*— you two root words of life, you are the straight and steep path to God, the gates to fulfilment, man's roads to himself. I hold to my old thesis: mankind nowadays largely not only lacks God, either having never known him or having shaken him off by its own decision—but its godlessness goes much deeper. Present-day man has fallen into a pattern of life in which he is incapable of susceptibility to God. All efforts on behalf of the humanity of to-day and of the future must be directed to making it susceptible to God once more and thereby susceptible to religion.

FROM LETTERS TO MUNICH FRIENDS

Beginning of September, 1944

One night, it was about the fifteenth of August, I almost despaired. Late in the evening, after being terribly beaten, I was brought back to the prison. The SS men accompanying me handed me over with these words. " Well, you won't be able to sleep to-night. You will pray, but no Lord God nor any angel will come to deliver you. But we'll have a good night's sleep and to-morrow morning we'll be as fresh as daisies and beat you up again."

When the alert came, I felt as if I had been saved, and I looked forward to the bomb, which might bring death or the possibility of escape. It brought neither. And from that night on I perceived the whole disastrous course of things. God has stationed me. Now it is a matter of living up to my post, come what may. I still believe firmly and confidently in the Hand that will take us and guide us. . . .

Gradually I am becoming disgusting—I am always writing only about myself. That is how egotistical one becomes as a " patient." Alas, how much I should like to be with people in distress! And now I myself don't count as a human being any more, only as a number—in this establishment, number 1142, cell 8-313. When shall I be addressed as Father Delp again? Do you believe in miracles? May you be blessed and protected.

For the time being, I entreat you, pray and hope with me. " Pound on God's doors "—isn't that what L. was always saying? God can still set things right. He alone. And he has actually put himself in the power of the people who believe and trust. God has let me win a fine space of inward freedom. God's reality is gradually dawning upon me as something very near and substantial.

E

Beginning of October, 1944

I don't know whether this is a farewell letter or not. That is something we never know in these days. I write these lines without knowing whether or when they will reach you, but not as a " last greeting." Somehow I believe firmly in life and in a new mission, although I am equally honest in saying that so far as human eyes can serve, I see very little possibility of this.

How am I? There is really very little to say on that score. Do not fear. I strive not to let them make kindling of me, even if the road leads to the gallows. For God's strength accompanies me in all ways. But sometimes it is a little difficult for me. Georg* has at moments been nothing more than a bleeding, moaning mass. But Georg has always tried to bring this moaning into proper relation with the only two realities that make existence worth while— adoration and love. All else is false. Believe me, these weeks have been like a bitter and inexorable judgment on my past life. But it is not past. It stands forth as a large question and demands the final answer, its definitive mould. If I should be permitted once more. . . .

Yes, if I should be permitted once more! God simply has completely cornered me. Everything that I undertook has failed. One door after another fell shut—even those that I thought would always be open. No help came from the outside. And so this is my present position—locked up and bound in a narrow cell. There are only two ways out—the one by way of the gallows into the light of God, the other by way of a miracle to a new mission. In which one do I believe?

The " kindergarten of death "—every day for an hour we are led about in the open, doggedly in a ring, well guarded by means of guns, etc. We go round in a circle, all fettered —officials, officers, workmen, diplomats, and business men. In some corners one can speak close up against the wall and

* Father Delp's pseudonym.

the person behind it will hear. That is how conversations are carried on in the " kindergarten of death."

May God keep you all. . . .

End of October, 1944

Again I write some words of greeting. Whether they will reach you I do not know, just as I know nothing about anyone except the people here in fetters, who every day become fewer.

I am so thankful for the Eucharist that I have had in my cell since the first of October. It breaks the solitude, although—be it said to my shame—I am sometimes so tired and broken that I no longer grasp this reality.

November 22, 1944

This week was in many respects a very agitated one. Three of us have gone the way that as a bitter possibility confronts all of us, and from which only God's miracles can cut us off and save us. Inwardly I have a great deal to do with the Lord God, I have much to ask him and much to tell him. But one thing is clear and tangible to me as rarely before: the world is so full of God. This realisation wells up towards us as it were from all the pores of things. But we are often blind. We remain enmeshed in the good and in the bad hours. We do not experience them through and through up to the point at which they flow forth from God. This holds true in relation to the beautiful as well as to wretchedness. In all things God wants to solemnise the encounter, and asks for and desires the adoring and loving response.

November 30, 1944

To-day is another very black day. God must really be very intensively concerned with me, in that he has thrown me so exclusively on my own resources. For some time now I have again been totally isolated. I am to learn what faith and

trust mean. . . . There are also good hours of plenitude and
consolation. But on the whole we are on a tight rope just
the same, and have to run across an abyss, and, on top of
that, they shoot at us, and constantly some fall off. Sometimes I tell the Lord God that I need a bit of consoling.
Then he has the strangest answers. Recently on such a day
the two Mariannes managed to get twenty cigarettes and
five cigars to me at one time. And then the precious gray
prayer book . . . and a few things that smacked so much of
Munich. Sometimes I also ask for a word of guidance and
consolation, and open the Scriptures at random. Just now
I opened to, " Those who believe will work the following
miracles," etc. . . . I made the " play " once more and this
time I opened to Matthew, chapter 20, again a word of
assurance.

Alas, how limited the human heart is even in the capacities
most characteristically its own—in hoping and believing.
It needs help in order to find itself and not flutter away like
some shy half-fledged birds that have fallen out of their nest.
Once in a sermon I said, " Faith as a virtue is God's
affirmation of his own nature in the freedom of man." And
that is the point to-day, precisely that. Pray and hope and
believe with me that the Lord will *soon* bring us to the other
shore and put us on firm ground once again. Let us no
longer consider it quite so firm as we sometimes have
thought it.

I wanted so much to write something coherent. But
reading and everything else is so haphazard. Even so, what
a blessing it is. And then with these shackled hands nothing
can be done in the way of writing. The few moments in
which we are freed are not enough. . . .

Beginning of December, 1944

To-day is a bad day. Sometimes all one's destiny gathers
itself into one load and weighs upon one's heart, and then
one really cannot tell how long one can go on exacting all
this from one's heart. . . . I believe in God and in life. And

what we pray for in faith will be given us. God has thoroughly tested me as to whether I will honour my previous declaration that only in alliance with him is it possible to live and to bear one's fate. . . . Forgive me for making such a begging plea to you recently for a word of faith. I really want to know whether you still believe in me and in my return. Sometimes I really want that, thus to escape from this solitude. I still believe in myself, but all the rest have given me up. I have been very sternly urged to take death more seriously and not to deceive myself as to the situation. That is what good friends have written to me. . . . I know that I am walking a tight rope. And I also know that without God's special help I cannot get across. But I do believe that he will help me, and I tell him so every day.

When the decision will come, is once again up in the air. Yesterday it looked as if the matter would drag on until Christmas. To-day the word is, it will come as early as next week. In any case, I now know what it means to live in His hand. That is what we should always have done. But often I have lived very much in reliance on my own powers and certainty—and by reason of this remain indebted for so much to so many people.

December 18, 1944

Well, it is certain now that the decision will come next week, on Tuesday or Wednesday. The miracle will have to consist in a reversal of the ready-made sentence of death that the presiding gentlemen will be bringing with them in their pockets. If nothing like that takes place, we shall stand on Wednesday before the eyes of God and, if he is merciful, within his light.

Even now I do not feel as if I were writing a farewell letter. Always, when the decision seems imminent, this calm certainty sets in. Throughout this entire time I have never had the feeling of being lost, no matter how often I was told that I was. Somehow, the whole phantasmagoric affair was an unreality that did not concern me. There would also come again the hours in which Peter took the wind and the waves seriously, and began to lose courage. I never would have thought that God would have to labour so arduously to clear the view to the summit for me.

Now everything is in God's hands. I shall defend myself as best I can. I hope that physically things will be in some degree bearable. It is a pity that we shall have to leave this place beforehand. Over there we shall begin starving again. And that is something really despicable—to have to bear up hungry and weary under that pressure and fury of assault. In the past I have sometimes said that a crust of bread is a great mercy. Now I know it from bitter experience.

How things will proceed I don't know. Up to now I have only the feeling that I shall come through. Even though I have no basis in reality for it.

Oh, how I wish that I could come to see you for just an hour. Not for my sake—I believe that I shall have a joyous Christmas. But to be with you and to be able to put a bit of Christmas into your souls—and to be allowed to do so. I shall send you a big blessing and shall entreat the Child, the great Mystery of the world, to be with you.

Now it is a matter of merely waiting further and of enduring. I have prayed very hard to God for a Christmas light. Perhaps he will have one of his nice surprises for me again. Oh, he has so many possibilities of setting us on our feet and leading us on a bit farther. How often I have experienced that in these long and anxious weeks. . . . I am of good hope. It is such a comfort to know that one is backed up by the prayers and the loyalty of one's friends. These are other realities, and with their help we shall succeed. God against might—God invoked by loyalty and love and trust.

I should like to kindle a few lights for you, my friends. You have accompanied me such a long way into my night, and have your own night still to undergo besides. We'll bear it all in common, let's say. Together we'll manage

another bit of the way, and in the middle of the night the
light will appear. It will. Let us help one another. . . .

After Christmas

Christmas was beautiful and quiet. I felt your help and
your nearness very much. Some day this Advent that began
in the summer will find its light, its consummation, and its
Christmas. Actually I had been afraid of these days. But
they were quiet and blessed. The Mass in the night was the
most beautiful Christmas Mass I have ever celebrated. I
had fairly well released myself from this affair and its cares.
And now and then I even permitted myself to dream of how
it would be if I were to return to Munich soon. I visited
my mother and you and other friends.

All good wishes for the New Year. God's blessing and
protection. Success and courage and strength and joy in
the Lord—despite everything. Until we meet again.

January 11, 1945

And now I have to write a farewell letter. Apparently the
Lord God wants the whole sacrifice, and the other road.
The death sentence has been demanded, and the air is so
filled with hatred and animosity that I no longer see any
way out. Hatred and animosity ruled the whole trial. In
its actual charges the case broke down. But from the first
word on I knew that the outcome was fixed.

Inwardly I am now in a quite peculiar position. Although
I know that according to the normal course of things I shall
die to-night, I don't feel as if I were going to die. Perhaps
God is being merciful and saving the fear of death for me
until the final hours. Or should I continue to believe in a
miracle?

January 14, 1945

I don't know how long I am going to be waiting here, and

whether or when I shall be executed. It is only a ten-minute trip from here to the gallows at Plötzensee. Usually one learns only shortly before that one is " coming up " that day, in fact immediately.

Don't be sad. God has helped me so wondrously and so perceptibly up to now. I am still not at all frightened. That is probably yet to come. Perhaps God has willed this waiting state as the extreme test of my reliance. I assent. I shall endeavour to fall into the furrow as fruitful seed for all of you and for this land and nation that I wanted to serve and help.

AFTER THE VERDICT

My life now is of a strange sort. One becomes used to existence so quickly again, and is obliged now and then forcibly to recall the death sentence to consciousness. That is the peculiar thing about this death: the will to live remains unbroken, and every nerve is alive until hostile force overpowers all. Hence the usual omens and harbingers of death are absent in this situation. One of these days the door will open and the good warden will say, " Pack up, the car is coming in half an hour." The thing we have heard and experienced so often.

Up to now the Lord God has helped me most splendidly and kindly. I have not yet taken fright nor broken down. The hour of the flesh will no doubt strike too. Sometimes a sadness comes over me when I think of all that I still wanted to do. For it is only now that I have become a human being, inwardly free and far more genuine and more truthful, more real than before. Only now have my eyes acquired a flexibility of range enabling them to encompass all dimensions, and the normality needed to take in all perspectives. The contractions and atrophies are disappearing.

Yes, and then there are the people who remain behind. To be perfectly honest, I still do not believe in the gallows. I do not know to what this is due. Perhaps to a great gift of mercy and help from God the Father, who is permitting me in this way to endure the desert without dying of thirst. During the whole of the trial, even when I realised that there would be no " miracle," I was far above everything and immune to all the proceedings and prospects. Is that the miracle, or what is it? In relation to God I am really at a loss, and must clear my mind about it.

All these bitter months of maturation and misfortune have had quite a peculiar law of their own. From the first moment on I was inwardly certain that all would go well. Over and over again God strengthened me in this certainty. In these last few days I have begun to doubt, and to wonder whether I have fallen victim to self-delusion, whether my will to live has sublimated itself in religious fantasies, or what else all this has been. But these many perceptible moments of exaltation in the midst of calamity; this certainty and imperviousness under all the blows; this defiance, so to speak, that has kept advising me that they would not succeed in annihilating me; the feelings of con-solation during prayer and sacrifice; the hours of grace before the tabernacle: these signs that I have always prayed for and that have been given and confirmed to me. I don't know whether I may set all this aside now. Am I to con-tinue to hope? Does the Lord God desire the sacrifice that I do not wish to deny him, or does he want an attestation of faith and trust to the outermost extreme of the possible?

And this is the second law that has governed these weeks of my life: everything that I have undertaken to help myself has gone awry. Not only that, but such efforts have actually turned out disastrously. The entire external course of the trial was frustration and shipwreck, impotence heaped upon impotence. And again, amidst it all, there is the quite peculiar manner of our misfortune: we remain in Tegel, and we are still alive to-day.

What does the Lord God mean by all this? Is it a school-ing for total freedom and complete dedication? Does he want the whole chalice, down to the last drop, and are these hours of waiting and of this unique Advent a part of it? Or does he demand an ordeal by faith?

The climate of things here is so ruined for me that even an appeal for clemency has no prospect of success. Is it folly to go on hoping, or illusion or cowardice or an access of grace? I often sit here before the Lord and merely gaze at him questioningly.

In any case, I must set about a thoroughgoing inward release and surrender myself. This is a time of sowing, not of harvesting. God sows; some day he will also reap again. I want to strive for one thing—to fall into the earth at least as a fruitful and healthy seed. And into the hand of the Lord God. If this is the way the Lord has chosen for me— and all visible signs point to that—then I must take it voluntarily and without bitterness. May others some day be able to live better and more happily because we died.

I ask my friends not to mourn for me, but rather to pray for me as long as I need help. And afterwards to rest assured that I have been sacrificed, not murdered. . . . To speak honestly and straightforwardly, I should like to go on living and more than ever now to go on working, to proclaim many new words and values that I have only now discovered. But matters have gone otherwise. May God sustain me in strength sufficient to measure up to his disposition and his pleasure.

My remaining task is to give thanks to many people for their loyalty and kindness and love. To the Order and the Brothers who provided me with a beautiful and genuine field of spiritual life. And to the many staunch persons whom I was enabled to meet. Those whom I have in mind will know. Alas, my friends, to think that the hour never struck, and the day never dawned, that would have permitted us freely and openly to associate ourselves with the Word and the work for which we were being spiritually developed. Remain true to the silent command that in our hearts summoned us again and again. Continue to love this nation, now spiritually so forsaken, betrayed, and helpless— and basically so lonely and confused, despite all the parades and declamatory self-assurance. If by reason of some man's existence a little more love and kindness, a little more light and truth have come into the world, his life has been of use.

And I do not want to forget those to whom I must remain a debtor. I owe a great deal to a great many. May those whom I have hurt forgive me. I have done penance. May those to whom I have been untruthful or insincere forgive me. I have done penance. May those to whom I have been proud or arrogant forgive me. I have done penance. Yes, indeed, in my hours of confinement underground, in the hours spent with hands, body, and spirit in chains, a great deal was broken. Those hours burned out much that was not worthy, nor valuable enough.

So farewell. My crime is that I had faith in Germany, a faith surmounting even a possible interim of desolation and darkness. That I did not believe in that insensate trinity of pride, arrogance, and force. And that I did this as a Catholic Christian and as a Jesuit.

And so, in conclusion, I shall do what I have done so often before with fettered hands, what I shall continue to do as long as I am still permitted to breathe: I shall give blessing. I shall bless land and people, bless this beloved German nation in its distress and inner anguish. I shall bless the Church, that its sources may flow within it once more, purer and clearer. I shall bless the Order that, honest and disciplined and free, it may remain loyal to itself by force of selfless loyalty to every true cause and to its every mission. I shall bless the persons who believed me and trusted me, bless those whom I have wronged, bless all those who have been kind to me, often too kind.

As for myself, however, I intend to wait here faithfully for the dispensation and guidance of the Lord God. I shall trust in him until they take me away. And I shall strive to see that even this release and its password do not find me small and despairing.

LAST LETTER TO THE BROTHERS OF HIS ORDER

February 2, 1945

Dear Brothers: Now I must in the end take the other road. The death sentence has been demanded, and the air is so filled with hatred and animosity that presumably it will be announced and carried out to-day.

I give thanks to the Society of Jesus and to the Brothers for all their kindness, loyalty, and help, especially as accorded me even in these last difficult weeks. I ask for forgiveness for many things that have been wrong and unjust, and I ask for some help and care for my aged, sick parents.

The actual reason for my sentence is that I am and remain a Jesuit. It was not possible to establish any connection with the event of July 20. Neither was the charge of a tie to Stauffenberg upheld. Other sentences demanded by the prosecutor, in cases actually involving knowledge of the affair of July 20, were much less severe and less biased. The air was so filled with hatred and animosity.

The basic tenet is that a Jesuit is *a priori* an enemy and an adversary of the Reich. Thus in the one aspect the whole thing was a farce; in the other, however, it became a *pièce à thèse*. This was not a trial: it was simply a function of the will to annihilate.

May the Lord God keep you all. I ask for your prayers. And I shall strive to make up from yonder for what I owe here.

About noon I shall once more celebrate Mass, and then in God's name I shall go the way of his dispensation and guidance. To you, God's blessing and protection.

Your thankful,
Alfred Delp, S. J.

ADAM VON TROTT ZU SOLZ

DIPLOMAT

As a member of the Kreisau circle, Adam von Trott zu Solz, born in 1909 in Imshausen, Hesse, made contact, in the course of trips abroad, with leading statesmen in London and Washington. But his daring attempt to gain the assurance of an honourable peace for a Germany freed of the Hitler dictatorship failed. After the events of July 20, Trott zu Solz, as a friend and collaborator of Count Claus von Stauffenberg, was sentenced to death by the People's Court. He was executed on August 26, 1944, in Berlin-Plötzensee.

FROM HIS FAREWELL LETTER TO HIS MOTHER

Königsdamm 7, Berlin-Plötzensee, August 26, 1944

Dearest Mother: There is after all, praise God, still opportunity for a brief line to you; you have always been, and are now too, very close to me. Thankfully and tenaciously I cling to that which is our bond for ever and ever. God has been merciful to me in these weeks and has given me a joyous, clear strength for everything, almost everything. He has also taught me how and in what respects I have failed. Above all I ask you too to forgive me for all this great sorrow, and for the fact that now, in your old age, I have had to deprive you of the support you had in me.

For the last, a grateful and loving kiss to you—until we meet again.

Your son who loves you very much,

Adam

" Unto Thy spirit, O Lord. . . ."

FAREWELL LETTER TO HIS WIFE

Königsdamm 7, *Berlin-Plötzensee, August* 26, 1944

Dear little Clarita: This unfortunately now is probably my very last letter. I hope that you have received my previous longer letter.

Before all else—forgive me for the great sorrow I have had to cause you.

Rest assured that in my thoughts I shall continue to be with you, and that I die in profound trust and faith.

To-day we have a clear sky, Peking blue, and there is a rustling in the trees. Teach our dear, sweet little ones to understand these signs from God—and his profounder ones —thankfully but also with an active and valiant spirit.

I love you very much. There would be still so much to write—but there is no more time.

May God keep you. I know that you will not let yourself be defeated, and that you will struggle through to a life in which I shall in spirit still be standing by your side, even if you seem to be all alone. I pray for strength for you— and please do the same for me. In these last few days I have found time to read the *Purgatorio*, as well as *Maria Stuart.* . . . Otherwise, I have had few things of this kind—but many things in my mind, which I have been able to turn over and clarify in quiet. Therefore do not grieve too much on my account—for fundamentally everything is very clear, even if very painful.

I should like so very much to know how all this has affected all of you practically. Whether you intend to go to Reinbek or whether you are staying. They will surely all be very kind to you, my beloved little wife. In my other letter I asked you to give my greetings to many friends—a matter that I have at heart. But you know about them exactly, and will transmit them correctly without help from me.

I embrace you with all my heart and know that you are with me.

God bless you and the little ones.

In steadfast love,
Your Adam

HANS-BERND VON HAEFTEN

DIPLOMAT

As early as 1933, Hans-Bernd von Haeften, born in Berlin on December 18, 1905, gave expression, in a letter to his wife, to his consternation at the transfer of power to " this Hitler with his robber-chieftain morality." His refusal to join the Party won him suspicion from those in power. When finally he had the temerity to unmask a wearer of the golden Party emblem* as a crook, the tension turned into open conflict. In 1940 he joined the Kreisau circle. As a devout Christian, considerations of conscience forbade him to lend support to the planning of the tyrannicide. Nonetheless, on July 20 he joined his friends in this supreme venture, because, like them, he could no longer bear the guilt involved in remaining a silent onlooker. In the hearing before the People's Court on August 15, 1944, he admitted his action. And the tensions of all the preceding years were released when, in answer to Freisler's question whether he realised that he had committed treason, he said: " Legally speaking, it is treason; actually it is not. For I no longer felt an obligation of loyalty. I see in Hitler the executor of the evil in history."

Hans-Bernd von Haeften was executed on the same day. Shortly before his execution he wrote the following letter to his wife.

August 15, 1944

My dear, dearest wife, my good Barbara: In a few hours I shall fall into the hands of God. Hence I want to take leave of you. Quickly, a few external matters. . . .

* Worn by Party members who had joined before 1933 (translator's note).

Barbara, in these weeks of imprisonment I have quietly submitted to the judgment of God and recognised my " unrecognised offence " and acknowledged it before him. " To do justly, and to love mercy, and to walk humbly with thy God "—this is the rule that I have broken. I did not keep holy the fifth commandment (although I once brought Werner* back from the brink), and I did not take seriously enough the commandment enjoining humility, and possessing one's soul in patience. Above all, I did not practise love towards all of you who were entrusted to me. For your sake, and for the sake of Mama and your parents, I should have desisted from everything. Please tell them, in giving them my deepest thanks for all their help and love, that I sincerely ask them to forgive me. Barbie, I did all this desiring to do right before God, and in the conviction that I was so doing. Actually I was disobedient, although I honestly implored him to lead me in his ways, lest my feet slip. They did slip. Why? Probably because amid all the doubts I did not wait quietly and patiently enough for him to declare his will unambiguously. Perhaps, also, it was his unfathomable, holy, and salutary decree that things should go as they have.

My dearest wife, I die in the certainty of divine forgiveness, mercy, and eternal salvation, and in the firm assurance that God in his immeasurable compassion will transform into blessing all the harm, pain, grief, privation, and loneliness that I have brought you—and that tears my heart out —and that his fatherly hands will lead you all on your earthly ways and draw you finally to himself. The Lord in his mercy to us will moreover gradually allay your suffering, soften your sorrow, and still your pain; your love will remain the same, for it " endureth for ever."

My good Barbara, I thank you from the bottom of my heart for all the love and all the blessing you have given me in the fourteen years of our marriage. Please forgive me any deficiency of love. I love you much more dearly than I

* His brother Werner was shot dead in Berlin on the evening of July 20, together with Stauffenberg, Olbricht, and Merz von Quirnheim.

have shown you. But we have an eternity ahead of us in which we can show love to each other. May this thought be a comfort to you in the affliction of your widowhood. I am certain—and you must be too—that we two will be united once again, together with all our loved ones, in the inexpressible peace of God (which is at once most perfect rest and most blissful activity in the service of God), in the adoration and immediate experience of divine love, in the marvellous shelter of the Saviour's mercy and kindness, in the bliss of redemption as God's children. Even now on earth you are a member of the body of Christ; this union is felt most deeply in the Sacrament received at the altar, in the presence of the Lord, who in marvellous fashion joins together all who belong to him—whether they stand on this side of the great transformation, or on the farther side.

Pray for me in the words of Psalm 126; it was the text of the last sermon I heard in our village church, on the day of my arrest. And along with it offer in prayer Psalm 103, give praise and give thanks.

My last thought, my dearest wife, will be that I consign you, my dear ones, to the mercy of the Saviour, and my spirit to his hands. I want to die thus rejoicing in my faith. And I would have you for your part, my dear Barbie, remain " the ever cheerful Frau von Haeften." Joke and laugh with the children, fondle them and be merry with them; they need your gaiety of spirit—and be assured that nothing could be *more* in keeping with my wishes.

So I salute you, my dear dearest ones, with the old greeting, " Rejoice! " " Rejoice in the Lord always: and again I say, Rejoice. . . . And the peace of God shall keep your hearts and minds through Christ Jesus."

Greet and kiss all our dear children for me, dear Janneman, good Dirkus, faithful little Adda, precious little Dora, and sweet little Ulrika. As for yourself, my dear, very dearest wife, my kind, most heartily beloved Barbara, I kiss you and embrace you and hold you to my heart with the deepest, and most prayerful wishes for time and eternity.

Your Hannis

KURT HUBER

Kurt Huber, born on October 24, 1893, in Chur, Switzerland, had been a professor at the University of Munich from 1926 on. It was impossible for this inspired and fascinating teacher to hide his deep antipathy to National Socialism. He became the central figure and counsellor of the student group that agitated for resistance by means of pamphleteering. After the incident of February 18, 1943, when Hans and Sophie Scholl dropped pamphlets into the main lobby of the university, the Gestapo stepped in. Huber was condemned to death on April 20. Meditation and prayer filled his time as he waited for the execution of the sentence, which followed on July 13.

LAST STATEMENT BEFORE THE COURT

As a German citizen, as a German university professor, and as a political being, I consider it not only my right but my moral duty to collaborate in the shaping of German history, to uncover evident abuses, and to combat these. . . . My purpose has been to rouse student circles—not through an organisation, but by means of simple words—not to any act of violence but to a moral discernment of existing grave evils in political life. A return to clear moral principles, to a constitutional state, to mutual trust among men—this is not an illegal aim; on the contrary, it means a restoration of legality.

I have asked myself, taking the point of view of Kant's categorical imperative, what would happen if this personal principle motivating my actions were to become a universal law. To this there is only one possible answer: it would mean a return of order, security, and trust into our political life. All morally responsible people would raise their voices in unison with us against the threatening dominion of naked might over right, of purely arbitrary will over the will of morality. The tenet that upholds the right of even the smallest ethnic group to self-determination has been forcibly suppressed throughout Europe, and no less so the tenet looking to the preservation of racial and cultural individuality. The tenets fundamental to genuine national solidarity have been annihilated by the systematic destruction of the trust between one man and another. There is no more terrible judgment on a national community than the admission, which all of us must make, that no man can feel safe in the presence of his neighbour, that a father can no longer feel safe in the presence of his son.

That was what I wanted, that was what compelled me.

There is an ultimate boundary beyond which all external legality becomes false and immoral—namely, when it becomes the cloak of cowardice, of a lack of courage to take action against notorious breaches of justice. A state that strangles all free expression of opinion and that brands any morally justified criticism, any suggestion for betterment, as a " preliminary to high treason," subject to the severest penalties, breaks an unwritten law that has always been alive in " sound popular understanding " and must remain alive.

I have attained this one goal: I am presenting this warning and admonition not to a small private discussion group but before the most responsible, the highest judiciary seat. Upon this admonition, this solemn plea for a return, I am staking my life. I demand that freedom be given back to our German nation. We do not want to eke out our brief existence in the chains of slavery, even though they might be the golden chains of a material abundance.

You have taken from me the status and the rights of a professor, as well as my doctorate attained *summa cum laude*, and placed me on a footing with the lowest criminal. No trial for high treason can rob me of the dignity of a university professor, or a man who openly and courageously avows his view of the world and the state. The inexorable course of history will vindicate my actions and my purposes; on this I rely with adamant faith. I hope in God's name that the spiritual forces that will vindicate them may be born in

good time from my own nation. I have acted as I had to
act in response to an inward voice. I accept the consequences in the spirit of the words of Johann Gottlieb
Fichte:

> *And you must act as though*
> *On you and your deeds alone*
> *The fate of German history hung,*
> *And the responsibility—your own.*

FAREWELL LETTER TO HIS FAMILY

July 13, 1943

In the middle of my work for you I was overtaken to-day
by the news that I had been long expecting. All you dearest
ones! Rejoice with me! It is for my fatherland, for a just
and more beautiful fatherland that will certainly emerge
from this war, that I am allowed to. . . .*

I shall be with you and our beloved little ones through all
the days, until you follow me to the place where there is no
parting any more. In your dear maternal hands I place the
fate and the education of our beloved children. I know that
they will think of their daddy and that they will bring their
mummy joy by anticipating her wishes in every way they
can. Beloved Clara! Think of the wonderful hours we have
had, of our life together with the children, and forget all
suffering. Place yourself, together with the children, under
the Cross, and everything else will come to you a hundred-
and a thousand-fold. And be proud that you are all bearing
your share in the struggle for a new Germany! You are
heroes just as are the wives and children who have lost their
husbands and fathers at the front. Beloved Clara, you have
shown me so infinitely much love in these hard months, and
you have lightened my time of suffering so much that I do
not know how I can thank you. If I did not know that I shall

* Here the writer either forgot or did not wish to write the word
" die."

be permitted to stand by you in the better world beyond,
I should be a beggar. As it is, however, I remain eternally
in your debt.

Dearest Birgit! Your life will be grave and dark at the
outset, but bright in the future. I know that you will
remain your mother's right hand and support. Your father
does not forget you and prays for all of you. God gave you
rich gifts. Use them, seek joy in music and poetry, and
continue to be the dear, good angel you have been for us.

Dearest brave little Wolfi! The whole of this beautiful life
lies still open before you. You will grow up to be a good boy
and an able man. Mother's protector and pride. And if at
times life becomes hard for you, always think of your daddy
who continues to care for his dear boy.

Dearest ones! Don't cry for me—I am happy and protected. The alpine roses, your last sweet greeting from our
beloved mountains, stand withered before me. In two hours
I shall enter into the true freedom of the heights, for which
I have been struggling for a lifetime.

All my beloved ones! One more brief hour! My last
wish:

> Lord, my Lord, I am prepared.
> Guided by the hand I go
> Joyously unto eternity!
> Bless thou this our German land,
> Bless my wife, my children too,
> Comfort them in all distress.
> Give to those I love below
> Heavenly peace—thy gift of love.

May Almighty God bless you and take you into his care.

ERNST VON HARNACK

GOVERNMENT OFFICIAL

Ernst von Harnack, born on July 15, 1888, in Marburg, was executed on March 5, 1945, in Berlin. A deep compassion for the poor and disinherited, and a sense of social responsibility, drew this idealistic civil servant, son of the great theologian Adolf von Harnack, into the camp of the socialists. Under the Third Reich he helped to create the liaison between the Social Democratic leaders and the military resistance; for this he paid with his life. He died not vanquished but as a victor. It was his wish—this was his request to a prisoner in an adjoining cell, who had a violin—to die with the sound of a Christian song of triumph in his ears, *Vexilla regis prodeunt.*

FROM A LETTER TO HIS SISTER*

Berlin-Moabit, December 7, 1944

You will surely win honours in your examination. Our whole generation has been undergoing a test for a very long time now, and a harder one than we ever dreamed of in the " gay, bright days." This is how I am getting through *my* test: the not inconsiderable leisure allowed to prisoners held for investigation I fill to the brim with thinking up films, working at hobbies for practical use here at Christmastime, with writing, reading, and yes, studying. Yet all this without tension, so that I can still always raise my eyes calmly from time to time, and look towards the future without horror. Because communication is so slow, there is as it were an insulating wall between me and the outside world, but I have adjusted myself to it. . . .

* Anna Frucht von Harnack, who was about to take an examination in theology.

TO HIS WIFE

October 28, 1944

I want to start this letter with the reassuring explanation that no danger whatever threatens you, the children, or other persons related to us, because of my imprisonment. . . . My situation is grave, but the stakes were high, and it was not thoughtlessness that brought me to my present plight. The external conditions of my life are tolerable—including the circumstances that during air-raid alarms I remained locked in my cell. But these things are nothing compared to the spiritual afflictions and trials. To endure and to overcome these is a difficult, difficult task that challenges all one's resources of soul, character, and mind. Up to now God has given me this strength, and you, my dear ones, have fortified them through your wishes and prayers, your efforts and gifts. Now take one more load from my heart by promising me that you will not trouble yourselves about me with that grinding anxiety which Jesus Christ wanted to lift from us for all time. . . .

You all have heavy burdens, and the coming times will bring new trials. Therefore it is my heartfelt wish that the thought of me should not additionally darken your lives, but that from my quiet cell a flood of comfort and strength should flow forth to you and all who are related to me. Not that I have already surmounted the things of this world. This renunciation will cost still many a bitter effort and many a trial of patience. And it may also happen that the angel of death, whose wings have often brushed me, may this time too give me a reprieve. But it would be foolish and unmanly to stake all my hopes on an earthly miracle. It is the miracle of grace that I am striving to attain. I have already felt a ray of its glory—otherwise I should not be able to write this letter—and I hope in God's name that his grace will lift me high above all fears regarding my external fate. In apocalyptic times like these, with their constant threat of danger and forfeit, the value of life comes to seem very small, while the worth of the soul shines forth resplendently. Let us reunite spiritually in a realm in which there are no bars nor gates of steel.

Berlin-Moabit, Christmas Day, 1944

I thank you and our daughters with all my heart for the lovely Christmas holiday you made and still are making for me. Your parcels helped me to soar as with the wings of an eagle over the spiritual reefs of this occasion, with its wealth of memories. And, last but not least, I give thanks also because by means of the twenty-three prizes for the twenty-three tickets of my " Moabit Christmas lottery " I was able to provide a real joy for my fellow prisoners. Your notes, your stationery, the lovely cards that the girls painted, and a few things that I had saved up, lay neatly wrapped, with numbers inked on them, on my tray (made out of folders, paste, and gilt paper) covered with the white lace cloth and a schedule for the drawing that bore as its emblem a Christmas star shining through a cell window. In the afternoon I decorated my little silver fir—I cannot thank R. enough for having got it for me—made a fine star for the tip, and fastened your Advent angel on it. Beside it, the little work table that I have been enjoying for some time now became, with its blossom-white paper covering, the gift table. Boxes of cakes and Christmas *Stollen* were grouped around the familiar carved crèche.

And books! The always delightful Mozart letters, the engaging, warm-hearted Timmermanns, and the *Thoughts on Art* by Carus . . . whom I have always wanted to read. In the evening I lit the candles and left only the wall light burning behind R.'s perfectly executed transparency of the manger. It was beautiful, perhaps too beautiful, for when I tried to look at the family pictures, something always got into my eyes and dimmed them.

Then the cell door was opened with a bang, and there appeared the prison commandant, a chivalrous man, who shook my hand and said that he was pleased about my work on behalf of my fellow prisoners and wanted to meet me. He had brought with him Theo, the most upstanding of the " trusties," along with my lottery tray, and then I received permission to conduct the drawing myself in a subterranean cell occupied by five trusties. I stayed there for some length of time and shall never forget the evening—not any more than I shall forget the Christmas Eve, a lifetime ago, in the unlighted train bringing us from the western front to Luxembourg, or that of a year ago, in the organ loft of the Fieberbrunn church. " Tangled destinies " were laid bare, and made me think of Father's roughshod but true saying, " Man's a tough rascal." And how much decent feeling, how much innate refinement, was still there, surviving after all those vicissitudes!

Thus I was diverted from my own cares and difficulties, and when I returned to my cell, I was able to spread out those pictures with unclouded eyes and bring back to mind the times out of which they came. Thanks welled up within me and eclipsed every access of sadness. . . .

With heartfelt gratitude,
Your Ernst

FRAU VON HARNACK TO FRAU VON S.

Zehlendorf, March 10, 1945

My dear A.: Now that fearful thing has indeed happened which we feared so much but which we were never really able to believe true.

Courageously and with head erect he went his way to the end, remaining true to his conviction. He died for his faith. He said: " The decisive thing is not attaining the goal, but rather holding to the right road."

For us who remain, life has become sad and empty. . . . Now we must fortify our hearts to bear our burden.

JULIUS LEBER

Julius Leber, born on November 16, 1891, at Biesheim in Upper Alsace, was editor-in-chief of the *Lübecker Volksbote* and a Social Democratic member of the German Reichstag. His prominence as a politician made him an object of National Socialist persecution, and he suffered years of imprisonment in a concentration camp. He held a leading position in the resistance movement. Because of his connection with the plot against Hitler's life, he was sentenced to death, and died on January 5, 1945.

LETTERS FROM PRISON

Lübeck Prison, June 24, 1933

Sometimes this thought comes to my mind: Who knows, perhaps destiny is wiser than we now suspect. Perhaps some day it will actually be found to have been a good thing that an end was put to that stage of my life which in itself had no further task and held out no prospect other than that of steering towards a sunny eve of life. In the last two or three years this prospect has often tormented me, and in view of the hopeless atrophy of our political structure I saw no other way out. Surely you know me well enough to realise that it is somehow rooted in my character to look on the struggle for a goal as the thing that matters supremely; the goal once attained means little to me. But what sort of goal was there still to fight for in recent years? Had this bitter dispensation affected only me personally, I should perhaps have had to look for the tragic fault in my own evolution through the last two years. But what is the evolution of an individual in comparison with the large historical process? And what indeed is even the punishment meted out to me as against the fact that my life's work is collapsing!

Lübeck Prison, July 26, 1933

There are all sorts of means by which fear can be instilled in a people. But love grows only by aid of a spirit of humanity and justice, and without love there simply is no fatherland. Sometimes I doubt that I myself shall ever see a fatherland in which justice reigns.

Lübeck Prison, August 4, 1933

At bottom life is beautiful only because of its tensions. Among my early " beautiful memories " I recall only a few rare occasions that gave me a joy as tense as that which fills me now in the expectation of your visit. And if that week goes by as rapidly as the present one, life will be nearly perfect. Yesterday when the inspector went through my cell and asked me how things were going, I could answer only that I am having a happy time under his administration. He thought I was crazy, of course. But this inward collectedness and concentration induced by confinement to the close quarters of a cell really creates a condition more auspicious for spiritual happiness than the dispersive haste of a free existence.

The situation is such that in this place each man must find his way, hold himself up, and develop strength by himself. " Here the heart is weighed in the balance, no one intercedes for him ": this holds true here much more than on the battlefield. For here all pathos and high passion are lacking. Here the heart is put into the scale without any makeweight. Here one can delude oneself about nothing, absolutely nothing, for one is always alone within four bare walls that in the long months become as bright as a mirror of the soul.

Sachsenhausen Concentration Camp, December 21, 1936

Christmas is on the threshold, the fourth since our separation. Destiny is severe with us, but not malign. Buffetings of fate, trials, and calamities hammer the inner man into shape and transform him. He learns to see and judge himself more clearly. . . .

No time in the life of a man is lost but that which he allows to flow past him unthinkingly and foolishly. Does that perhaps apply to the years of our long separation? Not at all. For they have formed us, and we have become beings different from the ones we were. A destiny which demands that of us does not only inflict wounds, it also gives us something.

AFTER THE ASSASSINATION ATTEMPT*

I have only one head, and what better cause to risk it for than this?

SHORTLY BEFORE HIS DEATH

The loneliness of the cell is by no means oppressively burdensome. I often think of the medieval monks who left the world to give themselves over to their thoughts within the enclosure of four small walls. Many of them found supreme happiness and deepest fulfilment in this. In a book by the old-time mystic, Angelus Silesius, I read this verse:

> *Men talk so much of time and place, of now and eternity:*
> *But what are time and place and now and eternity?*

I have been turning over many thoughts in the last few weeks, and I have at all events reached the conviction that the love of which the soul of man is capable, and which is stronger than anything else in man or in the world, shows that this soul must be of divine origin. And to be of divine origin means also to be immortal.

* Written shortly before Leber's arrest in 1944.

NIKOLAUS GROSS

Nikolaus Gross, born on September 30, 1898, at Niederwenigern on the Ruhr, came of a workman's family. As a young miner, he broadened his knowledge by reading and by attending evening courses. He joined the Christian Miners' Movement, and founded and led youth groups; he became secretary of his union and finally a newspaper editor. His Catholic faith and his political convictions made him an opponent of National Socialism. He took part in the preparations for the attempted coup of July 20, 1944. Arrested and arraigned before a People's Court, he was condemned to death on January 15, 1945, and executed on January 23.

FAREWELL LETTER TO HIS FAMILY*

Most dearly beloved Mother:

You dear, sweet children all: It is St. Agnes Day as I write this letter, which, if it reaches your hands, will inform you that the Lord has called me. Your pictures stand before me, and I am gazing long into each familiar face. There is still so much I wanted to do for you! The Lord has willed otherwise. The name of the Lord be praised. His will be done regarding us. Have no fear that in the confrontation of death, there may be great storm and stress within me. I have prayed daily that the Lord may give you and me strength to take upon ourselves patiently and humbly whatever he has decreed or sanctioned in respect to us. And I perceive what calm and quiet this prayer has brought.

My thoughts go back to you with ardent love and deep gratitude. How good God is, and how rich he has made my life. He has given me his love and mercy, and he has given me a dear, loving wife and good children. Do I not owe both him and you lifelong thanks for this? Thank you, my

* Written two days before his death.

dear ones, for everything you have done for me. And forgive me if I have hurt you or poorly filled my duty or my tasks in relation to you. Especially to you, dear Mother, I owe my thanks. When, a few days ago, we said farewell for life, I returned to my cell and thanked God from the bottom of my heart for your Christian fortitude. Yes, Mother, with your brave farewell you cast a shining light upon my last days of life. The closing off of our deep love could not have been more beautiful nor happier than it became, thanks to your courageous attitude. I know—it cost both you and me a great effort of strength; but that the Lord granted us this strength is something that we must remember thankfully.

Sometimes during the long months of my imprisonment I have worried about what would become of you when I could no longer be with you. I have long since realised that your fate does not depend on me. If it is God's will that I should no longer be with you, then indeed he has some other aid ready for you that will work without me. God abandons no one who is faithful to him, and he will not abandon you if you rely on him. Do not sorrow over me— I hope that the Lord will accept me. Has he not ordered all things wondrously? He let me stay in a house in which, even as a prisoner, I received a manifestation of love and human sympathy. He gave me more than five months— apparently a period of grace—to prepare myself to be taken home. Indeed, he did much more: He came to me in the Sacrament, many times, to be with me in all time of storm or distress, especially in the last hour.

All this could of course have been different. It needed only some small thing—then, as happened to many others after the attack of the sixth of October, I need only have been taken to another house, and many things, decisive things, would not have happened to me. Do I not have to praise God's wise and gracious guidance and give thanks to him for his kindness and fatherly care? You see, dear Mother, hard and painful as my early departure may be from the human standpoint, God has certainly thereby bestowed a great mercy upon me. Hence do not cry and do not mourn. Pray for me and give thanks to God, who has called me and taken me home to him in love.

I have prepared for each of you a saying or a little devotional picture inscribed with a personal last word. May it be a small remembrance for everyone; may these be for each of you a little remembrance, with the request that you do not forget me in your prayers. The crucifix and the rosary that you sent to me in my cell, dear Mother, have been a great joy to me. I wear the crucifix day and night on my breast, and the rosary too is my constant companion. I shall take care to see that both are returned to your hands. They too will be objects of loving remembrance for you. Now I have put my earthly affairs in order. The days and hours that remain to me will be devoted wholly to prayer. May God have mercy on my poor soul, and may he ever and always accompany you with his blessing and his mercy.

In the love of Christ, our salvation and our hope, I bless you—you, dearest Mother; you, Klaus; you, Berny; you, Marianne, and you, Elisabeth; you, Alexander; you, Bernhard, and you, Leni. May God reward you for every loving, kind thing you have done for me. Trusting in his mercy and kindness, and hoping for an eternal reunion in his kingdom of peace,

Your father

JULIUS FUCIK

JOURNALIST

Julius Fucik, born on February 23, 1903, in Prague, as the son of a workman's family, was among the leaders of the Communist resistance movement in Czechoslovakia. He was arrested by the Gestapo on April 24, 1942, and executed on September 8, 1943, in Berlin. An unknown person succeeded in rescuing the notes made by Fucik during his imprisonment. The last sentence he wrote before his death reads: " Mankind, I loved you. Be vigilant! "

ON A MEETING WITH HIS WIFE*

It was during the period of martial law. The middle of
June of last year. She was seeing me for the first time since
our arrest, after six weeks of suffering spent in solitude in
her cell, brooding over reports that announced my death.
They called her in to soften me up.

"Talk to him," the division chief said to her on con-
fronting her with me. "Urge him to be reasonable. If he
won't think of himself, he might at least think of you. You
have an hour to think it over. If he is still obdurate after
that, you will be shot to-night. Both of you."

She caressed me with her glance and answered simply:
"Officer, that's no threat for me, that's my last wish: if
you are going to kill him, kill me too."

TO HIS PARENTS AND SISTERS†

My dear ones: As you probably know by now, I have
changed quarters. On the twenty-third of August, just as
I was waiting for your letter in Bautzen, I received instead
an invitation to come to Berlin. The trial was held on the
morning of the twenty-fourth of August and by noon everything was all over. Things turned out as expected. Now
I'm sitting with a comrade in a cell in Plötzensee; we are
pasting paper bags, singing a little, and waiting for our turn
to come. We still have a few weeks; sometimes it even takes
months. Hopes drop away silently, gone limp like wilted
leaves. Poetic souls when they see this sometimes fall prey
to longing. Winter prepares man for its rigours as it
prepares a tree. Believe me this has taken nothing,
absolutely nothing, from the joy that is in me and that
heralds itself each day with some Beethoven theme or other.

* The interview took place under the eyes of police officials.
† Fucik wrote this letter under the immediate impact of having
heard the verdict of death.

Man does not become smaller even when he becomes shorter by a head. And my ardent wish is that when all is over you will remember me not with sorrow, but with precisely that joy with which I always lived.

Julius Fucik

TO THE SURVIVORS

Every man who has lived loyally for the future, and who has died for it, is a statue hewn of stone. . . .

I ask for one thing: you who will survive this era, do not forget. Forget neither the good men nor the evil. Gather together patiently the testimonies about those who have fallen. One of these days the present will be the past, and people will speak of " the great epoch " and of the nameless heroes who shaped history. I should like it to be known that there were no nameless heroes, that these were men, men who had names, faces, desires and hopes, and that therefore the suffering of even the least among them was no smaller than the suffering of the foremost whose name endures in memory. I wish that they may always remain close to you, like acquaintances, like kinsmen, like yourselves.

Yes, I wish that there be no forgetting of those who fought loyally and steadfastly, abroad and here, and who fell. But I wish also that there be no forgetting of those still living who helped us no less loyally and no less steadfastly under the most difficult conditions. Not for their glory's sake. But as an example for others. For man's duty will not end with this struggle, and to be a man will still require a heroic heart, as long as man is not completely man.

ALFRED SCHMIDT-SAS

Alfred Schmidt-Sas, a teacher and musician, born on March 26, 1895, dedicated himself as an educator and agitator to the struggle against the National Socialist movement. He suffered imprisonment in concentration camps several times over. On October 9, 1942, he was condemned to death by the People's Court; he was executed in Plötzensee on April 9, 1943.

WRITTEN IN THE DEATH CELL IN OCTOBER, 1942

As in the game of chess, so too in life it matters not
Whether the duel be fought with pieces carved of wood or gold.
How one plays, and what one plays for, that alone
Reveals the man.

Whether, upon post-mortem, menials hurry off the corpse,
Or obsequies of state consign one to a splendid tomb,
How one dies, and what one dies for, that alone
Reveals the man.

From Plötzensee

I am writing this on Monday, March 8 (1943). Even those terrible minutes around one o'clock in the afternoon when they fetch the evening's victims from their cells and the whole house holds its breath, those minutes too are over for to-day, and this day can be chalked up as won. . . .

March 21, 1943

To-morrow will be again a supremely critical day, and no one knows whether in twenty-four hours I shall be still in this cell, and whether in thirty I shall be still alive. But death has lost all its bitterness—not its sadness of course, but is this sadness not almost sweet? I feel that very strongly at this moment, when I am just finding my way

162

back to words and concepts after a deep, indescribable union with you. What is the origin of that force which magically touches our souls and draws them together? Why does this spring not flow constantly? ... I was sitting on my hard stool in my cell, as I had for the hundreds and hundreds of hours before, and yet I was, undivided and completely, a part of everything—nature, man, and art. The differences between death and life disappeared in the joy of being. ...

March 28, 1943

Half-past noon. Four martyrs have just been taken from their cells. ... Thus, three or four times a week, I am led to the edge of the abyss, and while I am forcing myself to look calmly down, I await the little push that will suffice to hurl me into it. ...

April 4, 1943

I am approaching a dawn again ... it is the dawn that heralds the morning and a new day—which I cannot imagine spending in any other way than with you, close by you, in you. ... It is five hours later; I have just been deferred to seven, that is, this evening; in another five hours I shall be executed.

A great peace fills me, and a feeling of great lightness. All that is heavy has fallen away. And never have I possessed your love and the love of the others so purely, so deeply, and so unflawed. I am happy in an inexplicable fashion. Keep me thus in memory. ...

LAST LETTER

In a high, pale-blue spring sky there floated a small white cloud. A few breaths later, it had dissolved in the all. Did it therefore exist any less than before? Nothing that once has been can pass away. The face of the world retains it.

A deep, liberating peace encircles me. An astounding emotion wells up in me and fills me wholly: the essential element in life and in man is not affected by death. And so I remain completely with you, and you with me. I die with an exaltation that does not tolerate even tears—just think, not even tears. I stand face to face with the world in inexpressible purity, I stand at its centre, and these last hours are in truth the zenith of life—the zenith of life.

What I still have to write now is of only two kinds—words of thanks, and words of my never-ending love for you. My imperfect verses are a weak reflection of things you originally gave me. In the measure in which I have become increasingly aware of your love (while it in turn has grown to the point of surrender of your life), in the measure in which I have learned to love you, to love you ever more deeply, in that measure I have become perfect, in that measure the bright glow of kindness has spread wider, the confusion of the world has cleared away, strength and happiness have grown within me, and I have become well-disposed towards all men and have loved our earth anew; this, my dearest, has been your handiwork. And there was a merciful dispensation in your last visit, our last sense-perceptible union; had we known the future, we might not have had strength enough. So I see you present to me as a picture of most beatific hope, and I die as though I were clinging to your lips in a kiss.

I cannot speak to you of my love; it has become so strong that it bursts asunder all forms of speech.

My plea is: Do not close yourself to the beauty of this world, surrender yourself to life; through your being, your art, through your voice, create joy, happiness, kindness, and peace. How much I should like to help you in that. Let all who have helped in shaping me know that these final hours and this death are the crowning of my life, and

that I remain completely yours

O strangely luminous life so close to death

Almost nine paces long
Is this my final whitened world.
Still nine days more, perhaps—
Then will fall
My head,
Which now still thinks and speaks and sees and hears.
The great sleep hovers very near,
With its dark pinion overshadowing
The blinding fire of wishes and of fears.
It mitigates the bitter, anguishful,
The longest moments of this human pain.

*O strangely luminous life so close to death.**

NIKOLAUS VON HALEM

Nikolaus von Halem, born on March 15, 1905, at Schwetz on the Weichsel in West Prussia, studied law and later made his career in business. Very early he recognised in Hitler a " harbinger of chaos " and sought contact with various resistance groups in Germany and Austria. The brilliance and force of his personality (it was hard to tell whether he was destined by nature to be a statesman, a scholar, or a poet) made him one of the most dangerous opponents of the régime. His arrest on February 22, 1942, put him out of action. The death sentence followed on June 16, 1944, and his execution took place on October 9, 1944.

LETTER TO HIS MOTHER †

My dearest, unfortunate one, that you must experience this great pain! Now autumn is coming—I hope it is not coming to break your heart. I am writing this two days before the hearing, prepared for anything and in a state of great inner

* Written with manacled hands.
† Written two days before the main proceedings.

peace. How consoling is the prospect that my sufferings are soon to end. Only the fact that your sufferings will then really begin and go on, oppresses and torments me.

Believe me, as regards the problem of death, I possess all the advantages that the Stoics ascribe to their teachings, even though I feel akin to them only as regards the form of their thinking, and worlds apart from them in respect to content. For whether we know it or not, we are all of us completely saturated with the spiritual essence of twenty Christian centuries. At this very time we seem to be entering upon a period in which this common background is becoming visible even in the apparently non-Christian thoughts of the European philosophers like Kant, Schopenhauer, Nietzsche.

Rightly enough—spare me here the answer to the why— we all fear death, above all because it usually overtakes us unexpectedly. The death of an eighty-year-old man is so mildly saddening only because its timing conforms to the cosmic scheme, hence it is definitely foreseeable. It is with good reason that the Catholic Church puts such great value on the preparation of a dying person, in which the external incidents and ceremonies represent only a means of inducing the mind to turn seriously to the thought of the approaching end, and in this mood to collect itself. He who is prepared need not fear death. I am almost ashamed in this connection to touch upon the mystery of grace, to which in a certain sense the high and holy mystery of death forms a vestibule. One step—and we have passed through.

I know that the customary consolations, especially those offered by the Church, will not find the way to the depths of your heart, and I would not be your son had I too not had to take other ways of my own. But since it is also proscribed to you, as a civilised being, to free yourself of your sorrow by means of lamentations, outcries and rending of garments, try again and again with all your acuity of mind to absorb yourself in the problem of the meaning and essence of life. Cleopatra said to Antony:

O infinite virtue, com'st thou smiling from
The world's great snare uncaught?

Only to a woman can freedom appear as the fruit of
courage.* But you can—as only a few of your sex can—
gain the strength of a spiritual freedom from the world and
with it also from the death of your son, so that you too may
be able to smile freely as I shall on my last road.

Read—and as you read it, think of me—the second
volume of *The World as Will and Idea*. *Nota bene*, the second
volume at least to begin with, quite contrary to your habits.
Browse about in it, and do not let yourself be intimidated
by the fact that Schopenhauer again and again demands
grimly that one should read everything that he has written.
You will see that he will lead you further, perhaps to
Leibnitz's theory of the monad, which Schopenhauer so
despised, and which I love so dearly. If I can, I shall help
you. When the waves have calmed once more, and when
you erect a memorial to me—perhaps at Father's grave—
add the words that even as a child moved me as though they
came from cosmic depths: "Fear not: for I have redeemed thee, I have called thee by thy name; thou art
mine." It is in Isaiah, exactly where I cannot tell you
from memory.

I believe that the war will end at the close of this year or
at the beginning of next. Oh, that like Moses looking upon
the Promised Land, I could discern, if only from afar, a
bright future lying before all of you!

Now adieu, my dearest, my heart's dearest! After so
many words it seems to me that the essential thing is still
unsaid. However, it is in truth inexpressible. Let us leave
it mute within our hearts, where both of us are inexpressibly
sure of it.

Once more, adieu. Do not think that you are losing me.
Thanks, a thousand thanks, my deepest love and tenderness
are all joined together in one last kiss.

Your son

* In the German translation of Shakespeare's text as quoted by the
writer, "virtue" is rendered as *mutt* ("courage").

A FEW MINUTES BEFORE EXECUTION*

Dear Mother: Now I have overcome the last little tremor
that seizes the top of the tree before it falls. And with this
I have attained the goal of humanity. For we can and must
endure consciously that which the plants undergo without
consciousness.

Adieu. They are coming to get me.

A thousand kisses.

Your son

TO KARL LUDWIG, BARON VON GUTTENBERG

June 16, 1943

My dear friend: I am afraid that I must regard the opportunity of writing this letter as if it were the last. If I
succumb in this affair, I shall be the victim of an injustice
that cries to heaven. The charges against me are extraordinarily grave, but mendacious in a most fantastic way
and—so it seems to me—at bottom not very convincing.
In any case they grow out of very low and despicable
motives, and are advanced with a truly disarming im-
pudence. I am completely in the dark as to what will
happen to me. The worst outcome is just as probable as a
good one. Therefore, it is in order to be prepared to part
soon and to become for my part too one of those persons
who, as you put it, my dear friend, are leaving you. For I
have always felt very close to you and believe indeed that
there is more of a tie between us than we ever admitted
to each other in the casualness of everyday life. And
precisely now, when perhaps my turn has come, I can
distinctly sympathise with you in that bitter yet thoroughly
ambivalent feeling of the survivor, so simply expressed
in your own words. But, believe me, for the other person

* Written with manacled hands.

the picture is very similar. The going does not seem difficult to me, but the leaving behind is a terribly bitter thing.

Thus in regard to myself I am completely unshaken and of good cheer, although prepared for the worst. If I must die, or be swallowed up without prospect of rescue in a pre-figuration of the nether world, I shall lose not myself, but, indeed, all of you to whom I am so attached. I cannot speak of the painful emotion with which I think of Victoria and the children, nor of how my anxiety about their future torments me.

Nothing remains to me but my trust in my circle of chivalrous friends, my trust that they will rally about these forsaken ones and afford them protection in their distress. Do not fail Victoria and the children—you and my other friends. Think of how much more difficult V.'s fate will be in such a situation than that of a war widow. Help V. to preserve my memory, and through your friendship assure my sons too that although my end was sad and without glory, it was without guilt or ignominy. See to it that in the life and thoughts of my sons, their father does not become a blot and a hurt, about which the less said, the better. Spare them at least this festering consequence of my mis-fortune, in the origin of which they have in no wise had part. Also see to it that Victoria remains in the " world," in relation to which she herself is indeed marvellously free and independent, but which, when I am no longer with her, she will need for the sake of the children. The family alone cannot do this, especially since it consists almost exclusively of women. Your friendship alone can save V. and the children from the drab mediocrity that so often engulfs widows and orphans.

How happy I should be, therefore, at the thought that you and the others will establish a relation with my mother. Moreover, I am in this pass, and obliged to endure great sufferings for the reason that I am one of you, and that malicious baseness hates not only a given individual but also his kind. Uphold the cause of our kind, which is your-

selves, likewise when it is threatened in the persons of my
small sons, and give them counsel, help, and encouragement,
and support. Teach them what even the best mother cannot
teach—" to hurl spears and honour the gods "—and beyond
permitting them to take my place in your midst, see to it
that they do. . . .

From the vantage of this place, my life appears to me as a
strangely winding path that now, however, seems to be
plunging altogether into uncertainty, into confusion. But
I look forward to the next turn with calm, no matter what
may lie round the bend. I believe that it is in Isaiah that
it is written: " Fear not: for I have redeemed thee, I have
called thee by thy name; thou art mine." But it is an
experience that penetrates to the very depths when this
foreground, the ego, begins to become so shadow-like. How
retrospection changes in character when suddenly it seems
advisable to resort to it as one's only perspective. How
much there is about which all at once I can now laugh,
quite merrily and placidly, for—thanks be to God—I have
not yet forgotten how to laugh; rather, I have, in a number
of situations in the course of my life, found new strength and
a new zest for laughter.

Yet my retrospection yields more shadows than light.
Only now do I see how largely my life has been only a
reaction to drives, needs, and affects; only now do I see
how little in the course of all this I have moved from the
spot, how little, in the sense of a higher reality, I have
achieved of progress. Thus the dark factor always emanates
from me, the bright element from other persons. And from
you too ! And if, despite all my scepticism regarding my
power to avert the disaster, I have no intention whatsoever
of letting myself fall defencelessly—if in the consciousness
of the scandalous injustice that has been done me, and of
my own rights, I search out with tense concentration and
undiminished energy every possible chance of tearing this
loathsome, strangling noose from my neck—it is above all
out of an ardent desire to do what remains undone, to
complete what is unfinished, to speak out what has been

given me for this purpose in the form of ideas, and to grow upward to a higher stratum of life.

For it is hard to perish in such a senseless manner, and it is worthy of every effort to strive for a better lot. I know very well that for the time being others can do little or nothing about it, and I myself not much more. All the more reason for me to seek to gather my strength and hold it in readiness for an hour that will call for more than enduring, persevering, resisting. But it would only weaken me were I in the meantime to lull myself with hopes and prospects that depend on help from the outside, or are based on the hope of unforeseen changes or on similar dream constructions. A great many innocent persons have been murdered, and these times indeed make especially plain the insignificance of a single destiny. . . .

Greet all my friends, and transmit my request to them. Take it upon yourself to hold them to it in some small measure. I think of all of you with the heartiest affection. Every peal of happy laughter still rings in my ears, every serious word still passes through my mind, every good counsel, every glance, every act of kindness is still present and distinct to me, they clothe me like a suit of mail against the thousand little miseries.

Who knows, my friend—perhaps some day we shall be sitting together once more over a good glass of wine, thinking of old times, laughingly and wistfully. But if not, I want to thank you to-day for the gift of your friendship and for the many pleasant hours we have spent together. From them according to their measure has accrued, as from few other things, the richness of my life.

Farewell, my dear friend!

Your devoted friend

HILDE COPPI

Hilde Coppi was arrested in September, 1942, together with her husband, Hans Coppi, because they belonged to a socialist resistance group. In prison she gave birth to a son, Hans. One month later her husband was executed; eight months later, on August 5, 1943, the mother, thirty-four years old, met the same fate.

LETTER TO HER MOTHER

My Mother, my dearly beloved Mama: Now the time has almost come when we must say farewell for ever. The hardest part, the separation from my little Hans, is behind me. How happy he made me! I know that he will be well taken care of in your loyal, dear maternal hands, and for my sake, Mama—promise me—remain brave. I know that you feel as though your heart must break; but take yourself firmly in hand, very firmly. You will succeed, as you always have, in coping with the severest difficulties, won't you, Mama? The thought of you and of the deep sorrow that I must inflict upon you is the most unbearable of all—the thought that I must leave you alone at that time of life when you need me most! Will you ever, ever be able to forgive me? As a child, you know, when I used to lie awake so long, I was always animated by one thought—to be allowed to die before you. And later, I had a single wish that constantly accompanied me, consciously and unconsciously: I did not want to die without having brought a child into the world. So you see, both of these great desires, and thereby my life, have attained fulfilment. Now I am going to join my big Hans. Little Hans has—so I hope— inherited the best in both of us. And when you press him to your heart, your child will always be with you, much closer than I can ever be to you. Little Hans—this is what I wish—will become hardy and strong, with an open, warm, helpful heart and his father's thoroughly decent character. We loved each other very, very much. Love guided our actions.

> *To him who strives with might and main*
> *We can award salvation's gain.*

My mother, my one and only good mother and my little Hans, all my love is always with you; be brave, as I am determined also to be.

Always,
Your daughter Hilde

LIBERTAS

"Libertas," born in 1913, the daughter of an architect, Professor Otto Haas-Heye, and of Thora, Countess Eulenberg, was the wife of Harro Schulze-Boysen, head of a resistance group known as the Red Band. This group, though largely dominated by radical elements, included men and women from all walks of life and of varying political convictions. In August, 1942, the Gestapo took action against them. In September Libertas was arrested and sentenced to death. She was executed on December 22, 1942.

FIRST LETTER AFTER HER ARREST

October 21, 1942

My beloved Mama: Before all else, thanks and thanks again for the strengthening given me by your thoughts and your sympathy. In the first difficult days, I was as though literally borne up by them. Your love, your constant nearness, mean something so tremendous to me that I can only hope with all my heart to be able still to repay you in this life. Please do not desist for one instant. Time does not make things easier; rather, it makes them harder, because they become more and more comprehensible. The assurance that I am never alone helps me so infinitely much.

Let it be a comfort to you to know that even now I value

this interval of time as something necessary and therefore positive, something that turns me wholly in upon myself and in the direction of a purifying, fortifying realisation of God. And I try to master my pain by assenting to it, by not afflicting myself with any guilt feeling, and slowly becoming filled with that invigorating confidence which crowds out the petty fear for my life and the great longing for freedom. Whatever comes will be the thing that is best for me. I am ready to bear it—" I have the will."

One more comfort. Everyone with whom I have come in contact is good to me. You can imagine how much that means. Moreover, I have begun to write poetry again—slowly the old kernel is shedding its husk—that will gladden you. How much more there might be still to write, but, praise be to God, we understand each other even without words. Take my thanks once more for your love, your trust, your strength, Greet all who think of me and thank them for it in my name.

With inexpressible love, always

Your child

November 30, 1942

My Mama: It is really difficult to write letters, because the " mail of thoughts " is functioning so well. Also, when one thinks of how many hundreds of times the recipient will be reading such lines, it becomes all the harder to say great and more than momentarily valid things. Therefore I say, as you have so often, " Have patience, do not demand too much."

Thanks again for your marvellous calm at our reunion. Please preserve it, for all our sakes! The after-effects of this reunion are so beautiful, hard as it was immediately afterwards. . . . This mutual tie that unites us all is really such a great boon, about which I never cease to feel gratefully happy. And over everything God holds his great warm hand. . . .

This is the way all the days are now—hard and big, full

of clarification, maturation, and faith. I am thankful for each of these days, since they give me time and calm for this struggle and this growing. And the pain, the living pain, is slowly making of me what I wanted to be as a child, " a poet." My childhood is indeed so near to me. Do you remember how, many years ago, at Christmas, I stood on the piano in the great hall and as the " angel of the Lord " was allowed to say to the shepherds, " fear not! "

This Christmas, which will make us feel bound to each other as we never have before, think of that—and think of my favourite childhood verse: " Hail to thee, Child! "

The room in which I live has become dear and familiar to me. At night the constellation of my childhood days, the Great Bear, looks in at my little window. Without having a clock, I sense the hour of twelve.* Thanks to the powers on high, my physical condition continues good.

This is important, for the trial is impending. . . .

And now, my beloved Mama, once again I entreat you, remain strong. I intend to remain so too. And whatever may come, I do not want to break upon it, for it is a part of *the holy task of God*, about whom I can no longer fall into doubt.

I enclose two little poems, one of which is perhaps a beginning. That sounds presumptuous, but sometimes I cherish a silent hope of finding a new and adequate expression for the hardly expressible, which means nothing other than writing poetry. But in order to reach this goal, there must still be much, much suffering.

Greet all the dear, loyal people who think of me, and do you likewise remain sound and strong in these times that demand such great sacrifices of so many, many people.

Always and for ever,

Your child

---

* Twelve noon had always been the common hour of prayer for mother and daughter.

WRITTEN ON THE LAST DAY OF HER LIFE

December 22, 1942

My indescribably beloved Mama: Since I am already living in a dream from which, fortunate as I am, I shall never again have to awaken to any horrible reality, words become difficult for me. In my heart you are with me. Oh, if only I could take you with me completely, thus to spare you the suffering that I have overcome.

It came quickly and unexpectedly, but the hours before the trial and even the present and the intervening ones have been so great that I have felt that nothing greater could ever be.

" O grace, to ripen from a youthful body "—you will find this poem among my things and you will feel its deep truth.

With every moment I am mounting higher heavenward. . . . When I know you to be smiling, full of faith, all is well. I am not suffering at all any more, and everything is humanly pleasant and without terror. . . . All the currents of my chequered life are flowing together, and all my wishes are being fulfilled: I shall remain young in the memory of all of you. . . . I shall not have to suffer any more. I am being allowed to die as Christ died—for mankind.

I have been allowed to experience over again everything that human beings are indeed able to experience, and more besides.

And—since no one dies before the fulfilment of his task—because of the conflict in my nature, it is only this death that has made it possible for me to achieve something great.

Darling, we remain together. We have found each other in the Light, and now I may draw you upward, grown to a new stature as I have, just as you drew me upward in the last weeks in the convent.

I love the world, I bear no hatred, I have eternal spring. Do not grieve over things that perhaps could still have been done, over this or that—destiny commanded my death. I myself desired it. . . .

As my last wish I have asked that my " substance " be consigned to you. Bury it, if possible, in a beautiful spot, in the midst of a sunlit countryside.

So, my darling, the hour strikes.

> *In unending nearness and joy,*
> *All strength and all light.* . . .
>
> Your child

SECOND FAREWELL LETTER*

Yes, my Darling, my strong, my only Mamushka: What I have been allowed to experience in these last days is so great and marvellous that words can hardly any longer describe it. . . .

Now I know about the ultimate truths of faith, and I know that you are strong and happy in the consciousness of our *eternal union.*

Your angel killing the Evil One with its spear (you sent it to me for my birthday) stands before me. . . . If I may ask one thing of you, tell everyone, everyone, about me. Our death must be a beacon.

All of you, you my little sister, my little brother, the children—you who are so close—in you I live on, and I say to you with all the gravity that marks this hour:

I have found my fulfilment, *my own death*; no greater grace could have been granted me than this. And—do not make it difficult for me " over there " with tears. Rejoice with me.

> *All is well with me,*
> Your child

---

* Written in the last hours of life, as Libertas was not sure whether the court-martial would forward the first farewell letter. This one reached its destination later through secret channels.

PETTER MOEN

Petter Moen was born in 1901, the son of devout parents. He was an actuary in Oslo, and, within the Norwegian resistance movement, director of the entire illegal underground press. As such, he was arrested on February 4, 1944, held in prison under the most stringent conditions, and after seven months deported to Germany along with four hundred other prisoners. In Skagerrak the prisoner transport struck a mine and went down, and Petter Moen lost his life with the rest. Statements made by one of the few survivors led to the discovery of his diary, which was retrieved from beneath the floor of his cell in the Oslo prison in the form of hundreds of rolls of paper with a barely legible script of pin pricks. Some excerpts from this diary follow.

7th day of my imprisonment in 19 *Möller Street*

Was interrogated twice. Was whipped. . . . Am terribly afraid of pain. But no fear of death.

8th day. Evening

Again in a state of fear. Wept. I have tried to pray. Problem—fear and responsibility.

9th day

Fear continually. I must overcome it. The pains of self-examination are great. Everything is inaccessible—will, reason, and morality. . . . Mother in your heaven, pray for me. Mother was good.

10th day

Loneliness is a heavy burden. *Quousque tandem, Domine?* Oh! Months? A year? O God!!!

It is Sunday, February the thirteenth, Mother's birthday
and burial day. May she be eternally blessed. To-day I
want to find peace in remembering Mother. Oh, if only I
had as brave a heart as she had! Then fear would lose its
power over me. Mother always thought of others. Therein
lay her strength. And in her faith in God. Mother, give me
your strength of heart and your faith! I am in such
desperate need of them. I want to try Mother's way. It is
almost calm in me now. How long will that last?

10th day. Evening

Should those fellows at the Victoria Terrace* hit upon the
notion of treating me very roughly, then. . . . To-night I
intend to pray to the God of my Mother that this may pass
me by. I have prayed. The guards make fun of me because
of my slow, rolling motions. The command is, "Head
up!" Fear lurks unceasingly within me. Lord Jesus, help
me! I kneel and I pray. My way to the recognition of God
must be made difficult. Only suffering can teach me. Or
salvation from suffering. I begin to apprehend the mystery
of suffering. It is evening. I have wept much to-day.

11th day

To-day I have reached the age of forty-three. I have misused my life and deserve the punishment that is now being
meted out to me at the hands of the unjust. My thoughts
to-day are grazing the periphery of the problem of happiness.
Never in my life have I been happy—not one single day.
But I have been unhappy many times, unhappy enough to
be drawn to the brink of suicide. From now on I shall *seek*
happiness. Perhaps it lies in faith, in sacrifice, in prayer?
Now I can kneel down and pray. Not that I believe, but
I pray for faith. Strange, strange—that this is I. Where
may this lead?

* Headquarters of the Security Police.

11th day. Evening

Within me all day long there has been such a strange
emptiness. Even fear has disappeared. Is that a result of
psychic fatigue, or is it really—help from Mother? I hope
that I shall be permitted to go on living and to take another
road, a road leading to good—away from violence, vanity,
and avarice. Tearfully I have prayed to God on behalf of
Victor and Eric, asking that they be spared suffering and
be permitted to live on. I myself also want to stay alive.
But what is much more important for me now is to find a
God. If he exists only in conjunction with death—then I
must die.

12th day

It may well be that this will be my death. Scatter my ashes
to all the winds and afterwards forget me, and then—let
things go as they can. Is faith more than a wish mechanism
of the soul? Can the reality of God be demonstrated by
anything other than that I believe in him? Pray, the pastors
say, pray to Jesus and he will give you faith or peace or
courage. But then, I maintain, the truth is probably that
prayer creates faith, peace, or courage. . . . If that is the
case, then reason tells me that I must pray *a great deal*.

Oh, if I only had someone with whom I could talk. But
here there is only the rattling of locks and the heavy key.
And I am a " criminal prisoner." Oh, how very much
David's prayer is my prayer: Lord, take the stony heart
out of me, and give me a heart of flesh. The stony heart
is the dwelling place of sin. Mother, dear Mother, I call
out to you: Give me your heart!

12th day. Evening

The future looks dark for us political prisoners. Besides
individual death sentences or death without prior sentenc-
ing, I fear there will be mass executions. May a higher

power defend us. On my knees I have prayed to the God of my father and mother. I prayed for my life and for the lives of my comrades. I weep a great deal. I am not brave. I am no hero. There is nothing I can do about it. I am only abysmally unhappy.

16th day

A few more words by the fading daylight. Is my " desire for God " honest? It could be an *argumentum ad hoc*—a product of imprisonment. It has been said that the belief in God is a creation of fear—the fear of nature and the fear of death. If that is the case, then I am on the right road. I believe that I can " find God " through suffering, fear, and prayer. Then have I played a trick on myself? Has spiritual exercise mastered my intellect? I cannot answer this question now. I only know that suffering and fear are terrible realities and that in the hour of suffering and fear I call out: Help me, God! This cry helps me. It stills the fear and occasionally keeps it away from me. Is it to be said, then, that God has helped?

32nd day

Again and again I have to ask myself: Can *you* believe? I am speaking of belief in the teachings of the church, or of sharing the faith of which Mother and Father used to say: Christ is the Son of God and died for us. Whoever believes in him will inherit eternal life. I know that outside, in freedom, I should answer: No, I cannot do it. My experience forbids it. Now I do not say a flat no. For I have had this additional experience, that in the hour of extreme need I cry out: Lord, my God, help me! Jesus, save me!

38th day

I have prayed to God, honestly and with tears, asking that

he grant me a grasp on the mantle of faith. I want to be
sanctified. The Word must acquire validity for me. To me
that means to reach down to the very root of everything
vulgar, dirty, unworthy, and worthless in my being, and to
combat it. In one word—sin.

42nd day

It is six weeks since I came here. I do not want to utter
any false profundities concerning this period of time. The
problem for me is: What is there left for me " out there "?
Do I really want to leave this place? I have not gone insane.
I am only touching on the deepest problem of my life. The
truth is that I am only very loosely connected with life.
There is very little out there that calls me, and none of it
calls me with a really adjuring voice. It is terrible, but that
is how it is. Like Hamlet I can say: " Who would these
fardels bear to grunt and sweat under a weary life, but that
the dread of something after . . . puzzles the will, and makes
us rather bear those ills we have than fly to others that we
know not of? "

For many years that was my profession of faith—indeed,
basically speaking, always. I can no longer count the many
times I faced suicide. I have never found a cure within
myself for this melancholy. Tantalus stooped down to drink
—but his lips remained as dry as before. Do you understand
now, my friends?

108th day

The transition from praying to cursing was easy and pain-
less. But my reflections now, a month later, are very
painful. It is that very complicated sorrow that Solomon
paraphrases in the words, " And he that increaseth knowledge increaseth sorrow."

HERMANN STÖHR

Dr. Hermann Stöhr, born in 1888, was a professor of political science and secretary of the German Union of Conciliation; his life was dedicated, through writing, organising, and teaching, to the ideals of social welfare and of peace inspired by his evangelical Christian faith. His historical study was concerned chiefly with the overseas relief work of the United States. In this he saw an exemplar of political policy transcending national self-interest and pregnant with possibilities for the future. Under the Hitler régime he refused to do military service, and on June 21, 1940, he was executed for " undermining the morale of the armed forces." He died staunchly upholding the principles he had laid down at the founding of the Union for Conciliation in 1914: " Love, as it is made manifest in the life and death of Christ, is the only power that can conquer evil and the only enduring foundation for human society. In order to establish a world order based on love, those who believe in this fundamental principle must themselves completely accept it. They must assume the consequences that arise in a world that does not yet recognise this order. That is why it is forbidden us Christians to wage war."

June 3, 1940

This is my situation: ever since March 2, 1939, I have been explaining to the military authorities that I could serve my country only with work, not with arms (Matt 5:21-26, 38-48) nor with an oath (Matt. 5:33-37, Jas. 5:12). And God's commandments have force for me unconditionally (Acts 5:29). For this I was sentenced to death on March 16, 1940, and the judgment was confirmed on April 13, 1940.

To be daily prepared to die is of course enjoined upon every Christian. Therefore this present state is for me a discipline. In the midst of it I rejoice in my leisure, which I use above all for Bible study.

March 19, 1940

Wherever there is still any shrinking from death, something is wrong. I have been thinking much about this recently and have studied the problem with the help of the Bible and the hymnal. From a purely mundane point of view, being sentenced to death is indeed the worst thing that can happen to us on this earth. But from the point of view of faith we say: What harm can come to us from men? With that we know that we are securely sheltered in the hand of the Almighty. . . .

There has been no dearth of more or less well-meant attempts to make me change my mind. But this has resulted only in strengthening me in my awareness that God has also commanded the nations to love and to help one another. But to lie in matters relating to an awareness granted by God, only in order to save my own paltry life— that was impossible. It would have meant contempt of God and basing my life on a lie.

A year ago Gertrude nailed over my bed a plaque bearing the motto, " Be thou faithful unto death, and I will give thee a crown of life." At first this saying seemed to me too harsh, because it made me think immediately of situations of the sort I am in now. I have worked a great deal at spelling it out and have finally given it assent. After all, a great promise lies in these words. If we really have the faith symbolised by Easter, faith in a resurrection of the body, it is precisely in the face of death that we are filled with a great joy that radiates towards us all the more brightly amidst earthly adversities. But if we let go this faith, then indeed it becomes dark around us. Therefore above everything I wish all of you and myself a never faltering faith in the resurrection of the Lord.

TO HIS SISTER

June 20, 1940

This evening I was informed that my appeal for mercy has been rejected, and so to-morrow, that is, June 21, about six o'clock in the morning, the sentence will be carried out.

This is, then, the will of God, who loves us all, and we who in turn love him must accept this too as for the best. It is for the best. And in so far as it may seem at the moment incomprehensible to you or to anyone else, we pray to the Lord that he may soon give us revelation.

For me as for others it holds true that Christ has freed us from the fear of death, and that perfect love drives out fear. Perfect love—that is HE. And he may draw us all into this love. And once we stand within it, all suffering must vanish for us, and we shall partake of great joy. Whatever we have to reproach one another for, let us forgive completely with the petition of the Lord's Prayer: " Our Father . . . forgive us our trespasses, as we forgive those who trespass against us."—And let us go thus to meet the day that will unite us all in eternity.

TO HIS BROTHER

June 20, 1940

Since we live in this grace, even this, my last journey, must frighten us. Christ has freed us from all fears, including this one. The execution out of this sentence is for me the will of God—God's benevolent and merciful will. And in obedience to him I want to make this last journey as it were to meet him. Greet my relatives, and heartfelt greetings to you in the feeling that we shall all see each other again in eternity.

Do not sorrow about this my departure and my home-coming; rather, rejoice with me, as is suggested to us in

I Peter 4:13-16. I should like to call out to everyone: Farewell until we meet again in the presence of that Lord who has summoned us to an eternal life.

MAX JOSEPH METZGER

(BROTHER PAUL)

Brother Paul, born on February 3, 1887, at Schopfhiem in Baden, founded the Brotherhood of Christ the King of the White Cross, which set itself a threefold goal—to do social welfare work and give spiritual aid, to foster Christian pacifism and peace among nations, and to promote the union of the Christian denominations (*Una Sancta*). The National Socialist state saw in him a dangerous enemy. In 1934 he was held prisoner for four weeks, and in 1939 for eleven months. On June 29, 1943, he was arrested again in Berlin; on October 14, 1943, he was condemned to death. He was executed in Brandenburg on April 17, 1944, a martyr in the cause of that peace to which he had dedicated the effort of his entire life. His last words were: "Father, I give my spirit into thy hands."

FROM HIS TESTAMENT

Nothing could give a more meaningful conclusion to my life, than to be allowed to give my life for the peace of Christ in the kingdom of Christ.

GREETINGS TO HIS FELLOW PRISONERS

Brethren: to be robbed of freedom is a bitter thing for all of us. But does not the poet speak of the man who is free, even though born in chains?

That man is truly free who is superior to every condition and who finds a reward in every lot. Can this be? The Apostle Paul, when he was himself in chains, said: "All things work together for good to them that love God." I have written this to you because I wish that you could all be as free and as happy as I am.

Your brother who shares your lot greets you.

Paul

A LETTER TO SISTER JUDITH MARIA,
MOTHER SUPERIOR OF THE BERLIN HOUSE

November 11, 1939

You have already been informed that a time of retreat has been imposed upon me. How long it will last, I do not know. I shall be happy if it comes to an end soon. But— this may seem strange to you, but I am speaking seriously —I shall not be at all unhappy even if it lasts longer, if it only becomes fruitful for me. And that is how I imagine it will be. Often I have longed for an interval of quiet concentration, removed from all demands of " business." I have never found the time nor the strength to tear myself away and go into the " desert," which proved a space of so much blessing for St. Paul. Now God has simply ordained a retreat for me. I accept it gladly. Indeed, I can say that it has been a long time since I have experienced such a feeling of happiness as in these days, since I live only for the word of God from morning till night. I believe I should become quite content if I were to be allowed at some time to devote myself to this glorious work for a longer period. Of course, I should like to have the human aids needed for it, a few books, some paper and ink! But even if this is not granted me, my joy shall not be taken from me. Indeed, I actually rejoice in the real poverty and obedience in which I live here, so that for once I can at least go about actually doing what I preach to others and perhaps do not seem to be accomplishing so completely myself. Here I can do it.

Have no fears for me. Rejoice with me in this time of blessing. Just think, here we actually have natural sleep. There is no light. Hence at evening, after partaking of our supper (porridge or a thick soup) in the dusk, we lie down on our pallets—and there we must stay until it is light again. It is about a quarter past six now—twelve hours. Of course, one can't sleep all that time. So we have time to remember all our loved ones individually and to commend them to God. Here I feel that material bondage does not enslave. He is free whose spirit is great enough to master all events. And that is possible only in God. Hence the " freedom of the sons of God."

Now I commend everything to the Lord God, in whose hands we are all safeguarded. May he bless you and all of us.

Brother P.

July 29, 1943

It is now a month that I have been in prison, and there is no prospect of returning to you very soon. I bear my fate with composure, joyful in the knowledge that I have served my people and my fatherland in accordance with my conscience. Everything else is in the hands of God. He will make proper disposition in all things. Have no anxiety. Even if the sky is overcast with clouds, the sun will rise again in its time. *Deus providebit.*

October 14, 1943
*Main proceedings before the People's Court, Berlin
Dr. Roland Freisler, President, presiding*

CONDEMNED TO DEATH!

Well, now it has happened. I am calm. I have offered my life to God for the peace of the world and the unity of the Church. If God accepts it, I shall be happy; if he grants me life for a further space, I shall likewise be thankful. As God wills. Give to all the brothers and sisters a last greeting, and do not be sad. The Feast of Christ the King will find you a little heavy-hearted, but just the same sing Alleluia! And remain true to Christ, your King.

Brandenburg, October 24, 1943

Now I am in Brandenburg-Görden. This is probably the last station, again a little more difficult, but God gives me strength and grace to say yea joyously to everything. What I miss most is the Word of God. How fortunate you are in having the holy Book always at hand. . . .

I am happy to hear that you are serving loyally and bravely. To serve is the meaning of the Christian life, to serve out of love. All of you must strive for this blessing, for yourselves as well as for the others.

And now I commend you to God! What he does is well done! Sing with me from the hymnal, " In the midst of life," and, " What God does is well done." What comfort lies in these two songs!

> Greet everyone most heartily, and do not forget, as one bound to you in life and in death,
>
> Your brother Paul

February 1, 1944

Just one more prayer. Holy, almighty God! My Father! In the greatest tribulation of my life I come to thee, in reliance on the promise of thine only Son and the blood he shed for me. With Christ Jesus, my Lord and Master, I beseech thee: " Father, if it is possible, let this cup pass away from me: Yet not as I will, but as thou willest."

Yes, I believe that whatever thy wise and good providence ordains for me will be for my salvation. Hence I respond in advance with the unconditional yea of my obedience. In Jesus' name I pray to thee: Give me the strength of the Holy Ghost, that I may abide to the last in this trustful obedience. Then I shall know that I am and remain thy child and the heir of thy eternally blessed life. Amen.

ROSE SCHLÖSINGER

Rose Schlösinger was born in 1907. Arrested on September 18, 1942, because she belonged to a resistance group, she was executed on August 5, 1943. Her husband, Bodo Schlösinger, an interpreter with the German military police, ended his life by shooting himself in a Russian farmhouse when he learned that his wife had been condemned to death.

A LETTER TO HER YOUNG DAUGHTER

My dear little big Marianne: I do not know when you will read this letter. I leave it to Granny or Daddy to give it to you when you are old enough for it. Now I must say farewell to you, because we shall probably never see each other again.

Nevertheless, you must grow up to be a healthy, happy, and strong human being. I hope that you will experience the most beautiful things the world has to give, as I have, without having to undergo its hardships, as I have had to do. First of all, you must strive to become capable and industrious, then all other happiness will come of itself. Do not be too prodigal of your feelings. There are not many men who are like Daddy, as good and as pure in their love. Learn to wait before giving all your love—thus you will be spared the feeling of having been cheated. But a man who loves you so much that he will share all suffering and all difficulties with you, and for whom you can do the same— such a man you may love, and believe me, the happiness you will find with him will repay you for the waiting.

I wish you a great many years of happiness that I unfortunately could have for only a few. And then you must have children: when they put your first child into your arms, perhaps you will think of me—that it was a high moment in my life too when for the first time I held you, a little red bundle, in my arms. And then think of our evenings of discussion in bed, about all the important things of life—I trying to answer your questions. And think of our beautiful three weeks at the seashore—of the sunrise, and when we walked barefoot along the beach from Bansin to Uckeritz, and when I pushed you before me on the rubber float, and when we read books together. We had so many beautiful things together, my child, and you must experience all of them over again, and much more besides.

And there is still another thing I want to tell you. When we must die, we are sorry for every unkind word we have said to someone who is dear to us; if we could go on living, we should remember that and control ourselves much better. Perhaps you can remember it; you would make life —and later on death too—easier for yourself and for others.

And be happy, as often as you can—every day is precious. It is a pity about every minute that one has spent in sadness.

My love for you shall accompany you your whole life long. —I kiss you—and all who are kind to you. Farewell, my dear—thinking of you to the end with the greatest love,

Your Mother

DIETRICH BONHOEFFER

THEOLOGIAN

Dietrich Bonhoeffer, born on February 4, 1906, in Breslau, was a lecturer at the University of Berlin and the philosopher among the pastors of the evangelical Confessional church. The intellectual sensitivity and world perspective of his religious life produced in him not weakness but clear-sightedness. When he saw both his church and his fatherland in mortal danger, the learned theologian placed himself in the front line of action. " When a madman is tearing through the streets in a car," he said, " I can, as a pastor who happens to be on the scene, do more than merely console or bury those who have been run over. I must jump in front of the car and stop it."

In 1942, as spokesman for both the Confessional Church and the German resistance, he tried unsuccessfully to win the co-operation of the British War Cabinet in overthrowing the Hitler government, and with this end in view he met in secret at Stockholm Dr. George Bell, Bishop of Chichester. Bonhoeffer was arrested on April 5, 1943. He died on April 9, 1945, in the concentration camp at Flossenburg.

Notes Entitled: " *Ten Years Later—At the Turn of the Year* 1943 "

GOD'S ROLE IN HISTORY

I believe that God can and intends to let good spring from everything, even from what is most evil. For this he needs human beings who know how to turn all things to the good. I believe that God purposes to give us in every crisis as much power of resistance as we need. But he does not give it to us in advance, in order that we shall rely not on ourselves but on him alone. In such faith, all fear of the future would necessarily be overcome. I believe that even our defects and errors are not in vain, and that it is no more difficult for God to deal with them than with our supposed good deeds. I believe that God is not a timeless *fatum*, but rather that he awaits and responds to true prayer and responsible actions.

ON SUFFERING

It is infinitely easier to suffer in obedience to a human command than to suffer in the freedom of an act undertaken purely on one's own responsibility. It is infinitely easier to suffer in community than to suffer in loneliness. It is infinitely easier to suffer openly and in honour than to suffer apart and in shame. It is infinitely easier to suffer by risking one's physical life than to suffer in spirit. Christ suffered in freedom, in loneliness, apart and in shame, in body and in spirit, and many Christians have since suffered with him.

ON DANGER AND DEATH

In recent years the thought of death has become increasingly familiar to us. No longer do we hate death as much; we have recognised in his features a trace of kindliness and have practically made friends with him. In our heart of hearts we know that we already belong to him and that each new day is a miracle. It would not be entirely correct to say that we would die willingly, though there is probably no one who has not known that lassitude—to which, however, one must on no account submit. The truth is that we are too curious still for that, or, to put it more seriously, that we should like to get a better view of the meaning of our confused life. We do not idealise death, either; life is far too great and precious to us for that. Above all we refuse to see the meaning of life in courting danger; for this, we are not despairing enough and know too well the benefits of life; we know too well what it is to fear for one's life, and all the other destructive effects of a persistent threat to existence. We still love life, but I believe that death can no longer surprise us very much. After the experiences of the war, we hardly dare to admit to ourselves that we should like to have death strike us not accidentally, violently, and irrelevantly, but rather in the fullness of life and at the stage of total commitment to existence. It is not external circumstances, but we ourselves that will each make of his death what it can be, a death by free consent.

Prayers for Fellow Prisoners: Christmas, 1943

MORNING PRAYER

O God, at break of day I call to thee:
    Help me to pray;
Help me to concentrate my thoughts on thee;
    Alone I cannot.
    Within me all is dark,
    But in thy presence there is light.

I am alone, but thou wilt not forsake me;
I am fainthearted, but in thee is help;
I am distressed—in thee is peace;
In me is bitterness—in thee is patience.
    I do not understand thy ways,
    But thou wilt know the way for me.

    O Father in heaven,
    Praise be and thanks to thee
    For the surcease of each day's night.
Praise be and thanks to thee for each new day.
Praise be and thanks to thee for loving-kindness,
For faithfulness to me in days gone by.
    Thou hast given me much of good;
    Let me now in turn
    Take the burden from thy hand.
    Thou wilt not weigh me down
    With more than I can bear.
Thou makest all things serve thy children's good.

    Lord Jesus Christ,
    Thou wert poor,
Wretched, imprisoned, and forsaken as am I.
Thou knowest all the misery of man.
    Thou dost abide with me
    When no man gives me aid.
Thou forgettest not, thou seekest me,
Thou wishest that I know thee,
    And that I turn to thee.
Lord, I hear thy call and follow thee—
    Help me!

    Holy Ghost,
Give me the faith to rescue me
From desperation, passions, vice.
Give me the love of God and man
That roots out hate and bitterness,
And hope that frees from fear, faintheartedness.

Holy, merciful God,
My creator and my Saviour,
My Judge and my Redeemer,
Thou knowest me and all my ways.
Thou hatest and requitest evil both
In this and in the other world,
Without respect to persons.
Thou dost forgive the sins of him
Who prays sincerely for thy grace.
Thou lovest good, rewardest it on earth
With conscience comforted, serene,
And in the world to come
Thou givest it the crown of righteousness.

Thy presence bids me think of all my kin,
Of fellow prisoners—of all those
Who work at heavy tasks within this house.
Lord, be merciful!
Award me freedom once again,
And then let me so live
That in thy sight and that of man
I can answer for my acts.
Lord, whate'er this day may bring,
Thy name be praised!

Amen.

EVENING PRAYER

Lord, my God, I thank thee that
Thou has brought to end this day.
I thank thee too that thou hast let
Soul and body find their rest.
Thy hand has hovered over me,

Preserved and sheltered me.
Forgive all littleness of faith
And all injustice done this day;
And help me to forgive all men
From whom I suffered wrong.

O let me sleep in peace and in thy care
And save me from assailments of the dark.
I entrust to thee my dear ones; to thee
I do commend this house,
To thee commend my body and my soul.
Thy holy name be praised, O Lord.

Amen.

PRAYER IN AN HOUR OF SPECIAL NEED

Lord God,
Great misery has come on me.
My weight of cares is crushing me,
I know not what to do.
O God, be merciful and help,
Give strength to bear what thou dost send,
Let fear not overwhelm me.
Grant thy paternal care to those I love,
My life, my little ones.

Merciful God, forgive me everything
In which I sinned towards thee or man.
Relying on thy grace, I place my life
Completely in thy hands.
Do thou with me according to thy will,
And as is good for me.
In life or death, I am with thee
And thou with me, my God.
Lord, I wait for thy salvation,
And for thy kingdom.

Amen.

August 23, 1944

Please have no cares nor misgivings about me; but do not
forget to pray for me, as I am sure you will not. I am so
certain of the guidance of God's hand that I hope to be
maintained always in this certainty. You must never doubt

that I walk thankfully and joyfully this path in which I am being led. My life in the past has been filled to overflowing with God's goodness, and above guilt stands the forgiving love of Him who was crucified. I am most thankful of all for the people whom I have known, and hope only that they will never have to sorrow over me, and that they too will gratefully always be certain only of the kindness and forgiveness of God. Forgive me for writing all this. Do not let it sadden or distress you for a single moment; let it make you really only glad. But I did want to get it said for once, and I do not know of whom I could demand that he hear it really only with joy. . . .

Now, from the depths of my heart, I wish you much outward and inward peace. May God keep you and all of us and may he grant us an early and happy reunion.

Thinking of you in gratitude, loyalty, and daily prayer,

Your D.

THEODOR HAUBACH

STATESMAN

The constructive forces at work among the German people under the Weimar Republic, only to be overthrown in the end by despair and fanaticism, were exemplified in Theodor Haubach, born on September 15, 1896, in Frankfort. From the First World War, in which he was wounded eight times, he returned home a confirmed Socialist. On obtaining his doctorate in philosophy at Heidelberg he served the hard-pressed cause of the German Republic in various capacities—as journalist, political worker, and government official. After the catastrophe of 1933, he became an object and finally a victim of National Socialist persecution. He was arrested time and time again, and had to suffer imprisonment for years in a concentration camp. As a member of the Kreisau circle, he was arrested again after the abortive coup of July 20, 1944, put on trial before a People's Court, and executed in Plötzensee on January 23, 1945.

The letters to his fiancée here reproduced were written in prison, in the face of approaching death. He had found the woman he loved only late in life, shortly before his arrest on August 9, 1944. This exhilarating experience lifted his spirit above itself and and loosed his tongue for words of gratitude, contemplation, and praise. *Ex captivitate lux.*

Berlin, July 7, 1943

You know that in the course of my life I have had to put up with many evil things; don't you feel, in the pit of affliction, how near God is, how very close to you? The " dear Lord " of whom we Protestants speak in a somewhat diluted and simple-minded fashion is very likely a bit neglected there. But that other God, that abyss of mystery and might, the God who speaks to Job out of the whirlwind, behold, he has placed his powerful hand on you: " From midnight cometh gold, and around God shineth an awful light." Hear how Hölderlin heralds him:

> *Near is the God, and hard to grasp.*
> *But where there is danger,*
> *The saving powers grow too.*
> *In darkness dwell the eagles. . . .*

Yes, this abyss of light is also an abyss of fire, and if we do not bend the knee—" Lord, Thy will be done "—we break. Bunny,* these are not meant to be unctuous words. All this is much more serious. Let us not try to get rid of pain by lying, nor of misfortune by dissembling: let us honestly take hard things hard—just as hard as they are. Only when, with heads bowed, we feel within ruthless force the presence of the thrice-holy Master, only then is the *De profundis* answered by the *Resurge te* of the angels.

Bunny, when misery assails you, do not resist, but give yourself up to it. Did not even Christ call out on the cross, " My God, my God, why hast thou forsaken me? " Yet he was God's son and very close to paradise. Only in the outer-

---

* The name of Haubach's fiancée was Schellhas; her nickname, " Schellhäschen," was a pun on the second syllable (playing on the diminutive of the German *Hase* " hare," i.e., Häschen " little hare ").

most night of misfortune does the voice of the angel answer
when you call on him.

And now, Bunny, it is late at night. I'll tell you very
softly—I intend to pray for you. In conclusion, listen to a
voice intoxicated with knowledge, the voice of Heraclitus:
" Whosoever hopes not, will not find the unhoped-for; for
otherwise it is impenetrable and inaccessible! " Learn that
by heart.

And trust in your good friend.

Theo

Gestapo Prison, Lehrterstrasse
November 23, 1944

You whom I love with all my heart, my beloved: In these
weeks in which the storm of love has come over me, I have
soberly tested myself and quietly and critically put to myself
—you know my way—the question whether I am not
responding with ardent feeling to your love and your
helpfulness simply because of my present plight, because I
am in dread and misery. Yes, I am clinging to you, bright
star in the night of despair—but that is exactly why I had
to ask myself whether this feeling that has awakened in me,
overpowering all else, is actually pure and genuine. It is a
terrible question: have I perhaps, with the faltering,
enraptured words I have written, deceived this girl
Anneliese, who is giving me all the tenderness and strength
of her great heart?

To-day I can say, freely and clearly, before God, the
almighty, stern Judge, whose justice I fear: Anneliese, I
love you, love you as much as it is really given human
beings to love. God has heard my prayer; he is in the act
of tearing out my heart of stone and replacing it with a heart
of flesh. I love you as much as you have loved me, for a
greater love than yours is inconceivable to me among
mankind.

In the wisdom of your heart you have inexorably rejected
the thanks I wanted to render you. Yes, more than that.

You have had to threaten to put an end to everything if I persisted in my thanking.

You are right. Here there could be no talk of thanks, for the issue turned on love, which, according to St. Paul, is the greatest of all the powers of heaven. You could only wait to see whether the call from on high that had reached you would touch me too: " Blessed is he that cometh in the name of the Lord." The call from on high reached you, because you showed a strength, wisdom, and generosity of heart possible for a human being only when he is awakened and guided by mercy and love from *on high*. You have shown a nobility in your humanity that is possible only when God's omnipotent might becomes powerful in us weak creatures.

That is why I also sense it when at times you are not completely in possession of this strength, when you, who brought me the summons to faith as a truly flaming command, have on occasion been in fear, misery, doubt. At first, at such times, I despaired too, being deeply troubled. It happened after all only once or twice; then I learned to understand that you too are only a human being, a daughter of Eve, and that the angels of the Lord must help you so that there may radiate from you what you now nearly always have—the light and the glory of strength and wisdom.

God has sent you to me that I may realise why man at certain times in his life must descend into the depths; first, that he may learn to call upon and cry out to God; second, that he may recognise his sins; third, that he may undergo a change of heart; fourth, that he may fear God.

What I love in you now has little to do with the erotic. Needless to say, I desire of you what every man desires of any woman who is pleasing in his eyes. But that is not it; it is your valour, your wisdom—yes, even your hardness. And just as you have now become what God *actually* wanted you to be when he created you, may the Lord grant that I too may recover the nobility designed for me when I came into the world in his image. I have not yet reached that point; in the long nights the adversary still assails me with fear, misery, and despair. I still need not only your strength —yes, your hardness, if it must be. But I need more—the stream of your love. I, a novice in matters of the grand passion, kiss you, you teacher and blessed one. May God permit you to help me further.

Theo

Gestapo Prison, Lehrterstrasse
November 28, 1944

Dear, dear, dear Anneli: Day and night now I think about you and me. What has occurred between us is really strange. Here was a girl, charming, gay, very gentle, not quite capable of coping with life, very scatterbrained, mixing up a thousand things in her little head, and that again was very delightful. This girl was called Schellhäschen. . . .

And now there is something else: a young, girlish woman, blessed with strength of heart, blessed with unparalleled courage, a woman who, in her love for me, lays claim to leadership, actually takes over leadership, a woman of almost masculine wisdom and resolution, a woman who, armed with the nobility of love, is capable of attracting heaven's powers to herself. What is left of the " bunny " now? And yet—it is still there too, but behind the gay or melancholy little rabbit there arises another figure, touched by the call from on high, a being who can stride over the waters and reach out her hand to a drowning man.

I do not know whether you know anything of this second being in you. Perhaps you hardly suspect her existence. But I see her, and that is why I love you so very much. That is why I revere you. And if you do not yet know it, I'll tell you: a new dimension has opened up in you, a new form has come into being behind your original one, and you are in the act of transforming yourself into what God actually wanted you to be when he created you.

" Therefore if any man be in Christ, he is a new creature:

old things are passed away; behold, all things are become new " (II Cor. 5:17). I kiss the hands of this new being in you, and when I call and cry out to God for help, it has a deeper meaning now than before; it involves you too, dear, beloved Anneliese.

December 2, 1944

To-morrow is Advent—the holy season of the year is beginning. . . .

Anneliese, dear, beloved Anneliese: Prize question: Which of us rejoices most over a little letter? You, when you hurry home with your aching leg through ruined streets in the rain-wet night, and the dear, familiar house on the Falterweg opens to you, with all its beloved people? Or I in the deep solitude of my cell? O little Anneliese! We shall not be able to decide, but that you bring more radiance and happiness into my life than I bring into yours —that fact, I think, cannot be argued.

December 4, 1944

A thousand thanks, you beloved, sweet, adored one! O Anneliese! Dearest beloved! When your Advent greeting arrived yesterday I was so overwhelmed with happiness, so overcome with emotion and joy, that—forgive my weakness —I gave way and wept out loud. Believe me, it was not nerves—they were tears of happiness and joy. And while you were still sitting downstairs, under the same roof with me, I set up the little candle before your picture, lit it, and thought with so much tenderness and longing about you! Yes, you are right. God has brought us together in such a marvellous way. " And the light shines in the darkness ": you my light, sent to me by God—you, consolation, hope, and strength in one! I may not thank you, I know—you forbid it. And so I pray that the blessing, the grace, the strength that are so visibly upon you may continue to pre-serve and protect you. Sometimes I have such anxiety for you—the darkness, the ruins in the city, and your poor ailing leg.

I kiss you, you dearest beloved, and think of you with all the longing of which my weak heart is capable. Dear, dear Anneliese!

Your Theo

December 7, 1944

You my beloved, whom I love with all my heart: How happy I am when I know that you are sitting below. Always hold Fritz up as long as possible, that I may feel your nearness. You lovely, dear beloved! But that you have been ill—I am terribly upset! And in the little picture, although you are laughing, you look so ill, so emaciated, starved, so tired and harried. And all that because of me!

With what a wealth of friendship I am blessed! How have I come to deserve it? This too is God's mercy, potent beyond all understanding. Little Anneliese! Beloved beyond everything else in this world! These weeks and months are for me a holy season. I am learning and experiencing who HE is, who is enthroned above all the heavens. "For thus saith the high and lofty One that inhabiteth eternity, whose name is Holy; I dwell in the high and holy place, with him also that is of a contrite and humble spirit, to revive the spirit of the humble, and to revive the heart of the contrite ones " (Isa. 57:15).

Therefore it is not crucial if the matter here goes on longer. If only it be granted me to see you ever purer and stronger in God. You wonderful being! I ask you for only one thing: take good care of yourself, eat better, rest a great deal! For I need you so very much, not only now, but for an entire lifetime.

I kiss you, you happiness, you light of Christmas shining into my cell.

A thousand times
Your Theo

December 13, 1944

O little Anneliese! You dear one whom I love with all my heart! You, my friend, comrade, beloved, affianced to me before God—and, I might almost say, mother. Sometimes I feel like a child who is very ill, and the mother comes in gently, cools his burning forehead, holds his fevered hand, and tells him about the kind and all-merciful God. And in still another sense—sometimes it seems to me that you are lying in pain, a woman's hour of ordeal, and that you are giving me life for a second time! Where would I be now without you?

December 14, 1944

Look, it is of course deep night around me, but the star of Bethlehem has risen, and very softly the promise of the angels penetrates to me also—" Fear not." If you did not exist now. . . . If you could come once again! What a thought! To be able to hold you, you once more in my arms, see your dear face—but let's not for that commit any follies or try to force anything that cannot be. I know that what you can do, you will do—even if you have to jump up from your deathbed.

I kiss you with such longing.
Theo

Did you receive my last little flower? (Picked in the prison courtyard.) How I love you!!! What blessing I have in you!!

Shortly before Christmas

O Anneliese! A time of tribulation and miracles! The Lord is passing over the earth again, to strike off what is rotten, to save what is ready. We do not know the designs of his justice. Therefore we must wait—that is difficult! Very difficult!

SISTER TERESIA BENEDICTA

(EDITH STEIN)

On her conversion to Catholicism, Dr. Edith Stein, born in Breslau in 1891, entered the Carmelite convent in Cologne. In 1938, to protect her from persecution in Germany, the Carmelite convent of Echt, Holland, took her in. In 1939, she asked to be allowed to offer herself as a vicarious sacrifice for true peace; her plea was finally granted. In 1942, after Holland had fallen to the invader, Sister Teresia Benedicta—this was the name she adopted on entering her order—was torn from the convent and died in the concentration camp at Auschwitz. " Truly blessed by the Cross, and blessed with the Cross, she became through her cross a blessing for many " (Bishop Roleffs, Münster).

FROM HER NOTES AND LETTERS

Let us not judge lest we ourselves be judged.
Outward semblances delude us all.
Enigmas are the pictures earth presents,
To the Creator only is true being known.

God demands nothing of man without at the same time giving him the strength to accomplish it. Faith teaches this, and the experience of life in the faith confirms it. The innermost part of the soul is a vessel into which the spirit of God flows when, by virtue of its freedom, it opens itself to him. And God's spirit is mind and strength. He gives new life to the soul and makes it capable of achievements to which of its nature alone it would not be equal, and at the same time he gives direction to its activity.

—*Finite and Eternal Being*

Passion Sunday, March 26, 1939

Dear Mother: I beg your Reverence to permit me to offer myself to the heart of Jesus as a vicarious sacrifice for true

205

peace, so that the dominion of the anti-Christ may, if possible, collapse without another world war, and so that a new order can be established. I should like to do it this very day, for the eleventh hour has struck. I know that I am a mere nothing, but Jesus desires it, and he will certainly call many more to the task in these times.

September 1941

It is good to reflect nowadays that the vow of poverty also includes readiness to leave even the beloved convent home. We have pledged ourselves to seclusion, but God has not pledged himself always to grant us seclusion. He does not need to, because he has other walls to protect us. It is just as in regard to the sacraments. They are for us the ordained means to grace, and we can never receive them fervently enough. But God is not bound to provide them. At any moment when we might, through external force, be cut off from receiving the sacraments, he could compensate us more abundantly by some other means; and he will do it all the more certainly and all the more bountifully, the more loyally we have previously held to the sacraments.

Hence it is our holy duty to adhere as conscientiously as possible to the rules of seclusion, in order to live with Christ unhindered, shut away in God. As long as we are faithful in this, even though we should be driven into the streets, the Lord would send his angels to encamp about us, and their invisible wings would enclose our souls more securely than the highest, strongest walls. We may well pray to be spared this experience, as long as we add earnestly and honestly: " Not my will but thine be done."

Dear Mother: If your Reverence has looked over the letter from P., your Reverence will know the tenor of his thought. I should not like to do anything more in the matter. I put it into the hands of your Reverence and leave it to your Reverence whether your Reverence desires to elicit a decision. I am satisfied with everything. The only way of winning a *scientia Crucis* is by feeling the whole weight of the Cross. I have been convinced of this from the first moment on, and from the depths of my heart I have said: *Ave Crux, spes unica!*

Your Reverence's grateful child B.*

SISTER M. MAGDALENA DOMINICA

DOMINICAN TERTIARY

From 1940 on Sister Dominica, whose secular name was Dr. Meirowsky, lived in the porter's lodge of the Trappist abbey at Tilburg and rendered valuable services to the cloister as porter and doctor. A victim of the policy of extermination directed against Germans of Jewish descent, she presumably met her death in the gas chambers of Auschwitz.

LAST LETTER TO HER FATHER CONFESSOR IN TILBURG

Feast of the Transfiguration, August 6, 1942

You probably know that we are here and awaiting deportation to Poland. To-morrow morning we move on. With me are two Trappists and the two Fathers and a lay brother of the abbey. On Sunday morning we were all fetched away and taken to the camp at Amersfoort. And on Tuesday, the feast of our holy Father Dominic, we were sent to Westerbork, near Hooghalen. I know, good Father, that you are sincerely living all this through with me, with all of us. Your spiritual child, Sister Judith, is here, as well as the Carmelite sister from Echt. For this very reason I want to send you a last greeting and to tell you that I am full of confidence and completely resigned to God's holy will. More than that, I consider it a blessing and a privilege to have to leave under such circumstances and in this way defend the word of our Fathers and shepherd in Christ.

* No indication of either date or place; presumably written August 6th, 1942.

If our suffering has become a little greater, our blessing is likewise doubly great, and a glorious crown awaits us in heaven. Rejoice with me. I go with courage and confidence and joy, as do also the sisters who are here with me; we are being allowed to bear witness for Jesus and to testify with our bishops on behalf of the truth. We go as children of our mother, the holy Church; we want to join our sufferings to the sufferings of our King, Saviour, and Bridegroom, and to offer them in sacrifice for the conversion of many souls, for the Jews, for those who persecute us, and thus before all else for the peace and the kingdom of Christ.

In case I do not survive, you will no doubt have the kindness to write afterwards to my beloved parents and brothers and to tell them that the sacrifice of my life was on their behalf. Convey to all of them my love and gratitude, and tell them that I ask forgiveness for every wrong and for the suffering that I have perhaps inflicted on them. Tell them also that my mother's sisters and my father's twin sister went to the camps of Poland full of faith, trust, and resignation. Tell Father Stratmann that he must not feel sad, but on the contrary join me in giving thanks to God for having chosen me, and sing a jubilant *Magnificat*. The work we began together* will come to consummation when, where, and as God wills it, and I shall collaborate as zealously and effectively as possible. Either through my insignificant suffering—and it is indeed nothing as compared with the eternity of joy that awaits us—or from beyond I shall always help him and stand beside him.

And now, sincere thanks for all the good you have at any time done for me, for all your merciful Christian charity. You have given me courage so often.

Now we do not even have holy Mass or Communion, that is the worst thing. But if Jesus does not want it, I do not want it either. He lives in my heart and walks with us and gives me strength—he is my strength and my peace. . . .

May Mary protect you and may the lost of God sanctify

* The work for peace.

you always. Once again I humbly ask for your prayers and your priestly blessing.

In Jesus and Mary,
Your sister M. Magdalena Dominica

JOCHEN KLEPPER

POET

In the night of December 10, 1942, Jochen Klepper, born on March 22, 1903, chose voluntary death together with his wife and stepdaughter, Renate, who were of Jewish extraction, in order to save them from deportation. He left behind him the fragment of a novel on Luther that he had been struggling for years to finish. In his diary, this work is referred to as *Katharina von Bora*; this was the name of Luther's wife. His death, as Reinhold Schneider wrote in a chapter of his autobiography dedicated to his friend,

was a human, a Christian, and an artistic tragedy. . . . His fate is explicable only in the light of his conception of marriage: he felt himself charged with the salvation of his wife and her children, with leading Judah home. For this is the word of the apostle, that the husband is to be a tool of salvation unto the wife, and the wife unto the husband. Klepper's mission was to lead his wife and children to Christ, and this task he fulfilled. But when crime enthroned as power no longer permitted him this union and this responsibility solemnly pledged, he took his wife and youngest daughter by the hand and hurried away to God, not waiting for him to call them. This was an act of faith: " Protect those whom I can no longer protect! " It was a suicide under the Cross, the symbol of love. The problem presents itself in a form that leaves no room for answer.

DIARY OF THE LAST WEEK

Thursday, December 3, 1942

Through the tender mercy of our God; whereby the dayspring from on high hath visited us. To give light to them that sit in darkness and in the shadow of death, to guide our feet into the way of peace.—Luke 1: 78-79

Again it was not until noon that the sun appeared, shimmering softly; and once more the garden lawn began to gleam. And otherwise it was another dark day, glooming away in twilight. I devoted the morning to the garden, making it finally ready for winter, once again removing basketfuls of dried leaves—the garden is really a small forest—and covering the tubers and bulbs.

Pitch-dark evenings. Preparations for Christmas and the drafting of testamentary codicils proceed hand in hand these days. . . .

Once again C. and F. have undertaken steps for Renerle: we hear that another influential personage is no longer as negative in his attitude as he was. We merely scan such reports by now; we have no faith and Renerle likewise puts no hope in anything awaited from this course.

Friday, December 4, 1942

> And the spirit of the Lord shall rest upon him, the spirit of wisdom and understanding, the spirit of counsel and might, the spirit of knowledge and of the fear of the Lord.—Isa. 11: 2

To-day too the sun came with noonday, remained, and transfigured the precious, scant bright hours, and sank clear and large behind the pines, clouds tinged with rose and gold floating in its wake. The beginning of the day stands under the sign of the slender, clear sickle of the waning moon. Under the page from the Latin choir book a large, soft spray of pine, a fir spray on the Renaissance cabinet in the refectory.

Hanni had Frau K. to tea; in the evening we drove to a lecture by Guardini. It was the first time that we—who are no sort of devotees of lectures and readings—had gone to a lecture. What is more, the wish to go in this instance was Hanni's, because Guardini when we were together had had such a great influence on her. And—something I had never done before—I took a notebook and pencil along; so great was also my expectation of him. Three halls filled to overflowing with the best element of the public and the best of the young people; the lecture had to be carried into two of the halls by means of loudspeakers. People stood closely wedged in; anyone who could, likewise took notes. . . .

Only music and the landscape can entice us out of our domestic quiet. But equivocal as are the rights and pros-scriptions for women in mixed marriages, we do not dare to go to concerts at all. A great, dark, clear night of stars.

Saturday, December, 5, 1942

If so be ye have tasted that the Lord is gracious.—I Pet. 2: 3

Another of those days when one has to steel one's heart and shut one's eyes, lest they fancy they see the dispositions of God. It must not, it must not be. . . .

Early this morning a telegram came from the Meschkes in Stockholm: "Katharina and Brigitte well."* So Brigitte's child is born and, just as Karl and Brigitte had long led me to expect, has been named Katharina, after Katharina von Bora.

How painful it is that one has to be so thankful that the child was not born in Germany, the Germany of the monstrous present.

In the morning a call came from A.: the Swedish foreign ministry had telephoned to say that Renate has been granted an entry permit.

We did not have the strength to keep this a secret from the child when she came home, although the most difficult step lies still ahead: a second audience with Minister Frick,† for which I asked immediately, and which will prove whether he is standing by what he said in October of last year in reference to Renerle's leaving the country. In the afternoon Renerle and I had an appointment with A. at the Swedish embassy. . . .

* Brigitte was the elder daughter, who had been able to leave Germany for England at an earlier date.
† Frick was minister of the interior.

A. rejects all thanks: he has been merely an instrument of God, he says. And again it is a matter of holding fast to one's courage. Baron E., who had part in it and who received the call from the Swedish ministry this morning, says also that something perfectly extraordinary has happened. It seems that C. once more—after a year's interval—interceded very vigorously on behalf of Renerle. . . . The entry permit, which is limited to three months only as a formality, is effective immediately. In view of the excessive increase of measures affecting Jews in Germany, we are advised to act with expedition.

Negotiations are under way with the British Ambassador in Stockholm to ascertain whether, besides, the Quakers can take Renerle from Sweden to England now.

Heaven only knows what the coming week may bring!

Despite the wartime winter, Renerle and I have been able to decorate the rooms beautifully for Hanni to-day, cyclamens and begonias. And the child was given her beloved finesiae. . . .

The morning was raw and windy (just a little above freezing), the evening rainy and windy. Hanni and Renerle did some sewing for Christmas. And when I look at them I can think only of whether I can stretch this new step with Frick to include a letter of protection for Hanni. My cares are measureless—really torture.

Will there ever be an end of our terrible self-accusations for not having sent Renerle to England with Brigitte in 1939?

December 6, 1942. Second Sunday in Advent

> And when these things begin to come to pass,
> then look up, and lift up your heads; for your
> redemption draweth nigh.—Luke 21: 28

Dark, stormy, and rainy—so gloomy that we have had to keep the lamp lighted for all meals. Went to the Advent service with Hanni. The first two Sundays in Advent have already brought the great, grave hymns and the joyous ones of this season. The Gospel of Luke on the second Sunday in Advent has always meant so especially much to us.

We had Advent callers, perhaps the best thing for us on this Sunday so full of tension. . . .

Hans N. and Ed. are going about in terrible anxiety over the deportation of Ed.'s mother. Only the circumstance that she was in the hospital with a contagious disease and was operated on immediately afterwards has saved her from deportation so far. Even Hans, hard-working and versatile as he is, can no longer write now—he too lives in a state of nothing but alarm.

And what a picture of peace this Advent Sunday was, in glimmering candlelight and the green of pine and flowers, with its quiet little celebration of Katharina's birth, of Advent, and of St. Nicholas's Day.

And in the evening Hanni wrote to the Meschkes for Brigitte—" and miserable with joy, excitement, and happiness." And nameless fear. And yet so collected and full of love and kindness.

Only to see the children saved—that fills Hanni now with a heart-rending passion.

Monday, December 7, 1942

> Blessed are those servants, whom
> the Lord when he cometh shall
> find watching.—Luke 12: 37

Dark and rainy.

We have found it a relief to have visitors helping us in the tension of yesterday and to-day to escape from the vicious circle of our thoughts. And in between and simultaneously, constant activity.

Saturday, after the news came from Stockholm, I wrote to Frick. To-day, when I came home from the office, I learned that the ministry had already telephoned in the morning that Frick was expecting me to-morrow at eleven o'clock, and the message was repeated in the afternoon.

All that amounts to a great deal; such promptitude was not to be expected. . . . These days are crowding together too many dispensations almost beyond reasoning out. How could I ever have hoped to work on *Katharina of Bora*, into which all that is condensed, while this thing, Hanni's fate, is still working itself out in the most disturbed, confused occurrences?

This is no self-assuagement.

God will have to perform miracle upon miracle, both inwardly and outwardly, before this book becomes a reality.

This book which has become something like a mortal crisis. And yet—what is even this book as against the fate of our child. And again and again we face anxiety over the question of Hanni's fate. Into what a rat race of fear we have fallen!

Tuesday, December 8, 1942

> When he shall come to be glorified
> in his saints, and to be admired
> in all them that believe . . . in that
> day.—II Thess. 1: 10

In the abyss that is now opening up before us, finally plain to our sight, will the second saying of to-day's watchword still reach me? " Take courage and fear not: God himself will come and save you."

I have seen Frick. He still remembers everything clearly. He, one of the most important ministers and in wartime the general head of the civil administration, stands by what he promised in October 1941: he wants to help Renate to get out of Germany. But here he can no longer protect her. No one can.

Nor can he any longer give me a letter of protection for Hanni, no matter how it might be paraphrased, as he did earlier in Renerle's case. Only the advice to let Hanni follow Reni to Sweden, and the assurance that he would facilitate her emigration.

" At the present time your wife is still protected by her

marriage to you. But efforts are under way to introduce compulsory divorce. And that means, after the divorce, immediate deportation for the Jewish partner."

These were his words. He was excited and harassed and paced up and down at his desk. " I cannot protect your wife. I can protect no Jew. By their very nature, such things of course cannot be put through in secret. They come to the ears of the Führer and then there's hell to pay." For him, who in his time made it possible in the first place for Hitler to be elected!

The talk about compulsory divorce would never have come up had I not asked Frick for an answer to my question as to whether I must undertake for Hanni the same steps as I had taken for Renerle. For he had already dismissed me, after calling in a police major and Counsellor Draeger, who was at once charged with initiating steps to get the Security Division, that new institution, the most feared element of the government secret police, to release Reni from the Jewish labour service and grant her an emigration permit. For now this is the new, complicating, insurmountable factor: Frick, as minister of the interior, can no longer issue such an emigration permit. This sphere of authority has been taken away from him. Counsellor Draeger tried in vain to reach by telephone for me the two men at the Security Division who would have competence in the matter. So we must go on waiting in the most dreadful suspense.

And now things have come to such a pass that I have had to go to the Swedish Embassy on behalf of Hanni and myself. Poor A. has a hard task; indeed, we had to declare that no relative of Renerle's would hereafter present a similar request. And now I have also had to pledge that Hanni would withdraw her application if it jeopardised Renerle's admission, and that I would withdraw mine if it added to the difficulty of obtaining approval of Hanni's.

For it is not in us to hold out against God's will to the point of not assenting to separation *without divorce*, frightful as the thought is that a German victory would separate *us* for ever, and perhaps eventually place Hanni and Renerle in danger as great abroad as in Germany.

God knows that I cannot bear to let Hanni and the child be taken away in this cruellest and most gruesome of all deportations. He knows that I cannot vow this to him, as Luther could in saying: " Take my body, my goods, my honour, *my child*, and *my wife*—" My body, my goods, my honour—yes!

But God knows also that I am willing to accept anything from him in the way of trial and judgment, as long as I know Hanni and the child to be minimally safe.

Renerle has renounced the thought of flight—many are fleeing now, and what terrible measures will be directed against them and their protectors! Should the Security Division, in spite of Frick's intercession, refuse to let her leave the country, she wants to die with us; then there will remain to us only a very short space of time in which to settle final matters, so near and so great will the danger be, now that the letter of protection is no longer backed by any authority and in the questionnaires newly filled out it was necessary to refer to it specifically.

Should Renerle's emigration go through, the child wants to go on living, in all her grief. Then we should likewise still have a short breathing spell, and I shall try to get from Draeger some last information about the timing of the divorce regulations, some remote, even if ever so guarded intimation.

·The final step has been discussed.

I write this still in the hope that some day, looking back over my life's course, over God's course in my life, I shall be re-reading it.

But what has now begun is no longer incomprehensible to us. In a terrible way it has completely penetrated our consciousness.

A dark, stormy, mild, dismal day—like a darkening, evanescent destiny.

God is greater than our hearts. May the Word accompany us even into death.

There is still one hope, one very faint hope.

Frick and Draeger (who is president of the German-Swedish Society) called Reni's Swedish entry permit completely inexplicable. Even Sven Hedin was turned down by his own Swedish government in an application on behalf of a protégé of his.

How, how is one to act in face of the other mixed marriages?

Should Hanni and the child die—God knows that nothing in me would any longer rebel against his will. But not *this*.

What a transformation our life has undergone all over again—in a single conversation.

Hanni is no longer capable of tears.

Wednesday, December 9, 1942

> Nevertheless when the Son of man
> cometh, shall he find faith on the
> earth ?—Luke 18: 8

In the morning Hanni was summoned to see A. at the Swedish Embassy for the registering of all personal particulars.

In the afternoon I went to see Eichmann of the Security Division, after Draeger had prepared the ground in the morning. He thought that Eichmann would grant permission—that he wanted to push the matter through quickly. Eichmann too raised the question of immediate departure. That is a hint of new and ominous measures. To-morrow I am to receive final word. It must still be determined whether the security police will give Reni clearance. He: " I have not yet given my definitive assent. But I think the matter will work out."

Under threat of security police measures I am under strict orders to maintain silence regarding steps that will follow if Reni departs.

Now I found myself in the world I had dreamt about; there were the people, the voices, the rooms.

I was in the centre of power.

The question was put whether Hanni would remain in this country.

I: " I have not as yet a clear idea of my wife's situation."

He: " Because joint emigration would not be permitted."

Puzzle upon puzzle. And the whole thing so inconceivable. A man in my position conferring with Frick, with the Security Division.

Do they regard Hanni as a hostage for Reni? Would they refuse Hanni as my wife what they will perhaps grant Renerle as my stepdaughter?

To-morrow at three o'clock I have another appointment with the security police. Since I can say so little over the telephone now, Hilde, who has taken such warm interest in this, came to see us in the evening after work. Now all that with which we had to burden her so much during the Advent season last year is so imminent.

These quiet, quiet, dark, overcast days. So gentle, so full of the tears of heaven.

" When the Lord brought back the captivity of Zion, He became like men comforted."

One more day of this torturous waiting. Yet everything is going so rapidly.

In the evening poor Hilde was with us for discussion of our will.

December 10, 1942

This afternoon the conference at the Security Division.

> *Now we die—this too abides in God.*
> *This night we go together into death.*
> *Above us in these final hours stands*
> *The imaged Christ, in blessing, who contends*
> *For us. Our life is ending in his sight.*

HEINRICH, COUNT VON LEHNDORFF-STEINORT

The staff of Field Marshal von Bock included a small group of anti-Nazi officers, of which Henning von Tresckow was the head and Count Lehndorff (born in 1909) an outstanding member. Scion of an ancient East Prussian family, devoted to the management of his ancestral estate, he embodied the finest features of the Prussian tradition—a tradition incompatible with Nazi ways and Nazi ideas. As a participant in the attempted coup of July 20, 1944, he was arrested after its failure, condemned to death, and executed on September 4, 1944.

ON THE EVE OF CONDEMNATION AND EXECUTION*

Most dearly beloved to me in all the world: This is probably the last letter you will receive from me on this earth. Although my thoughts have pursued an orbit around you day and night ever since our separation, and the contents of my heart could fill volumes, it becomes difficult nevertheless for me to write this letter. I fear that with everything I shall only pile a new burden upon your poor sorely tried heart. Nevertheless—you angel—you must hear and know everything about how I have lived, thought, and felt in the past weeks.

It is certain that, without having oneself lived through something of the sort, one imagines everything to be far worse than it really is when matters have become actual and there can be no more evading. My disposition, fortunate in this respect, and, above all, the help of God, for which I have always besought him and which he has bestowed on me in ample measure, have permitted me to overcome all trials in a way that I would never before have thought possible. A total transformation is taking place, in the course of which my previous life is gradually sinking away

* Written with manacled hands, September 3, 1944.

altogether, and completely new standards prevail. With all that, you have of course certainly had your little joys, and I too have had moments of happiness. Only the causes for them have changed altogether. A kind word from a compassionate human being, permission to read or to smoke, to be able to walk a few steps across a sunny court-yard on being led to a hearing, and various little things like that make one exactly as happy as some great event or festive happening formerly did. Since I have been nearly always a little hungry, I have rejoiced as much over a piece of dry bread or over thin soup as I once did over a hunt dinner. And they are at least equally relished.

My beloved, I am picturing this for you in such detail so that you will not think that your Heini has spent these six weeks close to despair, staring at the walls of the cell, or pacing up and down like a captive animal in a cage. Please do not imagine this time to have been like that. Of course, my one and only love, there have been also very sad and bitter hours, when my thoughts went their own way and I had to gather all my strength in order not to give way and to maintain composure. But I believe I succeeded. And even those hours were not purposeless, but surely necessary to lead me to the ground on which I stand now. I could not explain this condition better than by means of the saying from the Bible: " Be not afraid, only believe."

Before chatting with you now about ourselves, my darling, there are still two matters that I have to broach and explain to you, because I want you to be fully informed about their motivation. I committed two great follies. First, the flight from Berlin. It was more or less a spon-taneous and unreflective notion, carried out because a favourable occasion suddenly offered. I planned to get to the region of Conow and go into hiding on one of the estates there. I had not considered that I probably would be implicating the person involved. Therefore it is very likely a good thing that I was taken prisoner again by the militia shortly before reaching Feldberg. For I hear that all the estates there were already under surveillance. You see, I was overcome by such a powerful urge for freedom that I simply could not do otherwise than just take off.

To picture those four days to you in detail would take me too far afield. In any case, I had four days of freedom; I made my way by night, slept by day in the woods, and lived on berries, milk, and raw vegetables, just like the escaped Russian prisoners. So far as that goes things went marvellously, and I relished my freedom in every fibre. But there was one catch to the matter, and that was my low shoes, which of course shipped sand immediately, so that before long I had so bruised my toes in walking that I really could drag myself on only by summoning every effort. Except for that, they would not have caught me. At least not before I had reached my goal. But who knows what end this outcome has served. Afterwards the kindly gamekeeper who had stopped me even took care of me, and then I was brought back to Berlin by the police.

Up to this point the affair involved only me. But, as I have learned, my flight has also affected all of you. That, my one and only love, I had of course not taken into account. Besides, everything else, to have brought this further suffering on you and other loved ones is really very terrible for me. But I know that all of you will forgive me this rashness.

The second thing, my angel, for which I must also implore your understanding, but which is considerably more difficult to explain down to the last point, is this. On the day when I was seized at four in the morning, and then, after a not too pleasant time in an SS camp near Fürsten-walde, delivered about eleven o'clock to the prison on Albrechtstrasse, and immediately subjected to a hearing, it was suddenly really all up with my nerves. The four days of little food, the strain because of my feet, the agitation of being captured, the trip to Berlin, and the first interroga-tion, in which it immediately became clear to me that regarding myself there was nothing any longer to hide, because everything was already known through depositions —all this gave me a severe shock. After the hearing I was supposed to sleep a bit and then put into writing everything I knew about the " case," as relating not only to myself (for that was already established) but also to all my friends and comrades. When I woke up—and it was then that all the fatigue and desperation set in with a vengeance—the thought of now dragging in others too through my depositions reared before me as a simply insurmountable obstacle.

As a result of my condition I felt that I was no longer strong enough to withstand the assault; on the other hand, I told myself, I should lose all self-respect were I to give in before it. In this despondent state of mind, no longer fully in control of my senses, I tried to make an end of it all by cutting the artery in my wrist. The attempt never got to the crucial stage because it was observed. Beloved— please believe me—by the very next day this action had already become totally incomprehensible to me, and even to-day I still cannot understand how I came to entertain the idea at all. It is so alien to me. And please believe too that when I took this step, it certainly was with no thought for myself, but only in consideration of others. I had to tell you this, my dear one, for you shall and must know the context of things exactly. Up to now you have understood me in everything, and I firmly trust that in this matter too you will follow my feelings correctly. Inwardly I surmounted the incident very quickly, because somehow I never looked at it as relating to me. There, my most beloved treasure, now that you know everything I feel relieved.

Now to the two of us—poor you, my most dearly beloved. In some way everything that has happened is beyond comprehension. That meanwhile we have a fourth child, that I did not know of this until a week after her birth, and that I shall never in my life see this little human being, my own offspring—these things I simply cannot conceive. My only consolation is that everything went well and that you are in good health. Give the little mite a tender kiss on her little cheek from her unknown papa. She will suffer the least under all these sorrows.

Beloved, if I wrote when I began that there have likewise been difficult hours for me, they were mainly those in which I concerned myself with the fate of my little family that I love so ardently. I really cannot think about it. Let us not imagine everything in detail now. You know these things as well as I, and I cannot of course help you in any way. My beloved, that is the terrible thing about my situation— to be leaving all of you behind, helpless and unprotected, without being able to help even with a bit of advice. I rack my brain, but how can I give you any sensible advice when I do not know at all the conditions that obtain. My sole trust is my faith in you, in your courage, and in your strength of spirit in the hour of need. even in a single thought I deemed it possible that you could inwardly reproach me, I should go totally insane. You will always feel convinced that I did not recklessly destroy the future of all of you, but, rather, served an idea that did not, as I believed, allow consideration of family or personal interest. God and fate have decided against me, but I shall take with me to the grave the immovable conviction that you will not condemn me for this by a single thought. Nor can I let myself reflect on how such things would be had I acted differently, for over such reflections one goes to pieces. We cannot undo anything that has been done. Do you know, beloved—in the last few weeks it has become altogether clear to me that all our steps and our fate are in the end directed only by God. In my situation too I have from the very beginning had a quite definite feeling that everything is unfolding according to God's will. I press upon you a beautiful saying, because of its truth: " Be careful for nothing, but in everything by prayer and supplication with thanksgiving let your requests be made known unto God."

And if our entreaties are not granted, we must say to ourselves that God's ways are not our ways, and that we ourselves can never know what is best for us. My angel, such language coming from me will seem strange to you, but, do not doubt me, these weeks have made a true *believer* of me and I am endlessly thankful for it. The Christian faith and the belief in a " heavenly kingdom " are one's only recourse in the hour of need. Oh, my dear, how often I have thought of our explorations together, and how infinitely happy I should be to discuss all this with you now. But the road to that place leads indeed by way of sorrow only, and first everything must be torn from one by force. Only then can one become a new being.

Only now has it become clear to me what a sinful creature I have been. To hope that God will forgive me all this is asking a great deal, especially since I found my way to him only then when utter need set in. But I have often prayed to him for it and I believe that he has heard me. In any case, I shall die believing this, and without fear or trepidation. " Watch ye, stand fast in the faith, quit you like men, be strong "—this shall lead me to the last. It is my confirmation verse.

It was of great help to me that I was able to get a Bible in Königsberg, and in Berlin, that was my principal reading. This is my wish and good counsel to you, my beloved: Try seriously to become a true Christian. It is assuredly the strongest weapon one can have. And when one *wants* it and prays for it over and over, God does not withhold himself. He will certainly not deny himself to you, for your heart is so kind. My dear, I have pictured all this too in such detail because I want you to know exactly everything that has gone on in my mind up to my last day.

For the rest, I was nowhere really ill-treated; everywhere I found people who were good to me and concerned for me out of genuine sympathy. Sometimes I was deeply moved by this. There are evil people everywhere, but also many good people. Do you know, I have often thought of our conversations in which you sought to encourage me to gather more spiritual than earthly goods. How right indeed you were! Where have all earthly treasures gone? Vanished like a cloud of vapour. . . .

My beloved, I can do no more than point out all this. I

have of course much more to say to you all, but I can hardly write any more, and in any case I cannot say everything in this one letter, and I must not become sentimental now. The thought that we two, who belong so wholly to each other, shall never, never see each other again in this world, is beyond my grasp. Seven glorious years we lived together. Even now you have not once left me. I have always had the firm feeling that you are walking by my side, and I shall abide in this feeling up to the last second. Let us be thankful for everything that we have had in each other and with each other. For you, beloved, everything is of course much, much worse than for me. For my own person, you must feel assured, I do not fear death. I fear it only as it affects you and our beloved sweet children, and in my thoughts of you all. How will you ever explain all this to them? They are, praise be to God, still so young that they will probably not wholly understand. Moreover, who knows what the future will bring?

One thing I ask of you. You will be very sad in the time about to come—that I know, yet I cannot avert it. I know that you will certainly not forget me. But when you speak of me, do it with cheerful manner and not with that fixedly mournful bearing which people usually affect when speaking of the dead. I have lived my short life blithely (perhaps too blithely), and that is how I want to be remembered. You will understand how I mean this.

No person can say how your life will go from now on. Wherever I may be, I shall always pray for you. May God grant that you be spared greater sorrow. You are the very dearest thing that I leave behind me on this earth. If only we could at least have seen and embraced each other once more. It has not been possible. Please, please, do not consume yourself with grief over my fate. I know that when a beloved person has departed from us in this world, we try to imagine exactly how everything was in detail and what he suffered. But I have already told you: I have no fear, inwardly I have settled accounts with myself, I shall face everything proudly and with head erect, I shall entreat

H

God not to withdraw his strength from me, and my last thought will be you and the children.

" Death's moving image is not a terminus to the pious, nor a terror to the wise." I do not want to characterise myself as either pious or wise, but I do look upon the end in this light. (My lawyer gave me this nice verse to-day.)

My one and only love—you will not believe how hard it is for me to end this letter, and therewith our last conversation. But it simply must be. We shall go on loving each other beyond death as dearly as we loved each other in life. This letter will bring you pain, yet I did have to discuss everything with you just once more. God keep you and our children on all your paths. I embrace all of you and love you all above everything in the world.

Your Heini

RUPERT MAYER, S. J.

PRIEST

Father Rupert Mayer, born on January 23, 1876, in Stuttgart, resisted the National Socialist enemies of the Christian faith with inflexible courage. Scornful of compromise, he refused to belong to what was termed " underground " Germany. From the outset, in his first trial, he defended himself with the words: " It seems much more honest to me clearly to state what is afoot than to wind through a maze of phraseology. When I speak, people know where I stand and that I shall not budge."

From June 5 to June 10, 1937, Father Mayer was held under arrest in the Gestapo prison in the Wittelsbach palace in Munich, and from then until July 22 in the penal prison at Stadelheim. He recorded the impressions of his stay in the latter place as follows:

I have now passed through the most beautiful period of my life. One would not believe that possible. I have been happy, completely happy, as I have never before been in my life. In the course of these weeks the dear Lord has let me know—and I am a man of reason—that he is satisfied with me. That makes me happy; all else cannot disturb me. Prison is better for me than a thousand lectures on behalf of the Catholic community, on apologetics, on the Gospel—much better than if I were to lecture on heaven knows what. . . .

The day before yesterday I read a marvellously beautiful passage of Paul's in the Epistle to the Philippians:

> But I would ye should understand, brethren, that the things which happened unto me have fallen out rather unto the furtherance of the gospel; So that my bonds in Christ are manifest in all the palace, and in all other places; And many of the brethren in the Lord, waxing confident by my bonds, are much more bold to speak the word without fear. . . . And I therein do rejoice, yea, and will rejoice.

Is that not marvellous?

On June 22 he wrote to a Gestapo official:

> Once when you came to visit me in my lodgings at St. Michael's, you smiled when I told you that I should end up in prison. And now? And when I told you that my life would come to its end in prison—you did not wish to believe it, at least that is what you said. And yet that is the way it will be—unless I live longer than the present system, which you certainly do not think likely. But I am in no way unhappy about it. In fact, I feel spiritually very well and satisfied. I have completely reconciled myself. If people could only understand how little it takes to become truly happy inwardly! I have always known that God is good, but that he is good *in the degree* that I have been permitted to experience during the past fortnight, I should never have thought possible.

On January 5, 1938, he was again arrested and by order of the Gestapo brought to Landsberg on the Lech, because. it was said.

he had " fared too well " in Stadelheim. In the second week of
his confinement there, he sought permission to write a letter to
Reichsführer Himmler:

Since January 5, 1938, I have been under renewed arrest,
first in the Wittelsbach palace; on the 15th I came to
Stadelheim, on the 17th to Landsberg a.L., and am to
remain here until June 3. It seems that I have been sent
here because during the period in which I was being held
for interrogation I " fared too well " in Stadelheim. That,
it is said, was the pronouncement of the political police with
regard to my case. I was very much incensed at this talk,
because it is not true. I have never wanted to have better
treatment than others, poor devils that they are. In the
several prisons I have had only prisoner's rations. Whatever
kind people sent me in the way of food, drink, or tobacco
I gave to the doctor and the head jailer to be distributed
to needy sick persons, keeping a few apples for my own con-
sumption daily. How, then, could I have fared so well?
The only privilege I had was that, as a great exception, I was
permitted, in the period preceding my sentences, to have a
light later in the evening. Otherwise I shared the lot of the
others in everything, for all that sometimes it meant great
hardship.

It is true that I was treated decently, and that, too, in the
Wittelsbach palace. I have been in that prison twice, and
precise information can be obtained there regarding the
manner of my life. I have, moreover, the right, even as a
prisoner, to demand decent treatment, as long as I behave
decently. Even if I was treated decently, no one has the
right to assert that I fared too well in Stadelheim.

Therefore I ask you, Herr Reichsführer, to re-establish my
honour, now impugned, before the political police in
Munich and the prosecuting authority of that city.

In case it may interest you, Herr Reichsführer, I want to
inform you that here in Landsberg I am happy, without a
single wish. The ancients in their time used to say that it
is sweet to die, likewise to suffer, for one's native land. I

have been granted this latter experience in bounteous
measure and I should not wish to have lacked it in my life.
But it is even sweeter to suffer for the holy faith, and also
die for it. It is this that fills me with happiness here in
prison, and that in turn is fortifying so many thousands of
young people in Germany in their Catholic faith. That too
fills me with happiness. Oh, if only the authorities would
desist from their contention with the Church! How very
differently everything would unfold, more beautifully and
more calmly.

With German greeting,*
Rupert Mayer, S. J.

Father Mayer's replies in the questionnaires he had to fill out
on entering the prison at Landsberg are very revealing. The
concluding sentence of his *curriculum vitae* reads: " After a life rich
in rewards, but also rich in disappointments and ingratitude, I
have now landed happily in prison. But I am in no way dis-
satisfied with this lot. I consider it not a disgrace, but rather the
crowning of life." The prison chaplain wrote: " Father R. Mayer
lived like a saint during his imprisonment in the penal institution
of Landsberg am Lech. May the hour come when it will be
permitted us to hang his picture in the cells in which he lived,
and when we may hail him as the patron saint of prisoners."

On November 3, 1939, he was again arrested and taken to the
Sachsenhausen concentration camp near Oranienburg. Of his
stay there he wrote:

In that period, I dreamt one time that I was about to be
shot. At the same moment it became very noisy in the
prison. I was still completely enmeshed in my dream and
had no other thought than that they were coming to get
me. Now suddenly there came over me a feeling of bliss
such as I had never before experienced. I was utterly unable
to comprehend that I had been chosen to die as a martyr.
I had already got up, in order to be instantly ready—then

---

* People who wanted to avoid use of the *Heil Hitler* formula wrote *Mit
deutschem Gruss* as a sort of substitute (translator's note).

the sound of steps receded from my room. That was a great disappointment, but the whole episode has often heartened me, since I actually would have been happy to die for the faith. But there was one other good thing about this occurrence: I had now experienced in my own being how easy God can make things, through his own omnipotent grace, for those who must, or, better, are allowed to die for our holy faith.

LETTERS TO HIS MOTHER

January 16, 1940

I received your letter of December 22 last Sunday. That was a Sunday treat! I have, praise be to God, completely resigned myself to my fate. I am glad that of my own free will I have always pared down my wants to a minimum. That is of infinite help to me now. My absolutely essential needs are supplied, and I want no more. In spite of my enormous outward activity, I have always been more or less a solitary being, that too is of help to me. Now I really have nothing and no one any more except the dear Lord. And that is enough, indeed more than enough. If only people were willing to perceive that! There would be many more happy persons on earth. I try to shut out every thought of the past or the future and to concentrate completely on my daily work; then I am at peace. In this way one day follows another—incredibly fast! Thus I hope to be ready when the Lord calls.

I am closed off from everyone and everything and hear no more of the world. That is just as well, for after all I can be of no help, nor can I change anything. I try to pray and to sacrifice. More than that God does not now demand of me; otherwise he would have disposed differently. I have seen all this coming down upon me for a long time; I spoke of it often at St. Michael's. No one believed it. Now things have come about as I said. God knows the reason!

Dear Mother: You will understand that I can write

nothing about what has brought me back into prison again. I am indeed glad that for years I have had no contact with even my nearest relatives. Thus not even the faintest shadow can fall on any of them because of me. In any case, the circumstances have brought one blessing in their train: I believe that spiritually in these past quiet weeks I have come a good bit closer to God and that in the same degree I have in spirit moved away from all earthly things. I cannot be thankful enough to the Lord God for this. And so I do not have the slightest concern about my future. I put everything into the hands of God. Thus I am inwardly altogether calm and satisfied. I consider myself obliged to impart this to you, and to all who are dear to me, for the sake of your peace of mind.

I think of Father daily. After his death, you sent me his best coat. It has since rendered me innumerable services. In the first place for going out, then in the confessional, and now it constantly and loyally accompanies me to prison. Here it serves regularly to cushion my hard chair and make it fit for use. Isn't that touching? How happy I am that I shall soon see my good father again.

Because it was feared that Father Mayer would die as a martyr in the concentration camp, he was suddenly notified on August 6, 1940, that in half an hour he would be moved. He prepared himself in the expectation of death before a firing squad, and asked God for his help. But things went otherwise. Father Mayer was handed over to the monastery of Ettal, in order to let him disappear there. Under pressure from the Gestapo, the ecclesiastical authorities pledged themselves to see that Father Mayer should not in any way come into contact with the outside world nor engage in any religious services in the cloister. Thereupon a difficult time began for him. Following are his own comments.

Since then I exist in a living death; indeed, this death is for me, who am still so full of life, much worse than actual death.

I could not have done the Gestapo and the whole movement a greater favour—and still cannot—than quietly to wither away to death here. . . . If I have not in all this time packed up and left—they could then quietly lock me up or shorten me by a head—the thing that holds me bound here is consideration for the monastery, which is responsible for me, and, further, consideration for any order, for which I might have created considerable trouble by disappearing from Ettal. Consideration for a number of good, dear people to whom I would have brought great affliction had I again been handed over to a prison or a concentration camp or perhaps met death as a result of something like that. Regard for God, to whom I have come decidedly closer than I have ever been in my life, thanks to the Way of the Cross that I have been walking for years and my gradual liberation thereby from everything earthly and temporal. Should I now, through an arbitrary act, forcibly interrupt this straight line which, by the grace of God, I have held to all the days of my life? Looking at it from the standpoint of faith, I believe that the question must be answered with a flat " no."

So I intend to go on carrying my cross and to do penance and atone for my own mistakes and weaknesses, until such time as the dear Lord will intercede to lift this cross from me again. And likewise for the time to come, my watch-word shall be, " Nearer, my God, to thee! "

Father Mayer became very much a hermit. Only over the bridge of prayer could he reach out to human suffering and need. He himself said at the time, " Everything passes, nothing remains to us; our happiness lies only in God. And the dear Lord indeed pursues man until at last he can only cling to Him alone." And from Ettal he wrote to some acquaintances: " My future lies in the hand of God, and that suffices." Over and over again he recalled the words of St. Augustine: " Restless is our heart until it rests in God." His favourite prayer was:

> Lord, as thou wilt, so shall it be with me,
> And as thou wilt, so shall I take my way;
> Help thou that I may understand thy will.

Lord, whene'er thou wilt, the time has come,
And whensoe'er thou wilt, I stand prepared,
Today and into all eternity.

Lord, whate'er thou wilt, I will endure,
And what thou wilt shall be a gain to me;
It is enough for me to be thine own.

Lord, because thou wilt, it is good,
And since thou wilt it, courage comes to me;
My heart, O Lord, rests wholly in thy hands.

After the entry of the American troops into southern Bavaria at the beginning of May, 1945, Father Mayer's return to Munich was a foregone conclusion. Once again he was to be a father confessor and preacher, and an apostle of charity. On All Saints' Day in 1945, standing before the altar of the Chapel of the Cross in St. Michael's, he spoke his last words as he preached, thus surrendering his priestly work directly into the hands of God. He had started the Mass with the Introit: *Gaudeamus omnes in Domino*—" Let us all rejoice in the Lord." As he reached the end of his sermon, and was trying to say one more sentence, beginning, " The Lord . . . ," he was unable to go on: the sentence begun on earth was completed in heaven. And it ended, doubtless, with the words, ". . . is good! "

HANNSGEORG VON HEINTSCHEL-HEINEGG

The young poet Hannsgeorg von Heintschel-Heinegg stands out among the leaders of the Austrian resistance, which in 1939 gathered its forces into a unified organisation. He was arrested by the Gestapo in the summer of 1940, together with his friends, and died on December 6, 1944, in the court house of Vienna, under the axe of the guillotine. As he approached the last year of his life, his work as a poet was devoted predominantly to a project that he, joining with fellow prisoners of like mind, finally brought to realisation in the death cell of the Vienna prison. He founded an order called " The Knights of the Holy Ghost," which set itself the task of reconquering a secularised Europe for Christianity.

FAREWELL LETTER

November 4, 1944

My dear Uegi: Now I can no longer write to you in the usual way, since prison restrictions affect me also, but I earnestly hope that this letter too will reach you and comfort you within a reasonable space of time. For this is the very moment at which I want to send you a few lines—now, when I know you to be in the thick of dangerous struggles in which for you too the issue is, more than ever, to vindicate yourself in the face of death.

This is what I want to say: Everything that is inessential in us must fall away like ashes in a furnace, in order that the pure gold of our being, thus refined, may shine in the light of grace. The Lord holds you in his hand: know then, dear friend, that you belong to the Lord no matter whether you live or die. And who amongst us will not die, only to live the more fully afterwards?

Rest assured that I pray for you constantly, daily, and that I entreat God to preserve you, not for this world and its gods, but for his kingdom in this world. This does not mean that I want to force upon you an evangelistic mission for which you are perhaps in no wise called. Not at all. But all of us have been snatched from the powers of darkness along with Paul, and transferred to the bright kingdom of God's beloved Son. " Be you "—and that is all of us— " built thereon . . . a holy priesthood "; every one of us on whom the Holy Ghost has descended " as a wind blowing " is a fellow supporter and fellow defender of the Kingdom and a knight of Christ the King. We are locked in struggle with a formidable Satan who really exists and who was not invented by the clerics; we are fighting on many battlefields, within ourselves in the first place, in our environment, and over the entire globe. For you too, my dearest friend, a place must be reserved in this fight, in relation to which the battle you are now engaged in is only a purely external symbol and a very forceful preparatory schooling, strengthening, and hardening for the inner battle, the spiritual contest on behalf of Christ and his kingdom that is and remains after all the actual, ultimate struggle of man.

Accordingly, the Lord will reveal himself to you in profound mysteries and in simple events, even now in this bleak wartime, in order to herald and prepare the great struggle of love, that is, of divine love, for mankind. Our position in this struggle is the ultimately decisive factor. Therefore I wish very much that in this matter you too may see clearly and recognise in all finite things the breath of transitoriness, and that you may receive the breath of the inexpressible summons. For when we mature, we mature only by virtue of ardent living, and we mature not to the serenity of an earthly purification (for that would be at bottom a pagan wish for serene happiness on this earth), but rather in order to hold our ground all the better in a still harder struggle.

For the peace of the Christian begins only in death; however, it begins not with a pagan sleep and the mute night that perhaps follows, but with the inexpressible bliss of supreme life, which is supreme wakefulness, supreme activity, and supreme intensity, and at the same time deepest calm, deepest peace, and deepest security. Here on earth there is no " bourgeois happiness " for the Christian, except for that of a relative lull in the struggle, and of those hours of quiet introspection (which, indeed, are integrally necessary) and peaceful concentration in which we draw on all of God's holy sources (on the revelations of nature, of art, of humanity, of the Prophets, and, finally, of the " beloved Son," our Lord), and from which we draw strength for the final struggle, in which the Lord can waste and expend us for the honour of his holy name. Everything of ours that we give returns to us a hundredfold; and this is the hallmark of true love, that the more it shares itself and spends itself, the more does it spread by growth and the more does it draw up from the bottomless spring of grace.

Therefore think of what I have been saying here, dear Uegi, when you assert, as you sometimes do, that I, in contrast to you, already stand above finite things, that I am more serene and better balanced. For even if matters were as you say, then perhaps I have—on another plane—entered upon far more difficult battles, and a far greater struggle holds me in its grip. For each stage marks the beginning of a new battle, into which we enter with new weapons, and the higher we climb, the greater does our responsibility become, and the more embittered the evil enemy. And it is of course not just of pure chance that he attacks saints particularly with much more violence than he applies to the ordinary Christian; indeed, even the simple Christian is a red rag to the devil, inciting him to attack. And how much the more does each stage of a hard-won struggle towards perfection become a target of satanic hate, of ceaseless attacks (from within perhaps more than from without), beset by countless new pitfalls that open to view only from the vantage of the height.

But the consoling factor in this forbidding prospect is a twofold one. First, the higher we climb, and the harder we fight, the more do we participate in the work and struggle of Jesus Christ, whom the devil sought to confront in all manner of forms (in the desert, in the expulsion of the demons, through Judas, in Golgotha), and suffering thus with him (which means of course also fighting) and struggling with him, we become victors with him. Second, the higher we climb, and the harder we fight, the more grace, light, illumination, and strength and promise do we draw down upon ourselves—yes, draw down forcibly, especially the grace of the Cross and the grace of Pentecost, in other words, grace born of the suffering of redemption and of the struggle for fulfilment. " Draw down forcibly," I say. " And from the days of John the Baptist until now the kingdom of heaven suffereth violence, and the violent take it by force," says the Lord. Thus every struggle does indeed lead to greater bliss, to increase of love through increase of suffering, and in truth to eternal consummation.

Feast of St. Martin, November 11, 1944

Forgive me, but not until to-day have conditions permitted me to go on with this letter. The past week brought all sorts of excitements and disturbances. Thus once more several of us have passed through the dark gate of death, in that unclouded wakefulness and crystalline consciousness —so completely the opposite of sleep, which has mistakenly been called the brother of death—that hyper-alert consciousness which is probably peculiar to *this* kind of death. Moreover, last Sunday, during an attack on our city by over a thousand planes, a high explosive bomb struck one section of our building (the one I am living in now) and brought all sorts of confusion in its wake. But now at last I have nevertheless managed to find a relatively quiet hour in the late evening in which I can put your letter before me once more and, stretched out on my shabby pallet, try to add another word of friendship.

I yearn from the bottom of my heart for a long talk with you; for surely we have much to give each other out of inward and outward experiences of light and of darkness. In so far as I still can (my memory, my heart, and my nerves are by now badly impaired) I devote some time to the study of books whose spirit even here and now is valid and lasting. At present, for example, I have Guardini's studies on Pascal, and in the way of lighter reading, Fromentin's *Old Masters*, which I managed to have sent to me from home. My own creative activity has lain fallow for a year now. Destiny, as it streams down from God's hands upon me, is so vast that, like the basin of a spring, I can only receive, gush upward, or reflect, when the silent stars are shining. When one hears so much, one must refrain from speaking.

You have lost your property: I am sure that you have taken this loss as a call and borne it as a test. Perhaps you now feel less encumbered, and have likewise passed through a gate, plunged down to a new level of being, in face of which the old one no longer has any validity. In 1940 I similarly lost a not inconsiderable part of my manuscripts out of the years from 1938 to 1940. Indeed, we must suffer loss in order to be free for the inexpressibly greater things that we are to win.

I am glad that in trying times you have felt the nearness of God so comfortingly. He alone is great, the sole Praiseworthy One: in him we live, in him we create, in him we have our being. There is no hour in which he is not with us. He is always near to us; it is only we who move away, in order to " love the created light " (as Angelus Silesius says), until that hour of grace comes in which, out of suffering and purification, a ray of the uncreated light strikes us: " I am who am." Do you know, moreover, that since Easter I have been reading the breviary? One little voice more in the great mystical choir of the Church. How beautiful that is!

My dear friend, what more should I in all intimacy tell you? The great things are so simple that if I wanted to give you advice it would take on the form of commonplaces. Indeed, everything that is true is so simple. And can better advice be given than this: " Learn to suffer with Christ "— or, " Consecrate yourself to the most holy heart of Jesus." We skim over so much that is too familiar and too simple. But just reflect on this: " Whoever does not accept the kingdom of God as a little child will not enter it." To be a man means to be of God; to be a Christian means to be for God. Therefore let us begin altogether from the beginning —with him.

I surely pray a great deal for you, my dear Uegi, and have also offered up Holy Communion for you recently. The Lord will always give you the grace you need in order to believe in him, to hope in him, and to love him. He will always give you the strength you need in order to bear your cross through all suffering; he will always give you his support in the struggle with the demons within you and around you; he will always call to you as his beloved child, if only you listen. All else rests with you. No man is tried beyond his strength. Never give up, even if everything is dark. There is always a star lighting the way for us, and it always leads us to the manger in which God became man, in order that man might become God (St. Augustine). What matters it how hard the way may be. That is the lot of the pilgrim.

Stride on courageously, my dear friend, the quiet hours will come. Let all the noise of the world rebound from you, let all suffering build in you. Do not concern yourself with the judgment of men. I too have won little honour among them; I too have lost many friends in this year, often in a very tragic way. But I know that the separation is not for ever; there will be a reunion, a reunion in the eternal home that God has prepared for those who love him.

" All that is transitory is only an image." Speak, cease to be, and look upward to the stars that go in their courses in silent wisdom. What is worthy of our love? You alone, O God. What is worth our searching for, never again to leave it? You alone, O God. What is worth our never leaving it? You, my Lord, you alone. And in you we find everything again, and everything renewed—a new heaven and a new earth, all good human beings, and every glory in thousand-fold sweetness. Here we are reflected light, there we shall be the light itself. With the melody of an inexpressibly tender song let us wing upwards to the eternally echoing choirs of blessed spirits before the Lamb, who there are consummated in the Lord. In him I bless you and embrace you.

Hannsgeorg

JOSEPH MÜLLER

PRIEST

Father Joseph Müller was born on August 19, 1894, at Salmünster in Hesse-Nassau. He was arrested on May 11, 1944, in Gross-Düngen, on the charge of being politically unreliable, and executed on September 11, 1944, at Brandenburg-Görden.

To his elder brother who, as a Franciscan friar, was expelled from his monastery along with his fellow priests, he said: " Now your hour has come, the hour to which God has called you! Rejoice and follow him! "

At the last visit of his brothers and his sister he said: " If I must die, I shall go to my death with the words, *Credo in vitam aeternam. . . .*"

LETTERS WRITTEN IN PRISON

My Brothers and my Sister: I am so alone in my world. There is a room in which I am; in it I am completely alone, as in a grave. The icy breath of a hand forces me from afar into helplessness, into staring wordlessly at the prison walls that hold me fast. There is nothing here that brings joy or warmth. I only know that you are here, my God, you whom I have made God in my temple of suffering, companion of my solitude, my confidant in all my thoughts and desires. Thoughts and desires! Here in your creation stands a portion of your omnipotence, given me by you as part of my life, which I am to bring with me on my journey to you —man. You inhabit his spirit; you look at me through his eyes; he stands on every road I take—your creation, man. In my pastoral life you have given him to me that I should utterly immerse myself in him, feeling with him, living with him, and bleeding with him, as a redeemer jointly with you.

But among your human creatures there are also some in whom I may find repose as I do in you, among whom I may talk freely, and even cry—people who come filled with longing for me and depart filled with love. Among these your messenger-beings there are some who from the outset of my existence have been close to me and linked to me as brothers and sister. They are human souls for whom I long, and who want to join me in love. A feeling of sacred security is joyously shared between us as a greeting from you (in whom we are all met). In human terms I hold them more dear than the other pilgrims wandering on this your earth: the same bond of blood, the same parental love has been about us in our outward, bodily investment. More than that: within our hearts we have, through you, erected an altar on which you stand, offering the priestly sacrifice. This is why they are so very dear to me: looking at them, I recognise you, speaking with them, I hear your words, clasping their hands, I hold your gentle, warm hands, the hands of the Saviour, in mine. With me they walk behind you, pray in common, bear in common your burden, man, we rejoice in common and in common contemplate your wounds and whisper lovingly to you all the knowledge of mysteries granted us by mercy from on high.

Through you, we are full of joy, warmth, and love towards one another. When you rejoice, the light of it shines out to me from their eyes. Then all the comfort, all the joy, all the light that comes from you spreads over the bond of brotherly love. Surrounded by them, I spent the sunny days in my childhood home, had the energies of my mind aroused at school, pondered and planned to answer the call which one day was to find its outlet in works of love. We revealed to one another our human encounters, our moments of loneliness, our wrestling with demons, our happiness and our woe and our world, and also our experiences and encounters with you, O God.

We saw one another in storm and ascent, in love and struggle, when the will was lame and the soul numb, and when the body was weary and ill. Yes, we grew up together, matured into life together, the one becoming the sculptor of the other, hammering and chiselling and through prayer

instilling the love of you into brother and sister. If one of
us was depressed, labouring, and burdened, he could rest,
talk, pray freely and, if the need was bitter, weep freely in
the company of the other. And, when death came, we
could grant each other the gift of resurrecting in our hearts
the love that has grown still and wan, and putting it to rest
in your holy will.

For, in order to come to you completely, one must always
first traverse a zone of silence and weeping, for you are to be
found only on the paths of compassion and charity. Then
all at once you are the Father who walks among his
children, who rejoices and weeps with them, and who has
understanding even for their slightest trouble. If we
brothers and sisters close this door to your chamber you
simply will not open it. Such a merciful confluence of tears
and laments, of enduring and questioning, of weighing and
venturing, is more precious than any other help that you
deign to give us in our togetherness. It is your will, then,
that among brothers and sisters, each—the one thanks to
the other—should grow beyond himself and be led onward
to those eternal powers and truths for which, indeed, a
human being lives. Whoever has not seen your light shining
above brothers and sisters has never in his life seen your
most beautiful light.

What, O Lord, did you actually have in mind when you
brought us together as we are now? Brothers and sisters!
Does that not mean mutual possession and enjoyment,
mutual giving and relinquishing, and, as brothers devoted
to the service of God, the mutual sacrifice of separation.
Brothers and sisters! These words stand for mutual understanding and trust, for something deeply human, and the
heaven of a resplendent circle of light radiating upward
and outward—joy and sorrow both.

Yes, sorrow too is part of the cycle of the brother and
sister relation, because any great love always turns to
suffering. Brothers and sisters are always trembling for one
another, not in regard to their mutual love and loyalty, not
merely because of separations in space and time, at least

not acutely—for indeed these darkened the lights in our windows from early days on. No, what hurts most in the loving unity of brothers and sisters, the most aching nerve, is that the one must let the other suffer while for his part suffering the other's sorrow. There is always a stretch of the road that each must go alone, and that is precisely the most difficult and the darkest part of the road, on which lies the peak of the mount of suffering. Thither each must let the other go—all alone, and that is the personal Golgotha of the individual brother or sister. Let me tell you, Lord, of the sorrow that one brother has brought to his brothers and his sister and that has poured out towards them so overwhelmingly. Not in order to complain—no, only in order to build a bridge to you, Lord, and from you back to my loved ones, who are subject to the same will of God as I—the sanctification of the soul.

FROM A LETTER TO THE BISHOP AND THE VICAR-GENERAL

Hildesheim, May 14, 1944

In the warrant for my arrest, charges are brought against me that cast the most serious aspersions on my civic and my clerical activities. I beg you, your Excellency, and you, my dear Vicar-General, to help me in such a way that my honour as a German and as a priest may be vindicated.

For the time being I can no longer carry on my pastoral duties, but I am now about to walk with Christ in the way that may also help in the care of souls, the way of suffering and prayer. I do not yet know in what direction God intends to lead me, but no matter how and where, he will meet with no pitiable figure. But I too need, above all else, support from above. It will not, I know, be denied to me —and for this my thanks to your Excellency and all my confratres.

To-day at the altars we said, " Whatsoever ye shall ask the Father in my name, he will give it to you." Let us

try this together in unremitting steadfastness, with the help
of our patron saint, who on her feast day led me into
solitude. Even here she spreads out her mantle and helps
me, that the true character of my way of thinking may be
made clear, for to me as a priest no less than before, my
fatherland, for which I was allowed to fight and bleed
throughout the years of the last war, is now the same as
then, namely, Germany.

And once again my thanks, my heartfelt thanks, for your
help, sacrifices, and prayers. Each for the sake of the other.
We all bear one burden, which sometimes becomes very
heavy, and it is called Christ.

My greetings in God,
Joseph Müller

TO HIS BROTHERS AND HIS SISTER

Berlin-Moabit, June 20, 1944

In my situation it is a great comfort to know of all the
thinking about me, for an outsider cannot picture to himself
how a man longs for the Word here. . . . These have been
hard days, in which I have shared with all my priestly
memories—Pentecost, Corpus Christi, etc. In spirit I
participated in everything, and often questioning disturbed
my thoughts. " Take up your cross, and follow me."

Up to this time God has put his shoulder to all the heavy
burdens of my life, now he has stepped out from under the
load, and heavy is its weight, and bitter is its bitterness.
Now the watchword is: Bow down in suffering, love your
enemies, avoid your friends, be patient in the midst of
adversities. That is my cry now.

Give me your help generously now, so that God may make
my grief and my suffering bearable, so that I may wrest my
way to the very pinnacle of God's will: " Not as I will, but
as thou willest." May everything soon become clear to me
and to you. Out of these days of trial my prayers go with all
who are concerned for me; but especially for you, my dear

brothers and my dear sister, may God's protection always remain near. To you, all of my brotherly love.

Your Joseph

WRITTEN IN THE LAST DAYS BEFORE HIS DEATH

I long for your countenance, O Lord, and the tribulation of my life is that I do not find it. I know that you are. I know what you have said, and I know your will. I have called to you so often, but you did not reveal yourself to me. I have sung to you the melodies of my life, in rejoicing and in trembling, in thanksgiving and in entreaty, in sadness and in serenity, I have chatted with you, I have complained and scolded, I have at times lost sight of you, but always I have had to come back to you. Always you have waited for me—for you had left me my freedom. You know perfectly well I should come back. And now you have come very close to me, so that I feel your breath on my cheek, as it were. You my fountainhead, you my ultimate goal, you my heaven. And now I am homeward bound, into " life," into the " life eternal," into the " joy of the Lord," into the " kingdom." Now I shall say nothing more, but I want to hear what you have to say to me about this my heaven into which you wish me to come.

ON THE DAY OF DEATH

Brandenburg, September 11, 1944

On the Eve of the Feast of the Name of Mary.

My very dear brothers and sister, Ewald, Oskar, Ida—
My dear, good Bishop and all my dear Brothers, my dear Degenhardt—
My dear parishioners, children, youths, men, women—
My dear, good Fräulein Krawinkel, dear Sisters, dear folk of Heining, Lauterberg, and Wolfenbüttel—
And all other dear, kind people—

Now my last earthly greeting comes to you from my cell.
What shall I say in the circumstances? Oh, my heart is so
full of joy now that I am on the way home to the Father.
I have known all these days that my sacrifice would be
accepted. It is now eleven-thirty. In one hour I shall be at
home; I shall have left you so far as this earth goes, but
nothing can separate us from the love of Christ.

I send a farewell to your world with a countenance
glowing with gratitude. Farewell, you little hut, my cell,
poor and faithful, you my silent friend—you were my last
church and my last pulpit. Farewell, all that lies behind
me—you churches in which I served as a priest, you streets
and lanes with your kind and your stony people. Farewell,
my home, my last place of work, and say to everyone that
the priest who lived in you lies in his last chains and is now
about to die on his last journey as all men die whom
Christ's life and death have benefited. I have just read the
Twenty-second Psalm and said the *Profiscere anima mea*, as
my last earthly prayer for all who stand at my hard bier.
Like St. John I go forth with the greeting of grace.
Blessed be Jesus Christ in eternity. Amen.

Joseph
Victima Christi

LAST PRAYER IN FACE OF DEATH

September 11, 1944

*Hodie scietis, quia venit Dominus et videbitis hodie gloriam eius et
erit in illa die lux magna.*

 In Te Domine speravi, non confundar in aeternum.
 *Credo . . . in vitam aeternam!**

---

 * Know that to-day the Lord cometh and that to-day you shall see
his glory and there shall be a great light on this day. I trust in thee,
O Lord; in eternity I shall not be confounded.
 I believe . . . in the life eternal.

ALEXIS, BARON VON ROENNE

Alexis von Roenne, born on February 12, 1902, was a colonel of the German Army. From the moment of the establishment of the régime, he regarded National Socialism as a disaster for Germany. Considerations of conscience prevented him from taking part in the preparation of the attempted coup of July 20, 1944. But the ties of friendship that linked him with the leaders of the resistance served as sufficient ground for his condemnation. He died on October 12, 1944, in Berlin-Plötzensee, at the hands of the hangman.

FAREWELL LETTER TO HIS MOTHER

Berlin, October 11, 1944. Evening

My only beloved Mama: To-day for a very special reason the notion came to me to write you once again, although a short letter to you is enclosed with my previous letters of farewell. I know that in spite of your great longing and joy at the prospect of going to the Saviour, mortal fear at the thought of just the physical process of death torments you. And because of that I have wanted so very much to say to you that our Lord can *completely erase* this too, if we ask him to do so. So have no fear at all. Father used to tell me that our grandfather on his deathbed refused a soothing medicine with the words, " Everything must be endured." He stood so sovereign over death—it was quite magnificent.

For a week now I have been awaiting death from day to day; at this moment, for example, I expect it to-morrow, and the Saviour in his boundless mercy has freed me of all terror. All day I pray and think in *perfect calm* and almost exclusively about Him and at the same time of course about those dearest to me. I have a good appetite, I take pleasure in the sunshine, and I have tried to free myself from the world only in so far as I have given up reading and, as much as possible, keep my thoughts away from all military and political matters and at the disposition only of the Saviour. I go to bed early, with prayer, I sleep very peacefully and soundly like a child the whole night through, and immediately upon awakening I turn to Him; spiritually, with all this, I am completely free, and moreover, apart from thoughts about my little brood,* I am a completely happy man—a phenomenon that has often been found astonishing here and been explained by reference to Him.

At first I cast about by myself to find avenues of thought that would give me strength and a joyous mood for dying; then suddenly God showed me two means of help. First of all, I was to picture my death to myself in its full reality, and then to compare it with his death. That has helped me immeasurably: on the one hand the innocent victim, voluntarily suffering a death of many hours of martyrdom at the hands of those He had saved; on the other, an event of a moment's duration that in any case was bound to confront me at some time, perhaps in much more painful form, as in a long illness. I got this suggestion from two beautiful verses, " When strength one day shall fail me," and especially, " And let me see Thine image, crowned in Thine agony." Thereupon I was ashamed of all my inhibitions and became free of fear. And then he pointed out to me that the moment of death is at the same time of course the first moment of life in his blessed rest and in the peace of God. Keeping these thoughts firmly in mind, I have for days been looking forward hourly, in *complete calm and detachment*, with perfectly peaceful thoughts and quiet pulse, to my departure on the swift journey home, and I am fully confident that the brief final occurrence will be similarly irradiated by his indescribable grace.

I am writing this to you in such exact detail, my beloved Mama, because perhaps thereby I can, acting in his service, give you a bit of help. Ever since the beginning of this last exceptional period of grace (two and a half months) there has been no doubt in my mind that I owe all this un-

* His wife and two small children.

deserved mercy in very large part to your prayers of a decade, and words are not sufficient to express my thanks to you. I consider this intercession of yours as the greatest gift by far of your unending love for me, and in the life to come we shall be speaking of it often. But I beg you with all my heart for the rest of your time on earth to transfer these prayers to Ursula and my two little ones. Do it, I beg you fervently, with the same love and loyalty. It is an indescribable treasure that you will be giving to my beloved little brood that needs it so desperately. I am certain that you will fulfil my wish.

I have of course ceaselessly brought my dear ones before God in my prayers. I have recognised his work in several acts of grace even now, in gifts both large and small, and he has filled me with confidence that " whosoever believeth in him shall not be ashamed." But in my prayers I have at the same time never besought him to grant them a long life on earth, but only to give them strength, to preserve them from horror, distress, and want of charity, and then, of course, to give them a blessed death. Death now means nothing to me; yet how gladly would I have gone home *with* my little brood, whom I can no longer care for and protect. But whenever such earthly thoughts come to me, the Lord reminds me that according to human probability I should in any case not have been beside them in time of stress, and that, above all, he is a far better protection.

How good it is to know that I have such dear brothers and sisters, who will certainly stand by my family like a rock in whatever way they can. But they themselves are experiencing great difficulties at present. It seems to me that in the first place our beloved Lapienen* must by now lie within the battle zone. Being cut off from communication with you all has often been hard for me; at the same time it has increased my realisation of the supreme closeness of our union before the throne of God, and above all of the insignificance of our earthly life span. And my joy in anticipation of the happy immunity to separation that is to

* A family estate in East Prussia.

come has grown ever greater. How indescribably glorious it will be, and how happy I should be if only I knew those dearest to me and all of you to be even now in the peace of God, remote from all suffering.

To all of you, who are probably in Rönkendorf now, I send greetings with all my heart, commending you to the hand of God and to his blessing. May he lead all of you graciously by gentle paths into his kingdom, as he is leading me who, like the thief, " this day will be in paradise." I know that you will never abandon my dearest one, and that you will keep in mind especially her *infinitely tender heart, which has such great need of love* and likewise holds all of you so dear. For this, and for all the boundless love of nearly forty-two years, I thank all of you, and especially you, my indescribably beloved mother, from the depth of my heart.

No child has ever received a richer or deeper love from his mother than

Your Alecci

With infinite gratitude I thought to-day of the splendid childhood that your love above all else made for me in Mitau and Wilkajen. Everything is in a golden glory, with you at the centre.

LAST LETTERS TO HIS WIFE

July 25, 1944

My beloved darling:* You know what events are sweeping Germany and you can surmise their significance. In view of my position, it is easily possible that the wave will seize me too and draw me into its vortex. Therefore I want to speak a word of farewell to you now—though only for this time on earth—and of ardent thanks. First, you and the little ones are to know that I have had no part nor guilt in what has happened, no matter what may be said afterwards. All else is of no importance in comparison with this.

* This letter was written by von Roenne before his imprisonment.

However, this exceedingly grave time has brought me an enormous gain. I have returned completely into the open arms of our Lord and Saviour, which I had often enough forgotten in the pressure of events. I spend nearly all my free time in prayer, a prayer for strength for myself in face of everything that is to come, and for blessing and help for you, my most beloved, and for the children. And so I sense so clearly the gift of fortitude that has come to me that I embark on everything with the joyful assurance that it can end nowhere but close to the heart of God, in eternal peace. Then indeed all that has gone before seems quite unimportant and should not concern you at all. At each moment, my inner eye will see behind anything only the open arms of my Lord and Saviour. My firm comfort and foundation are the sayings, " And Him that cometh to me I will in no wise cast out," and, " Though your sins be as scarlet, they shall be as white as snow," and then the many other pregnant expressions of God's love as the profoundest reason for his attitude towards us.

I cling to these and gain strength and especially also the certainty that my ardent supplications for you will not be in vain. For my thoughts and prayers concern you before all else and encompass in the greatest love your entire life for the future. My very dearest one, in all sorrow you must perceive constantly that you are not facing life alone: He is with you every moment, and he may even be mindful of my entreaties on your behalf when he helps you—just as your prayers and Mama's smoothed the way for me. Then besides, there is the firm assurance that some day, together before his throne, we shall give thanks and praise for all undeserved mercies, of which the greatest is that he at one time brought us together—the greatest at least of the earthly gifts.

You must know with absolute certainty that my whole heart belongs to you only, by virtue of bonds that can be conferred only once in life, because they reach beyond life into eternity. And next to the thanks I render to the Lord, my most ardent, never-ending thanks go to you, dear heart, and will be yours to my last heartbeat. Thank you for the inexpressible love that you have unceasingly spread about me like a mantle of gold.

And now our two beloved children whom, by the will of God, I must leave bereft of me, but whom I know to be sheltered in his love and your care. Tell them that the ardent last prayers of their father and his great love accompany them through life, and tell them to give all their love to you and always, whenever they think of me, to do something especially nice for you as a greeting from me. What they will be and what they will do at some future day is of no importance. It is *how* they do it—that is, whether they do it under God's guidance—that counts. Their father has often failed in this respect, yet the hand of the Lord never let him go; it needs only to be sought with fervour.

Give my thanks likewise to all others whom I love—to Mama, my brothers and sisters, your parents. All of them, but especially my beloved Mama, have given me much, much more love than they have received, and thereby have brought much more sunshine into my life, which has been a full and happy one, than they have ever realised. To them likewise I dedicate the wish, " *One day, above in the light!* "

Königsdamm 7, Berlin-Plötzensee
October 12, 1944

My dearest beloved: In a moment now I shall be going home to our Lord in *complete calm* and in the certainty of salvation. My thoughts are with you, with all of you, with the very greatest love and gratitude.

As my last wish, I entreat you only to cling to Him and to have full confidence in Him; He loves you.

Any decision you may take for all of you, after prayer, has my complete sanction and my blessing. If only you knew with what inconceivable loyalty He is standing by my side at this moment, you would be armoured, and calm, for all your difficult life. He will give you strength for everything.

I bless both of our beloved children, and include them in my last ardent prayer. May the Lord let his countenance shine upon them and lead them home.

Heartfelt greetings and thanks to my beloved Mama, to your parents and my brothers and sisters. May they, safeguarded by Him, survive even difficult times in our ardently beloved fatherland.

To you, my very dearest of all, belong my ardent love and thanks to the last moment and until our blessed reunion.

God keep you.

ALSO AVAILABLE
IN THE FONTANA RELIGIOUS SERIES

LETTERS AND PAPERS FROM PRISON
DIETRICH BONHOEFFER

These documents, smuggled out of prison under the noses of the Gestapo, have a clear and shining unity.

LET MY PEOPLE GO
ALBERT LUTHULI

The autobiography of the great South African leader—awarded the Nobel Peace Prize in 1961.

LE MILIEU DIVIN
PIERRE TEILHARD DE CHARDIN

The author of *The Phenomenon of Man* discusses man also in his relation to God. A biographical essay is included.

GOD'S FROZEN PEOPLE
MARK GIBBS AND T. RALPH MORTON

'A most important and stimulating book . . . clear and revolutionary thinking about the role of the laity.'

Archdeacon of London

MERE CHRISTIANITY
C. S. LEWIS

'He has a quite unique power for making theology an attractive, exciting and fascinating quest.' *Times Literary Supplement*

THE PSALMS: *A New Translation*

'A very impressive rendering. I am filled with admiration for the translators' achievements and have nothing but praise for it.' *Professor H. H. Rowley*

PHOENIX AT COVENTRY
SIR BASIL SPENCE

'A rare attempt to see how the architect's mind works in solving complicated problems of construction, economics and theology.' ILLUSTRATED, *Times Literary Supplement*

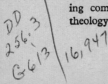